Writing the South Seas

Writing the South Seas

IMAGINING THE NANYANG IN CHINESE AND SOUTHEAST ASIAN POSTCOLONIAL LITERATURE

Brian Bernards

UNIVERSITY OF WASHINGTON PRESS *Seattle and London*

THIS BOOK IS MADE POSSIBLE BY A COLLABORATIVE GRANT FROM THE ANDREW W. MELLON FOUNDATION.

Publication of this book was also supported by a research grant from the University of Southern California's Advancing Scholarship in the Humanities and Social Sciences program.

19 18 17 16 15 5 4 3 2 1

University of Washington Press
www.washington.edu/uwpress

Library of Congress Cataloging-in-Publication Data

Bernards, Brian.
Writing the South Seas : imagining the Nanyang in Chinese and Southeast Asian postcolonial literature / Brian Bernards.
pages cm. — (Modern language initiative books)
Includes bibliographical references and index.
ISBN 978-0-295-99501-4 (hard cover : alk. paper)
1. Chinese fiction—20th century—History and criticism. 2. Southeast Asia—In literature. 3. Nationalism in literature. 4. Chinese fiction—Southeast Asia—History and criticism. 5. Authors, Chinese—Southeast Asia. I. Title.
PL2419.S58B47 2015
895.109'35859—dc23 2015025351

The paper used in this publication is acid-free and meets the minimum requirements of American National Standard for Information Sciences—Permanence of Paper for Printed Library Materials, ANSI Z39.48–1984. ∞

CONTENTS

PREFACE

From the 1850s to the 1940s, throughout a century that bore witness to the rise and fall of colonial empires, nearly twenty million sojourners made overseas voyages between southern China and Southeast Asia, a region the Chinese called Nanyang, the "South Seas." By and large, the sojourners and emigrants of this great migration came from the densely populated cities, towns, and villages of coastal southern China (Fujian and Guangdong provinces), a region with strong seafaring traditions. They embarked from Amoy (Xiamen), Swatow (Shantou), Hainan Island, semicolonial Shanghai, colonial Hong Kong, and other major ports. More than half traveled to British colonial Malaya (now Malaysia and Singapore), although roughly three million continued on to other destinations in the region, such as the rural plantations of Sumatra and other islands of the Dutch East Indies. Nearly four million sojourners, mostly from the Teochew (Chaozhou) region of northern Guangdong province (around Swatow), traveled to the Kingdom of Siam (now Thailand). Some hardy settlers, particularly Hakka (Kejia) peoples from the mountainous interiors bordering the South China coasts, headed for Southeast Asia's wilder hinterlands. They migrated for various reasons, but most common among these were poverty and famine caused by war, displacement, foreign invasion, overpopulation, political instability, and natural disaster.

Despite the diverse backgrounds of the Chinese travelers—not to mention the incredible diversity of places they traveled to in Southeast Asia—they imagined this region singularly as the "South Seas." Though this term is written with the same two Chinese characters, its pronunciation varies depending on the Sinitic language(s) one speaks, such as Nanyang (standard Chinese or Mandarin), Nam Yeung (Cantonese), Nam Yeo (Hokkien and Teochew), and Nam Yeong (Hakka).

For these migrants and settlers, the Nanyang was a "New World"—a pioneering frontier of opportunity and potential upward mobility—in spite of its dangerous and difficult environment. The vast majority (almost 90 percent) of the 7.5 million Chinese emigrants who settled abroad during this century of emigration did so in Southeast Asia (mostly in what are now Indonesia, Malaysia, Singapore, and Thailand), far outnumbering those who crossed the Pacific to North America during the same period.[1]

Other than its relative proximity to southern China, several factors made the Nanyang attractive to Chinese migrants. This region had already experienced centuries of Chinese influence. Even in the early fifteenth century, when the renowned naval admiral of the Ming empire, Zheng He (a Chinese Muslim also known as Ma Sanbao), navigated a massive armada of ships across the South China Sea and Indian Ocean to reach the eastern coastline of Africa, cataloguers of the fleet's seven expeditions noted communities of "Tang people" (indicating descendants of Chinese) already adapted to life in Java.[2] Though China's emperors never formally colonized the South Seas, and the Ming court abandoned maritime exploration following Zheng He's seventh mission, various kingdoms in Southeast Asia continued to observe the imperial Chinese "tribute system." During the Ming (1368–1644) and first two centuries of the Qing (1644–1911) dynasties, Southeast Asian kingdoms and sultanates such as Malacca (Malaya), Semarang (Java), Ayutthaya (Siam), Annam (Vietnam), Sulu (the Philippines), and Ava (Burma) recognized the authority of the Middle Kingdom through tribute payments, and in some cases they sought its military protection against neighboring rivals.[3]

China's age of oceanic exploration, military and technological supremacy, and tributary suzerainty is not coeval with its period of mass emigration: from the late seventeenth century, the Qing dynasty forbade emigration and commercial trade by an imperial decree that warned of execution to those who dared return.[4] Despite the ban, this was a phase of a smaller-scale "pioneer settlement" whose overwhelmingly male character led to intermarriages with indigenous (or sometimes other settler) populations and the formation of mixed-ethnic, creole communities in the early European colonies in the region, such as the Mestizos of the Spanish Philippines and the Peranakans of the Dutch East Indies.[5] On the Malayan peninsula, the Peranakan (a Javanese term meaning "crossbreed," or literally "of the womb") was also known as the "Baba-Nyonya," a name with a creolized etymology. Popular lore traces Peranakan ancestry to intermarriages between male castaways from Zheng He's fleet (mostly from Fujian) and indigenous Malay women in Malacca (now Melaka).[6] Indicating a male Peranakan, the term "Baba" came to Southeast Asia via West Asia and India, as it derives from a Persian and Hindi-Urdu honorific title for a man.[7] Denoting a married female Peranakan, the term "Nyonya" combines the Hokkien *nyo* ("young woman") with the Javanese *nyai* ("concubine," "madame"),[8] reflecting the indigenous origins of the female side. Speaking creole languages like Baba Malay, these communities differed culturally from the later wave of Chinese *sinkeh* (*xinke*, "new guests" arriving after 1850) and their "pure-blood" local-born offspring. In the colonies, the creolized communities served important roles as middlemen between indigenous communities, other Asian migrants, and the Western colonial regimes. The Babas, for example, formed an elite class of the British imperial bureaucracy in the Straits Settlements of Penang, Malacca, and Singapore.[9]

Along with revolutionary advances in steamship technology, the reconfiguration of global power in Asia following China's loss to Britain in the first Opium War, which forced the Qing government to lift the imperial ban on private overseas travel, allowed for an unprecedented outflow of Chinese labor and the proliferation of Chinese mercantilism abroad. Circular migration, or multiple sojourns and returns, characterized this period even more than permanent emigration, although both patterns were large-scale.[10] Those who eventually returned to China or migrated elsewhere took advantage of local, often short-term employment opportunities, especially during the peak years of migration in the 1920s, by which time economic, cultural, educational, and political networks between the Nanyang and China were well established. Despite popular caricatures, these Chinese sojourners were not merely "illiterate" migrant workers or "coolies" in search of subsistence, nor were they just "profiteering" merchants and venture capitalists hoping to expand their wealth in the colonial Southeast Asian economies.[11] They also included intellectuals, students, teachers, journalists, writers, political reformers, and dissidents who carried various agendas, ideologies, and worldviews, sometimes impressing them upon the local settler population.

Mainland Chinese historians have framed the mass exodus as one by-product of a "century of national humiliation" (*bainian guochi*) at the hands of Western (followed by Japanese) imperial powers dating from the Opium Wars to the founding of the People's Republic of China (PRC) in 1949.[12] Only national disintegration from excruciating poverty and political chaos could prompt one to abandon the ancestral homeland for a potentially perilous overseas voyage: even if one cherished hopes of return under improved circumstances, there was no assurance of that possibility.

Yet the modern history of Chinese migration and settlement in the Nanyang is not simply a narrative of national victimization and humiliation. It is also a tale of a Chinese settler colonialism fashioned from an economic collusion between China (the Qing dynasty followed by the Republic of China), commercial and industrial enterprises in the colonial and semicolonial territories of Shanghai, Hong Kong, and Southeast Asia, and Western imperial administrations in Asia. In Malaya, Borneo, Java, and Siam, Chinese merchants created a commercial niche (and in some cases a monopoly) as tin-mine operators, plantation foremen, tax collectors, "revenue farmers," bankers, government clerks, and wealthy financiers and industrialists, even while indentured Chinese coolies provided much of the manual labor force in a form of modern "paraslavery."[13] Chinese merchants were not fashioners of their own empires, but they played a key role as middlemen in administering Western imperial authority and managing the colonial economies of Southeast Asia.[14] This complex colonial history profoundly influenced the geopolitical trajectory of national liberation movements and developmental schemes in Southeast Asia from the mid-twentieth century onward.

Based on this historical narrative, the Nanyang encompasses more than a southern destination of Chinese overseas migration and settlement. More critically, the term maps a network—an archipelago—of cultural, political, and economic exchange. To imagine the South Seas is to remember the migratory passage, to recall the vast archipelagic network of cultural interchange this passage facilitated, and to address the lasting colonial legacies and postcolonial influences this network imparted in China and across Southeast Asia. Against the backdrop of Western imperialism and the formation of modern nation-states in Asia, Chinese migration, settlement, and intercultural exchange in the Nanyang left an indelible mark on the region's cultural and geopolitical landscape, shaping its postcolonial cultures and literary narratives. These narratives are the focus of the pages herein.

NOTE ON ROMANIZATION AND TRANSLATION

This book includes vocabulary from the non-Romanized scripts of Chinese and Thai. In the case of Chinese, many words come from Sinitic languages besides Mandarin. For ease of bibliographical referencing, all terms, titles, and names are transliterated using standard Chinese pinyin (based on Mandarin pronunciation). For authors or historical figures better known in (or who prefer to use) nonstandard spellings for their names (from Mandarin, Hokkien, or other Sinitic languages), those versions are used: pinyin is supplied in parentheses the first time an individual is discussed in detail. Terms from Sinitic languages besides Mandarin are Romanized to approximate pronunciation in those languages, followed by pinyin in parentheses. All Thai words (besides names more familiar in other spellings), including those transliterated from Teochew, are Romanized using the Library of Congress system (with most diacritical marks removed). The Glossary at the end of the book is alphabetized according to pinyin (for Chinese) and Library of Congress (for Thai) spelling: the list provides original script for terms, names, and titles not cited in the Bibliography. In the Glossary and Bibliography, traditional Chinese characters are used (except in the case of titles accessed in simplified characters). Unless noted by the citation, all translations from Chinese and Thai are my own.

ACKNOWLEDGMENTS

A project like this could never exist without the visionary work of authors who dared to "imagine otherwise," even when doing so put them at risk of public backlash, censorship, even persecution. Despite any personal repercussions they faced (or still face), all the writers discussed herein bravely challenged the customary boundaries of their assigned cultures by reconciling with their cross-cultural experiences, giving expression and visibility to their alternatively imagined communities. From the modern Chinese writers Xu Dishan, Xu Zhimo, Lao She, and Yu Dafu to the postcolonial Southeast Asian authors Ng Kim Chew, Pan Yutong, Chang Kuei-hsing, Yeng Pway Ngon, Chia Joo Ming, Suchen Christine Lim, Botan, Praphatson Sewikun, and Fang Siruo, this book was inspired by a diverse collection of creative voices who discovered in the South Seas a platform for "imagining otherwise." Of these writers, I especially wish to thank Yeng Pway Ngon, as well as his partner Goh Beng Choo, for welcoming me to their Grassroots Book Room in Singapore, where they enthusiastically discussed and shared their work with me.

As a comparably courageous gesture to "imagine otherwise," Shu-mei Shih's articulation and inauguration of Sinophone studies was a critical intervention in the customary boundaries of several scholarly disciplines (including modern Chinese literature, diaspora studies, and postcolonial studies), which provided vital intellectual inspiration to this book. For Shu-mei's mentorship, friendship, and patient dedication to the development of my own intellectual vision over the years, I am profoundly grateful. I would also like to acknowledge the vital role played by David Wang in enhancing the transpacific visibility of Sinophone studies. With the emergence of this exciting new field, I have benefited from the trailblazing work of scholars writing about Sinophone Southeast Asian literature in English, namely E. K. Tan, Alison Groppe, Andrea Bachner, Chien-hsin Tsai, and Tzu-hui Celina Hung. I have enjoyed collaborating with each of them.

Several research grants facilitated fruitful overseas trips to Asia to locate sources and participate in conferences: I would like to acknowledge the University of Southern California's Advancing Scholarship in the Humanities and Social Sciences Program, Fulbright-Hays, the University of California Pacific Rim Research Program, and the UCLA Asia Institute for the critical funding they provided. For hosting me as a visiting scholar from 2008–9, I am grateful to the National University of Singapore's Asia Research Institute. I also wish to thank Wong Yoon Wah, Chua Chee Lay, and Kho Tong Guan for hosting my June 2014 visit to the Malaysian Chinese Literature Centre at Southern University College in Johor, as well as Patipat Auprasert, who met with me at Mahidol University in Bangkok the following month and aided my research on Sino-Thai authors. Whenever a question arose in the research process, the guru to whom I most often turned was Tee Kim Tong: though we conducted most of our correspondence via email, he never hesitated to kindly share his wisdom with me.

Laurie Sears and Lingchei Letty Chen generously read and commented on an earlier draft of this book: their insightful suggestions at a manuscript review hosted by the USC East Asian Studies Center were invaluable to the revision process. For organizing the review, I would like to thank David Kang and Grace Ryu at EASC. I also wish to acknowledge my USC colleagues for their commitment to my scholarship, particularly David Bialock, Bettine Birge, Dominic Cheung, Youngmin Choe, Geraldine Fiss, Akira Lippit, Sunyoung Park, Satoko Shimazaki, and Duncan Williams, as well as Christine Shaw and all the staff in the Department of East Asian Languages and Cultures. For affirming my work's contribution to Southeast Asian studies, I am grateful to Geoffrey Robinson and George Dutton at UCLA.

Collaborating with the University of Washington Press has been a smooth process due to the expert assistance of my editors, Lorri Hagman, Tim Zimmermann, and Tim Roberts. The two anonymous reviews solicited by the press were incredibly helpful in preparing the book's final draft. I am additionally grateful to the Modern Language Initiative for supporting its publication.

I would like to thank Kirk Denton and The Ohio State University for kindly permitting me to revise and reprint material in this book from my article "From Diasporic Nationalism to Transcolonial Consciousness: Lao She's Singaporean Satire, *Little Po's Birthday*," *Modern Chinese Literature and Culture* 26, no. 1 (2014): 1–40. I also thank Taylor and Francis (www.tandfonline.com) and David Martin for permission to revise and reprint material here from "Beyond Diaspora and Multiculturalism: Recuperating Creolization in Postcolonial Sinophone Malaysian Literature," *Postcolonial Studies* 15, no. 3 (2012): 311–29. Harry Tan Photography generously granted permission to use its beautiful image of a triptych mural from the Tanjong Pagar Railway Station for the cover design of this book.

I have learned much from my dedicated graduate students at USC: in this regard, I would especially like to thank Keisha Brown, Melissa Chan, Li-ping Chen, Jier Dong, Yunwen Gao, Viola Lasmana, and Yu-kai Lin.

Long before I conceived of this project, my parents instilled in me a curiosity about the world beyond. With over thirty years of service as a physician to the Native American community in Minneapolis, my mother modeled endurance, effort, and a commitment to social justice complemented by a playful, songbird spirit. I am ever thankful for everyone in my family, which expanded when I met and married the love of my life, Lalita. Through all the variables in the journey that was the writing of this book, she has been my one constant. Reading over drafts and listening to my incipient ramblings, Lalita helped me cut through the noisy flow of thought to distill my voice, reminding me to always write from a place of joy, love, truth, and compassion. She is my blessing, and I dedicate this work to her.

Writing the South Seas

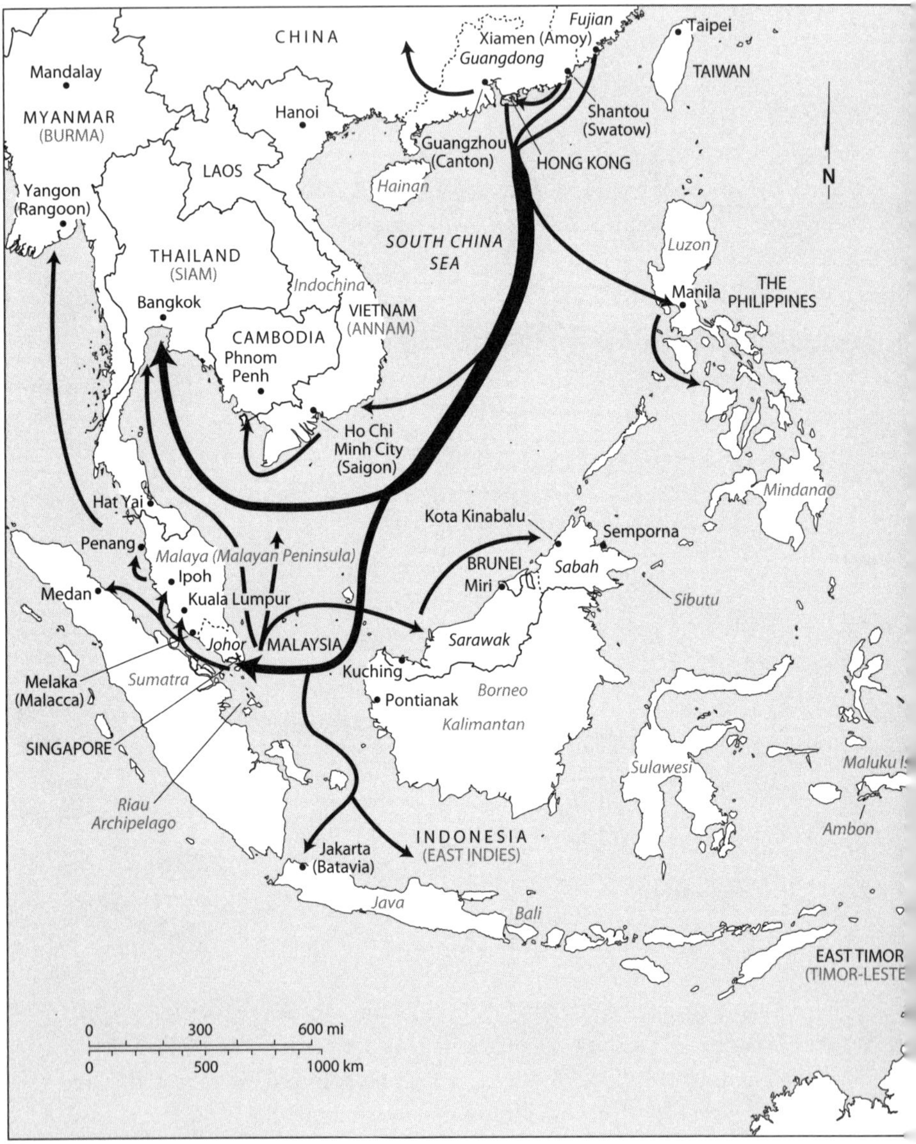

The Nanyang: Trajectories of Chinese Overseas Migration to Southeast Asia, 1850–19
Contents adapted from "Chinese in Southeast Asia," in *The World Today: Concepts a*
Regions in Geography, 5th ed. by H.J. de Blij, Peter O. Muller, Jan Nijman, and An
nette M.G.A WinklerPins (New York: John Wiley, 2011), 397.

Introduction

If the Nanyang can produce a great master—an author who puts the South Seas at the heart of his works, composing them effectively by the tens or hundreds—then Nanyang literature—a literature with a local South Seas flavor—will naturally succeed.

YU DAFU, "Some Questions" (1939)

Oh South Seas, you are my mother's native land.

NG KIM CHEW,
"Back Inscriptions" (2001)

We Nanyang Chinese in Southeast Asia are their [China's] married daughters. Married out already.

SUCHEN CHRISTINE LIM,
Fistful of Colours (1992)

When Grandpa decided to leave his home in Swatow, hop ship, and try his luck in the South Seas, his parents worried that he would be so charmed by the women of a foreign land that he would ultimately forget his birthplace.

PRAPHATSON SEWIKUN,
Through the Pattern of the Dragon (1989)

The four passages above highlight specific moments, contexts, and articulations—explored throughout this book—in the evolution of the Nanyang, the "South Seas," as a postcolonial literary trope of Chinese travel, migration, settlement, and creolization in Southeast Asia. In the first excerpt from a 1939 Singaporean newspaper editorial, Yu Dafu's reference to the potential of a "Nanyang literature" marks an important gesture by an author from China to legitimize the culturally generative space occupied by Sinophone literature in colonial Southeast Asia as distinct from the modern Chinese literary tradition to which the author belonged. This recognition denotes an evolution of the Nanyang imagination in modern Chinese literature, deviating from a barbarous realm in the imperial Chinese worldview to represent a maritime New World that births its own creole cultures through localization, adaptation, and intercultural contact. In colonial Malaya, Yu Dafu bore witness to a Sinophone literary movement that had already experienced two decades of maturation: he acknowledged the Nanyang as affirming its own historical subjectivity, neither "tributary" nor derivative of Chinese perspectives of the region.

An iconoclastic pioneer of literary modernity in 1920s China, Yu Dafu came of age as a writer while studying in Japan and suffering the ignominies of Japanese imperialism: his canonical fiction probes the melancholia of "national humiliation" haunting Chinese intellectual minds at the time. Nearly two decades later in Singapore, after fleeing the Japanese invasion of eastern China, Yu used his prestige as editor of newspaper literary supplements not only to advocate anti-Japanese activism but also to advise local Sinophone authors. He opined that the merits of a Nanyang literature could not be reduced to the degree of "local color" exhibited in a given work, nor to the faithfulness of an author's appropriation of modern Chinese literary trends, as both pursuits reflected an inferiority complex not entirely dissimilar to the colonized psyche of the young protagonist studying in Japan in Yu's inaugural short fiction.[1] He proposed that the Nanyang's literary development hinged on the abilities of local writers to cultivate honestly their lived experiences and individual perspectives.[2] Yu's judgments brought controversy, as they inadvertently implied that a Nanyang literary "master" could only arrive when a Chinese master from the "homeland" recognized his appearance. Yu's vision of a Nanyang literature never came to pass, as the South Seas never achieved the geopolitical unity necessary to constitute its own category of cultural production: instead, Sinophone literatures in Southeast Asia were mobilized around their respective colonial and emergent national contexts. In hindsight, Yu Dafu's New World vision of the South Seas serves as a conceptual bridge between modern Chinese and Sinophone Malayan literatures as anticolonial literary projects: it highlights the Nanyang's transcolonial signification as a maritime network of exchange between a postimperial China seeking "national salvation" and a prenational Southeast Asia.

Though the dream of a culturally integrated Nanyang receded with the hardening of geopolitical boundaries in Southeast Asia, its significance as a literary trope did not vanish from the postcolonial formations of Sinophone literature in the region, where the South Seas remained an important motif evoking the creolized origins and maritime lineages of the modern nation and national culture, a history often suppressed by official state discourses. This is particularly evident in Malaysia, where the British legacy of racialization—segregating colonial subjects into immutable indigenous or immigrant ethnic categories—and its designation of the colony as "Malay land" inform the autochthonous politics of postcolonial nationhood. Following ethnic rioting in 1969, the Malaysian government asserted Malay as the national culture and language, purging nonindigenous contributions to the nation from the revised history textbooks in the compulsory education curriculum.[3]

In the second excerpt above—from a 2001 short story entitled "Back Inscriptions"—the Sinophone Malaysian author Ng Kim Chew evokes the Nanyang to allegorically "reinscribe" Malaysia's purged historical texts of creolization. The excerpt alludes to a revolutionary song sung by migrant Chinese laborers in wartime Malaya against the looming threat of Japan's southward advance into Southeast Asia: "Oh South Seas, you are my beautiful native land." In the contemporary setting of Ng's story, the line is sung in "broken Mandarin" by an old man whose native tongue is Hokkien. The verse is also tattooed in ancient-looking Chinese characters across the man's back. A professor researching the history of Chinese migrant labor discovers the tattooed verse and wonders how it got there, since the old man is illiterate. The professor also notices that many of the characters are miswritten, making the line appear to read "mother's native land" rather than "beautiful native land." An investigation reveals that the characters were inscribed decades ago by an aspiring British writer who quit his colonial post in Singapore to pursue his fascination with the Chinese script: essentially, he purchased coolies as "textual bodies" onto which he imprecisely mimicked ancient Chinese writing.[4] The bodies of the old coolies are traces of a dehumanizing violation and misbranded racialization. In postcolonial Malaysia, they become symbolic texts of creolization absent from the sanitized history curriculum, voicing the longtime struggle to survive, adapt, and assert the place of settlement as the native homeland.

Ng Kim Chew's rewriting of the Nanyang as the "native land" (*guxiang*), which for descendants of Chinese settlers typically implies China (the ancestral land), also satirizes the diasporic consciousness and pursuit of "Chineseness" in Sinophone literature. Alienated by the political denial of their participation in defining "national culture," many Chinese Malaysians have sought communal belonging through expressing their ethnic difference or Chineseness. The suppression of Sinophone education in postcolonial Malaysia, compounded by the denial of Sinophone participation in its national literature, has prompted the "remigration" of many Sinophone authors, including Ng, to Taiwan for higher education and expanded access to publication. Despite the comfort of a majority Sinophone society touting its continental Chinese heritage, the experience of Taiwan—especially as the island undergoes a post–Cold War identity crisis—reroutes the trajectory of cultural discovery for these writers toward their "Malaysianness." Ng Kim Chew's "Back Inscriptions" alludes to this rerouting: the search for the origins of what appears to be an ancient Chinese writing practice only leads to a "language" beginning from a traumatic contact between Chinese settlers and Western colonizers in the South Seas. This literary return to the Nanyang destabilizes the hegemonic articulations of Chinese civilization and Malaysian indigeneity: the character for "land" or "village" (*xiang*), inscribed in blue ink on the coolie's back, is "written with too many strokes, so that it had become a blue blob." By obscuring "land," Ng Kim Chew undermines both the agrarian image of continental Chinese civilization and the idyllic motif of indigeneity (the Malay kampong) in Malaysia's national discourse. Many of the back inscriptions, including "mother" (*mu*), are graphic derivations of the character for "sea" (*hai*).[5] Evoking Malaysia's creolized history of maritime contact from a Taiwan grappling with its own "islandness," Ng Kim Chew reinscribes the sea as maternal womb. This process reflects the Nanyang's transnational signification in Sinophone Malaysian literature as an archipelagic trope linking postcolonial Malaysia and post–martial law Taiwan.

Whereas Sinophone Southeast Asian writers frequently appeal to other Sinophone literary centers—such as Taiwan and Hong Kong—for publication and recognition (requiring their familiarity with the Chinese literary canon), Southeast Asian authors educated in other languages who evoke the South Seas in transliteration and translation allude to the dominant literary discourse in their languages of composition. For Anglophone writers from Singapore, this entails not only engaging an Anglo-centric (predominantly British and American) literary world at large, but also an Anglophone history of Singapore that officially promotes "proper" English as a language of globalization and denies the localization of creoles like "Singlish." For Suchen Christine Lim, an author based in Singapore who studied abroad in Scotland and the United States, engaging Anglophone hegemony does not undermine the imagined cultural capital of the so-called Chinese motherland (as her reference to the "Nanyang Chinese" in the third passage above implies), only that she approaches this capital with different presuppositions about it.

In Lim's 1992 novel *Fistful of Colours*, the protagonist, an artist who migrated to Singapore from her Malaysian childhood home, expresses her resentment over the state's interpellation of her "Chinese" identity based on racial criteria. Hearing her university classmates from mainland China welcome her to visit the "motherland" as if she were "a married daughter coming back to visit her parents" reminds her of how Singaporean national discourse construes her every time she reads official slogans stipulating that to be "Chinese" is to speak Mandarin, not "dialects" (her first language is Cantonese). The artist regrets that Anglophone education has only reinforced this superficial racialization while disconnecting her from the culture of her Southeast Asian neighbors, teaching her "more about Henry VIII and his six wives than about Rama I of Thailand." Rather than acquiescing to demands to improve her Mandarin and learn "all about the Chinese emperors and philosophers," the protagonist prefers to locate her roots in the Nanyang, a region that she considers "more home to me than China." Lim's novel scorns the present "age of cultural lobotomy" in which Singaporeans blindly accept a narrow equation between race, culture, and language while forgetting the intercultural processes that shaped the island since British colonization.[6] Illustrating how postcolonial Singapore "haunts" the protagonist with her Chineseness,[7] Lim's Anglophone transliteration of the Nanyang bears the burden of racialization but also the potential for rearticulating "Singaporeanness" through regional, de-racialized cultural affiliations.

The Anglophone allusion to the Nanyang critiques affixing cultural expression to (often distant) ancestry over (local) history. Instead of racialization, the final non-Sinophone example—from a 1989 popular novel by Praphatson Sewikun entitled *Through the Pattern of the Dragon*—addresses Thailand's national narrative of Chinese integration. The narrator recounts the biography of her grandfather, a revered clan patriarch who leaves his Teochew home alone, penniless, and determined to create a better living in Siam circa 1927. Covering the turbulent second half of the twentieth century, this rags-to-riches tale of an industrious immigrant serves as a reminder to his privileged descendants to express gratitude for the prosperity they enjoy in their new homeland on the "golden peninsula" while honoring their virtuous heritage.[8] For a Thai readership, the novel asserts that the contributions of "merchant lords" were as critical to the development of the modern nation as those of kings, noblemen, and military and civic leaders. Written by an award-winning, part-Portuguese Thai author who does not claim Chinese ancestry, the novel encourages readers to imagine "Thainess" not as the successful assimilation of normative ethno-national standards, but as the flexibility and ingenuity of the nation's multiethnic population in creolizing those standards. Although the Anglophone Singaporean and Thai-language novels carry different tones (one a lament, the other a celebration), they both evoke the South Seas (in English transliteration as "Nanyang" and Thai translation as *thale tai*) to critique orthodox visions of national culture (racialization and assimilation). This reflects the Nanyang's translingual signification in Singaporean and Thai literature as a trope mediating between local Sinophone and non-Sinophone postcolonial contexts in Southeast Asia.

Like the Chinese sojourners and settlers in Southeast Asia themselves, the literary trope of the Nanyang crosses colonial, national, and linguistic borders to express cultural affiliation through the multiple trajectories of migration and creolization. Authors evoke the Nanyang to explore divergent migratory itineraries and relations to the dynamic environment of this tropical region. Implicating multiple readerships and discursive interlocutors, these authors endow the Nanyang with creative cultural, political, and ecological significance. With an archipelagic organizational principle, the Nanyang evolves from signifying a space of "southern barbarians" in the continental Chinese imagination to indicate a New World network of affiliation for settler communities (and their descendants) in postcolonial narratives on and from Southeast Asia. *Writing the South Seas* traces the transcolonial expression of the Nanyang in modern Chinese literature and explores its transnational and translingual articulations in postcolonial literature from Southeast Asia. Countering exclusionary and homogenizing stipulations of national culture, Chinese and Southeast Asian authors invoke the Nanyang to recognize national cultures born of settler-indigenous contacts and place-based political and ecological commitments. Their narratives "write back" to colonial and national authorities that repress or elide these creole histories under discourses of race, indigeneity, diaspora, assimilation, and even multiculturalism.[9]

ON NATIONAL CULTURE AND THE ARCHIPELAGIC IMAGINATION IN POSTCOLONIAL LITERATURE

Modern Chinese literary studies are increasingly committed to concepts of "Chinese literature"—such as "world literature in Chinese" or "global Chinese literature"—that divest the term "Chinese" of its limiting national and geographical connotations (as an adjectival China).[10] Apace with trends in comparative literature to critique "national literature" as an outmoded, politically tainted, artistically impoverished project,[11] these studies show how Chinese ethnic, linguistic, or regional/dialect affiliations transcend national boundaries of culture, language, and political citizenship to produce transnational or diasporic networks of literary production, circulation, and appraisal. It is primarily within this context that scholars writing in English have drawn upon Sinophone examples from Southeast Asia (usually Malaysia) to analyze how authors of Chinese descent form literary alliances (scales of "literary governance") that circumvent national ones,[12] redefine Chineseness by situating it between their local experiences and an imaginary homeland,[13] articulate cultural duality through a transnational circuit of Sinophone cultural and literary discourse between Shanghai, Hong Kong, Taipei, and Malaysia,[14] and creatively reimagine Sinophone writing from the "margins of the Chinese tradition" to unhinge it from a monolithic script politics.[15] Indebted to these critical contributions, *Writing the South Seas* does not prioritize a singular transnational framework for a Chinese or Sinophone literature organized around ethnic or linguistic criteria, but explores how the Nanyang as a literary trope moves between different national literary contexts to renegotiate the boundaries of (but not disavow) national literature as a meaningful postcolonial project. The Nanyang trope does *not* appeal to an ethno-linguistic Chineseness that supersedes the assimilatory or marginalizing force of the nation, but instead draws attention to the creolizing processes behind the formation of *multiple* national cultures: it is just as capable of expressing Malaysianness, Singaporeanness, and Thainess as it is Chineseness.

Locating the Nanyang at the historical confluence of multiple imperialisms, *Writing the South Seas* follows its postcolonial evolution as an archipelagic concept intervening in the discursive production of various national cultures and literatures. Emerging from their respective encounters with colonialism, several of these national literatures are typically conflated with an ethnicity or language constituting a national majority, yet this majority is not itself the nation. In this book, "modern Chinese literature" is the postimperial project of national literature in China whose boundaries are not coterminous with "literature in standard Chinese" or writings by individuals of Chinese descent. "Southeast Asian literature" denotes a regional moniker for a collection of national literatures from the member states of the Association of Southeast Asian Nations (ASEAN), which herein include Malaysian, Singaporean, and Thai examples.[16]

Certainly, one language or ethnic group may dominate in defining the terms, allocating the resources, and constructing the canons for its national literature, purporting to be *the* national language or *the* orthodox model of national culture. Emphasizing each nation as a modern response to or outgrowth of various colonialisms (semicolonialism, settler colonialism, continental and maritime imperialism), this study assumes no national literature is an exclusive or completed project and does not foreclose the possibility that multiple languages and differentially aligned collectivities (including disenfranchised ones) share a stake in the nation and its national literature. Open to contestation and renegotiation, national literature remains a horizon of possibility continually reshaped by the evolving interaction and particular admixture of the multiple languages (pidgins, creoles, dialects) and subcultures (indigenous, regional, colonial, settler, immigrant) that together constitute the national culture.

This definition harkens back to Frantz Fanon's 1959 decolonial exhortation to the Second Congress of Black Artists and Writers in Rome, "On National Culture." Fanon's definition of national culture as "the sum total" of a nation's "expression of its preferences, of its taboos and of its patterns," as well as "the result of internal and external extensions exerted over" it, recognizes that this "sum total" cannot stagnate as "custom," as this represents "the deterioration of culture."[17] Once the colonial power departs, a national culture confronts its residual knowledge structures still governing the nation both internally/psychologically (evidenced by the marginalization of populations by race, sex, gender, class, caste, language) and externally (evidenced by economic dependency on neocolonial capitalism). In the postcolonial context, the scope of national literature expands beyond the "revolutionary" canon that Fanon describes as the "body of efforts made by a people . . . to describe, justify and praise the action through which that people has created itself and keeps itself in existence."[18] Reflecting on national progress since independence, postcolonial authors may no longer sing the nation's praises but rather express disillusionment with its ossified customs. Postcolonial literature rethinks "national liberation" as an unfulfilled promise, reinvigorates national culture by imagining new bonds of strategic antihegemonic alliance (or reformulating elided ones), and revitalizes the national literature by forging new creative vistas with language, content, and form.

Fanon's formulation of national culture emerges from his own dissatisfaction with pan-African negritude as a viable response to Western imperialism. Fanon recognizes the need to dignify the subjectivity that the colonist did not disparage as "Angolan" or "Nigerian" but only as "Negro," yet cautions against the reactive impulse to identify one's struggle using the same racial idiom and geographic imagination imposed by the colonizer. For Fanon, to fight "on the field of the whole continent" and racialize claims by speaking "more of African culture than of national culture" leads African intellectuals "up a blind alley."[19] As a Francophone Caribbean intellectual from Martinique who became committed to the anticolonial struggle in Algeria, Fanon observed in his address to black audiences in postwar metropolitan Europe that the struggles uniting them also aligned them with liberation movements across the colonial world, and they should not contrive a primordial territorial or racial basis claiming to transcend their cultural diversity.

Like his Caribbean counterpart, the Anglophone Jamaican cultural critic Stuart Hall recognizes that the history of colonialism, in its "global and transcultural context," renders "ethnic absolutism an increasingly untenable cultural strategy."[20] Hall points to the underlying conditions that brought about an African diaspora: the "uprooting of slavery," transatlantic passage to the Americas and the Caribbean, and "insertion into the plantation economy" unified African peoples "across their differences, in the same moment as it cut them off from direct access to their past."[21] Though he critiques ethnic essentialism, Hall does not discount the imaginative capital of Africa as a necessary referent for Caribbean writers and artists in expressing their national cultures, calling it a "displaced 'homeward' journey" that is not an actual return but a fictional return to the Africa "of the Caribbean imaginary."[22] In this sense, the continental imagination of "Africanness" remains an important literary trope, yet it is given new articulation and signification across colonial, national, and linguistic boundaries in the Caribbean.

Western colonization of the Caribbean not only uprooted and transported African populations from the continent but also cut the various islanders off from each other: the displacement and extermination of indigenous seafaring populations resulted in a scattering of "balkanized" plantation societies across the archipelago. In *Caribbean Discourse* (*Le discours antillais*, 1981), Edouard Glissant, the late Francophone author and critic from Martinique, writes that colonialism in the Caribbean "divided into English, French, Dutch, Spanish territories a region where the majority of the population is African: making strangers out of people who are not."[23] Like Hall, Glissant acknowledges the importance of honoring the Caribbean's repressed African presence, but he warns against "reversion"—the ideal of continental return and "obsession with a single origin" negating histories of contact—and "diversion"—the ideal of French citizenship and "unfulfilled desire" for the West. For Glissant, reversion and diversion are insufficient cultural strategies that alienate transplanted colonial subjects from their environment and defer ambitions to "claim this new land for themselves." He suggests that the liberation of a national literature in French-controlled Martinique requires regional "reintegration" through a "painstaking survey of the land" and a "cultural self-discovery" of the island's "Caribbeanness" (*antillanité*).[24]

Inspired by Martinique's shared ecology and comparable colonial histories with other islands in the archipelago, as well as the Caribbean's hydrography as the "estuary" of the New World, Glissant defines this Caribbeanness as a "multiple series of relationships," with submarine roots, in which each island or nation "embodies openness." Caribbeanness is the "cross-cultural imagination" of the emergent national literature, one that embraces its continual becoming rather than essentializing its being. Against a "monolingual imperialism" of the West that defines national culture according to an ideology of "one people, one language" (a framework that reinforces the cultural segregation of the Caribbean's Francophone, Anglophone, Hispanophone, and Creole-speaking communities), Glissant's national literature is guided by a multilingualism embodying "the passionate desire to accept and understand our neighbor's language."[25]

In the decolonial forging of a viable national culture and literature (particularly for the "small countries" in whose future Glissant is invested),[26] reimagining and revitalizing regional networks and exchanges across the Caribbean (the archipelagic imagination) is just as necessary as retracing the region's African connections (the continental imagination). A similar imperative informs postcolonial literature from the Pacific Islands, where Western imperialism contrived disparaging racial genealogies for colonized cultures, stereotyping "brown islanders" as primitive, isolated castaways, cut off from time and civilization, whose ancestors arrived by "accidental" landfall. Confronting a continental US neocolonial discourse rendering the small and scattered Pacific Islands as economic dependencies, the Tongan/Fijian author Epeli Hau'ofa embraces the interdependency of Oceania as a "Sea of Islands" in which the sea enables, rather than impedes, mobility and agency: through a precolonial legacy of indigenous seafaring and defiant persistence of interisland exchange, "water ties" (routes) bind the region as much as "blood vessels" (roots).[27] Here, the archipelagic imagination enriches the national literature in "small countries" by overturning the perception of subordinate, dependent relationships and affirming symbiotic, interdependent ones.

In expressing national cultures, the archipelagic imagination conceptually differs from the continental imagination, prioritizing contact, exchange, heterogeneity, and creolization instead of racial, ethnic, or linguistic uniformity and singularity. Intervening in the continental projection of the nation as a "fortress and landmass" safeguarding internal homogeneity, the archipelagic consciousness imagines national "oneness" as a "fluid and open" network of "change and exchange" between lands connected (rather than isolated) by seas.[28] Postcolonial authors not only reenergize the archipelagic imagination of the national culture but also revive transcultural affinities that cross and transgress the boundaries imposed by colonial and national regimes in their regions.

As an archipelagic trope that Chinese and Southeast Asian authors deploy to rethink colonial and national paradigms that contrive their cultural genealogies, the Nanyang imagination speaks to these broader conversations in postcolonial criticism. To date, such criticism concentrates primarily on literature written in European languages (especially English and French) and on archipelagoes whose nomenclature (such as the Caribbean and Pacific Islands) is a legacy of Western imperialism. "Southeast Asia" is likewise the product of Western naming, but the term does little to inspire an analogous "archipelagic rethinking" of national culture and literature in the region, much of which is written in non-Western languages. This has generally left Southeast Asia and much of its literature (with the exception of Anglophone examples) beyond the purview of postcolonial critique, even though a multilingual, "multisited" close reading of Southeast Asian literary texts provides insights for postcolonial studies.[29]

Southeast Asia's instability as a regional concept and daunting diversity may ultimately prove useful as it prompts ongoing disciplinary self-reflection seldom seen in other area studies programs that take for granted their cultural and geographic cohesiveness. Somewhat like the Caribbean, Southeast Asia can, as John Bowen suggests, be reconceived as "a geographical and cultural openness, toward all the seas, distributing throughout the archipelago and the mainland a panoply of cultural forms," which for centuries have creolized and indigenized Indian, Chinese, Arabian, Persian, Portuguese, Spanish, Dutch, British, French, American, and Japanese influences. Shifting the perspective of Southeast Asia from its geopolitically defined, contiguous-and-asunder landmasses to the interconnected seas that flow through the region to touch the shores of each nation (except for the landlocked Laos) elasticizes its boundaries northward (the South China Sea), westward (the Indian Ocean), and eastward (the Pacific).[30] The "central body of water," which the islands and peninsulas of Southeast Asia "bracket and encircle," becomes its "focal, unifying element" and "common heritage."[31] Yet Southeast Asia is not an "Asian Mediterranean" (a single, land-encircled sea), but rather a chain of seas, straits, and gulfs—contoured by their island and peninsular coastlines—that flow eastward and westward, according to the seasonal monsoons, into the vaster Pacific and Indian Oceans.

Allowing for a tidal flexibility in Southeast Asia's boundaries encourages scholars to revisit archipelagic designations applied from within and beyond the region, such as the "East Indies." This invites comparison to other archipelagoes, such as the "West Indies," to potentially inspire novel analytical frameworks challenging assumptions that concepts emerging from the historical experience of one region, such as creolization, defy adaptation to the other.[32] This "nautical approach" also encourages analysis of regional designations in non-Western languages whose spatial imaginary, unlike Southeast Asia and the East Indies, predates (and is not contiguous with) colonial or national boundaries: these include Nusantara (Javanese: "Archipelago"), Suvarnadvipa (Sanskrit: "Golden Islands/Peninsulas"),[33] and Nanyang, as well as its Japanese counterpart, Nanyō.[34] These are archipelagic concepts that downplay terra firma, emphasizing the centrality of the seas in connecting cultures across the region. To call them "archipelagic networks" is not to suggest that they represent a scattering of small islands in a vast sea (as "archipelago" commonly connotes), but rather to invoke the Greek etymology of the term (literally meaning "chief sea") to underscore their defining feature of maritime interconnection and exchange. The archipelagic etymologies of Suvarnadvipa, Nanyō, and Nanyang prioritize particular interregional relations and exchanges in Southeast Asia—with India, Japan, and China—and their various commercial, military, or imperial motivations. Emerging from a continental, China-centric perspective, the Nanyang bears the legacies of such motivations, yet as a postcolonial literary trope, this archipelagic network has evolved to signify new relations that deviate from earlier connotations.

IMPERIAL ETYMOLOGIES OF THE NANYANG

Comprehensive Chinese dictionaries define the Nanyang as synonymous with Dongnan Ya (a literal translation of "Southeast Asia"), though the term appeared long before the Western moniker was adopted.[35] The idea of the Nanyang originated with imperial China's vision of a seascape off its southeastern coastline. For millennia, the Nanyang represented all that was anathema to an agrarian, sedentary civilization (Zhongyuan, the "Central Plains" of the Yellow River delta) prioritizing continental expansion and consolidation: as a maritime realm, the Nanyang lay "outside civilization" (*huawai*) and "beyond the four seas" (*sihai zhi wai*) that insulated the empire (Zhongguo, the "Middle Kingdom").[36]

Yet for South China's coastal populations, the Nanyang has long denoted an overseas *itinerary* of trade, travel, migration, and refuge seeking. Although the Nanyang posed little concern to the rulers and military generals of the Middle Kingdom, commercial port cities in southeastern China like Quanzhou thrived by welcoming traders and navigators from West, South, and Southeast Asia who arrived by way of the South Seas. As early as the Han dynasty

(206 BC–220 AD), Chinese merchants and sailors from Fujian and Guangdong "descended to the South Seas" (*xia Nanyang*) along the "Maritime Silk Road" to engage in trade (or to abscond from the law or flee calamity). Like their Southeast Asian counterparts, they stayed for extended periods according to the monsoonal winds, leaving behind traces of Chinese settlement. Not backed by imperial authority (and unable to appeal to it for military assistance), Chinese merchant ships were frequently vulnerable to plundering and looting by pirates in the region, leading to a common practice by the thirteenth century of keeping "one or two of the natives" from among their Southeast Asian trading partners onboard as hostages for the return journey.[37]

As China's rulers tried to assert their authority over maritime activity on the southeastern shores, the Nanyang was absorbed into an imperial "xenology," or "knowledge of the Other," which since antiquity had differentiated the uncivilized "barbarians" on China's territorial boundaries according to the four cardinal directions. Unlike the land-roaming nomads to the north and west, whose constant threat of invasion catalyzed the construction of a border defense, the category of the "southern barbarian" (*man*) designated many distinct communities that the empire divided into more docile groups that could be absorbed into Chinese civilization and more hostile yet subduable groups from whom tribute payments could be exacted.[38] These "southern kingdoms" (*nanguo*) on the continental frontier (at the intersection of what is now Guangxi, Yunnan, Vietnam, Laos, and Burma) were, beginning in the Han dynasty, the target of expansionist military campaigns of "pacification."[39] The desire to expand China's tribute system into the Nanyang introduced to the imperial cosmology another brand of "southern barbarian" (*fan*) whose kingdoms were subdivided into various rankings based on China's strategic maritime interests. In the early Ming dynasty, the rationale behind expanding the tribute system into the maritime realm by taking advantage of China's naval capabilities was to "show that no one was outside" (*shi wu wai*) its world order. Speculation about the intentions behind the Yongle emperor's (r. 1402–24) sponsorship of the seven oceangoing missions of the admiral and palace eunuch Zheng He ranges from the "enlightened" desire to peacefully showcase the grandeur of Chinese civilization and retrieve knowledge of the outside world to a more sinister desire for maritime "imperial expansion" following unsuccessful attempts at "land-based colonialism" in

Vietnam. Regardless, the overall effect was that many new Southeast Asian kingdoms entered into China's tributary system.[40]

The Zheng He voyages brought the Nanyang more squarely into the popular imagination of imperial China. Inspiring tales of exploration, adventure, and the fantastic, they were mythologized in much popular fiction, such as Luo Maodeng's three-volume novel, *The Voyages of the Three-Jeweled Palace Eunuch upon the Western Seas* (*Sanbao taijian xia Xiyang ji*, 1598).[41] Luo based his tale on travelogues from the expeditions, including Ma Huan's *Overall Survey of the Ocean's Shores* (*Yingya shenglan*, 1433), which surveys the political and military affairs of each locale Zheng He visited, listing exotic products offered as tribute to the Ming emperor. *Overall Survey* also comments on the Ming's strategic interventions in the affairs of maritime Southeast Asian kingdoms. Ma Huan contrasts the Muslims and the "Tang people" (Chinese settlers) in the South Seas with the "people of the land," who are depicted as having "very ugly and strange faces," going barefoot, and "devoted to devil-worship." He depicts the Siamese Kingdom of Ayutthaya as a volatile threat led by a warmongering king and full of "noisy and licentious" people, whereas he portrays the Sultanate of Malacca favorably, noting how the king and his people "all follow the Muslim religion."[42] Though Ma Huan, like his commander, was a Chinese Muslim (and Arabic and Persian translator), his espousal of Malacca over Siam suggests more than religious favoritism: Zheng He offered naval assistance to Malacca against Siamese invasion beginning in 1409, bringing the sultanate under "the imperial domain" as a special protectorate similar to that of a "tribute-paying province."[43] Stationed at arguably the world's most coveted seaway for commercial trade in the fifteenth century, Malacca was a strategic stop for Zheng He to solidify tributary relations.

Overall Survey occasionally forays into the realm of the fantastic: Ma Huan describes a dense jungle island near Java where an "old male monkey" lords over "thousands of long-tailed monkeys," receives gifts from the "childless women" of the village, and copulates with a female monkey in a "very remarkable" ceremony to bless the women with pregnancy.[44] Appropriating such "animal kingdom" exotica from the travelogue, popular fiction from imperial China conjures Nanyang adventures that test the bravado of Chinese strongmen. During the Qing dynasty (following Manchu conquest), when private overseas travel and emigration were prohibited, such tales projected loyalist desires onto the South Seas with nostalgia for virtuous, benevolent leadership. An early Qing sequel to a fourteenth-century classic of Chinese fiction, Chen Chen's *Water Margin: A Sequel* (*Shuihu houzhuan*, 1664) continues events alluded to in the original work: in chapter 119 of *The Water Margin* (*Shuihu zhuan*), Li Jun, one of the 108 rebels of Mount Liang, escapes from China, sails for foreign lands, and is alleged to have become lord of Siam. In the course of Li Jun's overseas ascension, he and his fleet subdue an enormous sea serpent, a despotic tyrant and "cave-dwelling barbarian" who abducts native children, and an evil minister who, fearing the Chinese rebels are a threat to Siam's sovereignty, enlists Japanese help to usurp power from the Siamese king.[45] This leads to Li Jun's enthronement as new king, whereupon his Siamese kingdom (inaccurately imagined as an island) becomes an "overseas" Mount Liang. As Ellen Widmer observes, the novel is an imperial fantasy in which "true heroes from the field and marsh" can set things right after "dynastic incompetence" and Manchu invasion "have set them wrong" in China.[46]

In this loyalist imagination, which not only longs to reassert "orthodox" Chinese rule over the empire but also to exert that authority overseas, the Nanyang obtains a preamble to its modern New World signification. Yet it is only with the post–Opium War downfall of the Chinese imperial order in Asia in the mid-nineteenth century—and its replacement with an industrialized Western one—that the Nanyang takes on its modern signification as a route of mass migration and network of exchange between China and Southeast Asia. Although Chinese emigration and colonial capitalism's penetration into Asia indelibly transformed the connotations of the Nanyang, the older worldview embedded in the trope did not entirely disappear: using a commonplace idiom, even impoverished migrants referred to their Nanyang journey as "travel overseas to [the land of the] southern barbarians" (*guo fan*). Western encroachment did not eradicate popular Chinese perceptions of Southeast Asia as an inferior domain.[47]

Historical transformations of the late Qing (c.1860–1911) give the Nanyang its second definition in standard Chinese dictionaries: through the early Republican period (c. 1911–30), Chinese administrations distinguished between Beiyang (the "North Seas," indicating the northeastern coastline of Liaoning, Hebei, and Shandong) and Nanyang, which indicated China's southeastern seaboard in Jiangsu, Zhejiang, Fujian, and Guangdong.[48] This less common definition highlights a key connotation of the Nanyang trope: the interconnectedness between the two areas referred to as the Nanyang (Southeast Asia and China's southeastern seaboard) during the peak years of Chinese emigration from the mid-nineteenth to the mid-twentieth century. As a maritime passageway, the Nanyang not only connected China and Southeast Asia but also served as gateway to the West: passenger steamship travel between China and the West required layovers in the South and Southeast Asian colonies, from British India, Burma, Malaya, and the Dutch East Indies to French Indochina and the Spanish/American Philippines. Here, the South Seas motif converges with Western imperialism: the implied China-centrism of the Nanyang, as a North-South demarcation between civilization and heathendom, confronts Western Orientalism (an East-West distinction) as knowledge production about the Asian Other to legitimize imperial domination.[49]

Traditionally demarcating a continental empire/civilization's maritime southern frontier, yet evolving to denote a route of migration and exchange between specific ports in China and Southeast Asia (such as Swatow and Bangkok) throughout the West's peak "age of empire,"[50] the Nanyang bears multiple imperial etymologies. Its postcolonial recuperation in Southeast Asia inherits but also deviates from these origins, particularly as it confronts local processes of nation building. With the mid-twentieth-century foundation of the People's Republic of China, the Cold War realignment of international relations, and the disruption of immediate contact with the ancestral homeland among Chinese settler communities, the Nanyang comes to signify divergent experiences of minoritization and assimilation across national borders in the region. By sustaining, establishing, or simply imagining new relations between islands (Borneo and Taiwan), capitals and port cities (Kuala Lumpur, Singapore, and Hong Kong), or regional centers (Hat Yai and Penang) that transcend national boundaries in the archipelago, the postcolonial Nanyang becomes an alternative network of affiliation to circumvent official national policies and dictates.

As an archipelagic trope of symbiotic, interdependent relations, the postcolonial Nanyang imagination defies demands for uniformity, homogeneity, and dependency based on racial, ethnic, or linguistic criteria. It provides an alternative to the continental imagination and cultural capital of China as ancestral homeland, a bounded Chineseness as its racial idiom, and standard Chinese as its monolingual expression. The cooptation of an "imagined China" by ethnocentrism and diasporic nationalism relegates creole communities to a perpetual positioning as "Overseas Chinese" (forever elsewhere) until the fulfillment of the diasporic homeward journey. By contrast, the archipelagic imagination of the Nanyang expresses the ongoing formation of multisited, multiethnic, and multilingual cultures. Within the four national literatures addressed herein, the Nanyang as archipelago remaps the prioritized itinerary and organizational principle of diaspora by historicizing and claiming place-based cultures of creolization.

SINOPHONE CREOLIZATION: TRANSCOLONIAL, TRANSNATIONAL, TRANSLINGUAL

A central concept in *Writing the South Seas*, creolization is not merely synonymous with hybridity, intermixture, and syncretism, but more broadly denotes a cultural process and practice informed by the multisited and multivalent historical expressions of the "creole" (including its checkered past). This connotation encompasses an early history of creolization in the Portuguese and Spanish colonization of Latin America and the Caribbean that foregrounded "adaptation and acclimatization" on the part of European colonists, even in the context of their violent subjugation and displacement of indigenous populations. The creoles (Portuguese: *crioulo*; Spanish: *criollo*) were the offspring of European settlers "born and raised in the New World"—distinct from Iberian-born *peninsulares* (Spanish) and *renóis* (Portuguese)—who reacted against metropolitan accusations of their physical and moral degeneracy, conditions supposedly resulting from "astral and climatic influences" and not necessarily intermarriage or "genetic mixing" with indigenous or non-Western populations.[51]

Addressing the significant role of "creole pioneers" in the prehistory of New World nationalism, Benedict Anderson in *Imagined Communities* applies the term to both Latin America, where settlers embraced creole identities, and North America, where Anglophone settlers never identified as creole but stressed localization as their cultural distinction (sometimes by appropriating tropes of indigenous cultures) in rebelling against the British. If early creolization (prior to the advent and spread of racialist doctrines in the nineteenth century) emphasized localization and downplayed miscegenation, it did not necessarily exclude the latter process, especially among early settlers who were overwhelmingly male. Anderson notes this ambiguity:

though the creole referred to "a person of (at least theoretically) pure European descent but born in the Americas," the "growth of creole communities, mainly in the Americas, but also in parts of Asia and Africa, led inevitably to the appearance of Eurasians, Eurafricans, as well as Euramericans, not as occasional curiosities but as visible social groups."[52] Anderson's observations have influenced Southeast Asianists who apply the term not only to Eurasians but also to communities tracing ancestry to "pioneer" male Chinese settlers (prior to the late nineteenth century) that married indigenous women, such as the Peranakans in Indonesia and the Baba-Nyonyas (Straits Chinese) of Malaysia and Singapore.[53] Downplaying the question of mixed ancestry, such groups define themselves more by their long-time localization.

Creolization's affinity with hybridity can be traced to the championing of *mestizaje* among creole nationalist movements in nineteenth-century Latin America, where creole "became compatible and overlapping with mestizo."[54] In this sense, creolization approximates *mestizaje* and *métissage*, described by Françoise Lionnet as a symbolic interweaving of cultural forms that "demystifies all essentialist glorification of unitary origins." Whereas *mestizaje/métissage* draws its inspiration from the historical presence of "distinct but unstable" racial categories blurring boundaries between colonizer and colonized like *mestizo* (Spanish) and *métis* (French),[55] creolization's primary historical analogy lies with linguistic transformations in the New World. In the Francophone Caribbean (where ethnic referents of the creole are more variable), "Creole" referred to local varieties of French spoken by slaves on colonial plantations. French colonists condemned Creole as "bad" French (incapable of conveying abstract thought and knowledge) and forbade students from speaking it in school. As a linguistic term applied more broadly (beyond the Francophone context), a creole denotes the next stage of code mixing in an emergent language after a pidgin or patois.[56]

Encompassing (but not limited to) histories of ethnic and linguistic mixing, creolization, according to Thomas Eriksen, refers to the "cultural phenomena that result from displacement and the ensuing social encounter and mutual influence between/among two or several groups, creating an ongoing dynamic interchange of symbols and practices."[57] The Cuban poet Nancy Morejón describes creolization as a "constant interaction, transmutation between two or more cultural components whose unconscious end is the creation of a third cultural whole—that is, culture—new and independent."[58] These definitions invite analogies to hybridity and multiculturalism, yet there are salient distinctions. By requiring the "pure" cultures of the colonizer and colonized to blend into a singular culture, hybridity "presumes the existence of its opposite for its conceptual force."[59] While both hybridity and multiculturalism describe interactions between distinct or separable cultures, hybridity supposes the production of a third, whereas multiculturalism—"predicated on homogeneity" or the "impermeability between different ethnicities and cultures"—assumes the components retain their distinctions in the process.[60] By contrast, creolization recognizes culture as an ongoing process that cannot be reduced to a singular outcome, offering neither a finished product (hybridity) nor a composite portrait of separate, immutable entities (multiculturalism).

As an aesthetic practice, creolization must reconcile with its emergence from brutal, traumatic contexts: like diaspora, it alludes to historical displacement or uprooting (whether by migration or colonization). Unlike diaspora, which evokes cultural collectivity through allusion to a presumably singular ancestry based on an original site of dislocation, creolization eschews primordial origins to recognize culture as an ongoing formation in the present.[61] As an unfinished process, it may mobilize positive changes that defy or transcend historical traumas: Supriya Nair writes that "the inevitably incomplete reconciliation and the lack of homogeneity between different elements is precisely what makes creolized cultures innovative, inventive, and unique." She also distinguishes between "hierarchical" and "lateral" creolization, with the latter referring to cultures emerging from intermingling between "various subordinate groups."[62] These lateral affiliations form the basis for Edouard Glissant's theory of Relation as the "conscious experience" of cross-cultural contact in which "all cultures are equal" and "each and every identity is extended through a relationship with the Other." For Glissant, creolization (as an "unceasing process of transformation" open to "infinite" variation) approximates Relation, and "the archipelagoes in the Caribbean and the Pacific" are its "natural illustration."[63]

As a postcolonial literary trope, the Nanyang is a natural illustration of creolization that reframes the *category* of the "Chinese diaspora" as a *network* of variable cultural relations in Southeast Asia: it connotes a shift from the impulse to "reversion" (continental return and obsession with Chineseness as singular origin) to highlight localization, adaptation, acclimation, and ethnic and linguistic interchange. Among the many creole communities lumped into the category of the "Overseas Chinese" are those whose Sinophone ethnic self-denotation is "Hua people" (Huaren). This term—and its historical difference from "Chinese people" (Zhongguoren)—is the legacy of diasporic Chinese nationalism in the early twentieth century, when settler communities in Southeast Asia became targets for sojourning Chinese intellectuals rallying support for China's national revolution. Their ethnic unification relied not only on an imposed monolingualism (standard Chinese/Mandarin) but also on internalizing the racialist ideology of Western colonizers who categorized settlers as belonging to a singular Chinese race, regardless of year of settlement, language spoken, or degree of creolization.[64] This history marks an important difference between the significations of "Chinese" (Zhongguo as the national idiom of China) and "Sinophone" (Hua as the creole idiom of the settler society).[65] Shu-mei Shih defines the Sinophone as "a network of places of cultural production outside China" or "everywhere immigrants from China have settled," where "a historical process of heterogenizing and localizing of continental Chinese culture has been taking place for several centuries."[66] The Nanyang specifically illustrates Sinophone creolization in its multisited and multigenerational formations in Southeast Asia. Local Sinophone expressions for the various cultural referents of "Hua" bear traces of these processes, such as Ma Hua (Chinese Malaysian), Xin Hua (Chinese Singaporean), Tai Hua (Sino-Thai), and Tusheng Huaren (Peranakan: literally "native-born Hua"), terms that prioritize trajectories of localization over presumed ethnic intermixture or single ancestry. As a literary trope, the Nanyang is not a singular "Chinese" motif, but one that traces archipelagic routes of Sinophone creolization, which "write back" to that idea of totality. Observing the Nanyang trope appropriated across colonial, national, and linguistic boundaries brings these creolizing processes to light: these are the transcolonial, transnational, and translingual contexts of literary articulation that compose the organizational chronology of this book.

Chapters 1 and 2 examine the transcolonial signification of the Nanyang in modern Chinese literature written by authors who traveled to colonial Southeast Asia in the first half of the twentieth century. The term "transcolonial" was coined by South Asian historians as an analytical framework to "decenter empire" by focusing on "the multiple networks of exchange that arose from the imperial experience, networks that connected colonies to one another . . . and stretched across the geographical and political boundaries that normally delimit such inquiries."[67] The transcolonial shifts the postcolonial's prioritization of a temporal rupture to a defining spatial movement "from the colony to elsewhere" or between colonies.[68] The first two chapters demonstrate how this physical movement can produce a transcolonial consciousness, a way of thinking across colonial or semicolonial spaces in Asia, imperial regimes, and modes of colonization that give rise to distinct anticolonial nationalisms. Arising after the postimperial founding of the Republic of China, the transcolonial consciousness in modern Chinese literature critiques certain presumptions about what China should be—a modern nation under a concept of (Han) majority-rule—and what it previously was—a feudalistic imperial state run by an aristocratic, minority (Manchu) elite—to comment on the intertwined ideals of enlightenment and nationalism defining the emergence of a national Chinese "New Literature."

Chapter 1 examines how the enlightenment aspiration of New Literature provides a new context for imagining the Nanyang. When "southbound authors" from China travel to (or through) colonial Southeast Asia in the early twentieth century and deploy "South Seas color" in fictional travelogue, they do so in a way that alludes to and critically diverges from the imperial Chinese worldview of the Nanyang and the "southern barbarian." Their firsthand impressions reveal a problematic intersection between the gendered China- and Western-centric stereotypes of the Other, producing a kind of "Nanyang Orientalism." Emphasizing itinerary and the traveler's subjectivity as opposed to destination, these narratives imagine the South Seas as a cultural "cross-waters" where one can glean from and syncretize the best of humanity's spiritual traditions to cope with otherwise crippling conditions of colonial modernity. This endows "South Seas color" with a discrepant cosmopolitanism that transcends the limited China-West-Japan view of the world commonly ascribed to New Literature's pursuit of enlightenment.

Chapter 2 analyzes how southbound authors imagine the Nanyang to interrogate the ideal of nationalism. Viewing China from the vantage point of Southeast Asia, rather than from the metropoles of Japan and the West, provides insights into the ethnocentric orthodoxy of modern Chinese nationalism. In the Southeast Asian colonies, diasporic ethnocentrism directs itself not only against the imperial power but also toward other colonized peoples, thereby reinforcing the West's divide-and-rule strategy. Southbound authors cannot simply write off such ethnocentrism as old-fashioned feudalism, since it expresses the same sentiments that inspired the diaspora to lend loyal support to the revolution that overthrew the Qing in 1911. These authors imagine the Nanyang to critique an ideologically interconnected Chinese ethno-nationalism in China and Southeast Asia, revealing its failure as anticolonial strategy in both contexts and calling for distinct national literary projects free from ethno-linguistic prejudice.

The foundation of the PRC and subsequent Cold War radically reconfigured geopolitical relations between China and the newly independent nations of Southeast Asia. With the consolidation of national boundaries and official impediments to crossing them, the intimacies of the once vibrant maritime network between mainland China and Southeast Asia dissolved. These dynamics transform the Nanyang as a literary trope, as Southeast Asian authors who grew up in the postcolonial era invoke the term to articulate alternative networks of cultural affiliation. While authors necessarily rethink Chineseness (just as Caribbean authors create an imagined Africa) as an ethno-linguistic signifier of diasporic cultures marginalized under (post)colonial policies in the region,[69] they also move beyond "reversion" by invoking the archipelagic imagination of the South Seas to affirm Malaysianness, Singaporeanness, and Thainess as creolized expressions of national cultures.

Chapters 3 and 4 examine how a new pattern of international migration from postcolonial Malaysia to Taiwan catalyzes the transnational rewriting of the Nanyang in Sinophone Malaysian literature. By the 1970s, Malaysia's implementation of nativist cultural, educational, and economic policies favoring Malays inspired disillusioned Chinese Malaysian students to seek higher education in Taiwan. Though many students initially imagined their journey as a return to Chinese cultural roots, they confronted Taiwan's evolving geopolitical status in the late 1970s, when the island republic's claim to the continental mainland was delegitimized and Taiwanese nativism arose. As writers, they came of age precisely as Taiwan began reexamining its own colonial history and national culture, balancing its dominant continental orientation with revitalized interest in the island's archipelagic heritage. In a post–martial law environment of cultural pluralism after 1987, Malaysian authors garnered the critical attention and acclaim of Taiwan's Sinophone literary establishment through their imaginative "return" to the South Seas.

Chapter 3 explores this return in the short fiction of a Malaysian author whose "Taiwan experience" compels him to reassess diasporic subjectivities, belatedly recuperating from postcolonial elision a creolized Malaysianness that informs his Sinophone modernist aesthetics. This creolization is not merely a reflection of longtime localization, intercultural appropriation, and multilingual code switching, but a metacognitive parody of the political conditions of colonial racialization, indigeneity, and interethnic friction that simultaneously shape and repress these processes. By satirizing episodes of incomplete cultural assimilation and religious conversion, these short stories make the Sinophone itself a "blasphemous" marker of a transgressive creolization that desecrates both the official boundaries of Malaysian multiculturalism and the presumed insurmountability of one's Chineseness.

Chapter 4 examines how the transnational context for imagining the Nanyang also inspires an "ecopoetic" mode of Sinophone modernism by authors whose narratives imaginatively return to Malaysia's marginalized island frontier, the Borneo rainforest. These authors invoke tropical biodiversity to cultivate a formal ecocritical poetics, giving the Borneo rainforest an umbilical, life- and language-giving subjectivity as "motherland" that disconnects Sinophone writing from its singular, patrilineal "descent" from the "ancestral homeland." The creative pilgrimage from metropolitan Taiwan to rustic Borneo traces an archipelagic network of affiliation between the two islands, reframing the dominant ethnic-oriented paradigms of national culture and literature in Malaysia and Taiwan.

Moving from a transnational context of imagining the Nanyang to one that emphasizes relations between two languages of literary production in a single nation, the final two chapters explore the translingual function of the South Seas trope between Sinophone and non-Sinophone fiction in postcolonial Southeast Asia. In literary studies, the "translingual" typically denotes an author who either publishes in more than one language or in a language that is not considered one's "mother tongue." Recognizing that "linguistic maternity" is often multiple, making it "difficult to determine precisely which is the mother tongue," Steven Kellman notes that the translingual also implies "a writer who resides between languages."[70] Though composed in a "primary" language, translingual texts highlight creolization by revealing "traces of their authors' other tongues."[71] Here, "translingual" not only refers to the author and a creolizing language practice (a feature of practically every text analyzed in this book), but to the trope of the South Seas itself as produced in different literary languages (translated or transliterated) that partake of the same national culture: it connotes the interactions between Sinitic and non-Sinitic languages of literary evocation, such as Mandarin and Malay, Hokkien and Singlish, Teochew and Thai.

In Singapore, as Chapter 5 demonstrates, the Nanyang trope engages a national policy of "multiracialism." As part of postcolonial Singapore's socially engineered self-makeover as a global financial hub, multiracialism attempts to sanitize, but not eliminate, cultural and linguistic diversity, giving it legible boundaries by discouraging interethnic creolization and eradicating intraethnic plurality. Responding to multiracialism's demands for the global legibility of one's cultural and linguistic expression based on dual proficiency in (and clear separation of) "proper" English and a racially designated "mother tongue," Sinophone and Anglophone Singaporean authors recuperate the Nanyang as a translocal, transethnic, and translingual referent to de-racialize the assigned boundaries and prescribed modes of cultural affiliation for Chinese Singaporeans.

In Thailand, as Chapter 6 argues, the South Seas imagination of both Sinophone and Thai-language popular novels reframes the historical tension between assimilation and biculturalism in the national "success story" of Chinese integration. The assimilation narrative suggests that by evading Western annexation, Thailand was able to assimilate upwardly mobile Chinese immigrants to indigenous cultural standards, ones that rigidified into national orthodoxy throughout the military dictatorships of the Cold War period. A post–Cold War environment of civic pluralism prompted revision to this assimilation narrative, insisting upon the historical persistence of Sino-Thai biculturalism. Examining the creolizing processes between Teochew and Thai signified by the South Seas trope in popular Sinophone and Thai-language narratives, Chapter 6 argues that this biculturalism is not the mutual embodiment of two distinct cultures but rather an ongoing process of creolization within and between two languages that together contribute to and produce Thainess.

Across its varied contexts of articulation, the Nanyang imagination reveals an imbricated Sinophone postcoloniality in Southeast Asia that confounds reductive articulations of national cultures based on dichotomous power structures of colonizer/colonized, native/settler, or center/periphery. Such complexity does not imply that efforts to imagine national origins and collectivities based on ethnic or linguistic criteria (especially from the traumas of colonization and dislocation) are fraught simply because they must inevitably encompass great heterogeneity and unequal distributions of expressive agency. While this study exposes the fraught formulations of *certain* origins and collectivities, it also recognizes and lends credence to less hierarchical ones. Despite the expanse (but not exhaustion) of literary terrain covered, the selected texts convey strategic affiliations that expose the hierarchies, elisions, and reductionist caricatures of the status quo. In its transcolonial, transnational, and translingual signification, the Nanyang imagination retraces histories of migration, settlement, and creolization to articulate an archipelagic vision of national literature and culture as open and interdependent.

CHAPTER 1

Modern Chinese Impressions of the South Seas Other

By most historical accounts, modern Chinese literature was born of the New Literature movement, one of the broadly based, often iconoclastic cultural transformations that began within the decade following China's 1911 national revolution and continued through the 1920s.[1] Collectively known as the New Culture movement, these transformations were catalyzed by the 1919 May Fourth movement, a massive student demonstration in Beijing both against the West (namely the victorious Allied nations following World War I) for having ceded the former German possessions in Shandong province to the Japanese at the Paris Peace Conference that year (instead of returning them to China) and against the provisional government of the Republic of China whose envoy to the conference complied with the terms of the treaty.[2] Citing the dual failure of the 1911 revolution to impede the aggressive encroachment of Western imperialism (dating back to the mid-nineteenth century) and to emancipate the new Chinese citizenry from subservience to feudalistic authority, the May Fourth movement called for an inward critical reevaluation of Chinese culture through an outward-oriented quest for "enlightenment."[3]

Regardless of how they approached the classical canon of Chinese literature, and irrespective of their internal diversity, the major writers of New Literature shared a common trait: they actively sought creative inspiration in a literary universe whose cultural, linguistic, and geographic boundaries transcended that canon. Their interest in different intellectual, aesthetic, and literary trends beyond China inspired them to not only consume imported texts and translations from abroad, but compelled many of them to physically venture beyond China in search of this knowledge and to then "translate the world" for readers back home. For many, the experience of living and traveling abroad itself motivated them to become writers. Against the bleak outlook of a newly established Chinese republic ravaged by internal and external conflicts, New Literature confronts (and reproduces) a "colonial modernity" simultaneously oppressive and emancipatory: while paving the way for humanist liberation from the bondage of "feudal" traditions, this modernity also exposes the dehumanizing material conditions of global industrial capitalism.[4] Tempered by a sobering cynicism regarding these conditions, the sojourns of May Fourth authors and their creative works beyond China—as well as their selective discovery and appropriation of the "foreign"—produce an idealized dream of modernity as cultural enlightenment.

As a principal impulse of New Literature, the quest for enlightenment and humanistic emancipation transformed the South Seas as a Chinese literary trope. From a primitive, feminized, and fantastical realm of "southern barbarians" in the patriarchal worldview of imperial China, the Nanyang now came to symbolize the simultaneously binding and liberating conditions of colonial modernity that inspired the overseas voyages and outward orientations of modern Chinese authors. Many of these authors traveled to (and through) colonial Southeast Asia: whether a long-term destination or a short stopover to points elsewhere, the Nanyang left enough of an impression to be worthy of creative composition. These travel narratives are New Literature's works of "South Seas color" (*Nanyang secai*). Though literary histories might remember them otherwise, canonical authors such as Xu Zhimo, Xu Dishan, Lao She, and Yu Dafu were all at one point "southbound writers" (*nanlai zuojia*; literally "writers who came south").

Not to be written off as New Literature's detour into exoticism, the impressionistic South Seas color in the short fiction of Xu Zhimo and Xu Dishan is integral to modern Chinese literary enlightenment. It suggests a broader conception of and inquiry into "the world" than typically attributed to the New Culture movement. South Seas color encompasses exchanges with, and sometimes misreadings of, manifold "others" who inhabit or navigate the cultural cross-waters among East, South, Southeast Asian, and Western experiences of colonial modernity. As narrative content, South Seas color denotes both an object of representation—typically a colonial Southeast

Asian environment and South or Southeast Asian peoples—and a subjectivity of expression: the modern Chinese transoceanic traveler. The interaction between the traveler and his (as the authors, narrators, and protagonists are mostly male) object of representation (often female) produces local impressions—flavors, textures, colors, and sensations—that, although superficial, fleeting, and sometimes "indescribable," prompt serious reflection and self-examination. As narrative form, South Seas color implies a travelogue style, even in the genre of short fiction. In the short stories of Xu Zhimo and Xu Dishan, the Nanyang is an itinerary as much as a destination of travel. This itinerary is noncanonical: it produces a brand of cosmopolitanism through historically overlooked axes of cultural comparison. This "discrepant cosmopolitanism" is shaped as much by the transcolonial network between China and Southeast Asia as it is the canonical blend of Chinese, Western, and Japanese elements attributed to the global paradigm of Chinese literary modernity.

NEW LITERARY ENLIGHTENMENT: BEYOND THE CHINA-WEST-JAPAN PARADIGM

New Literature is informed by two intertwined goals of the May Fourth movement: "national salvation" (*jiuguo*) and "enlightenment" (*qimeng*). The enlightenment ideal is rooted in the failure of the 1911 revolution (which overthrew the Qing dynasty and inaugurated a republic under the Nationalist Party, or KMT) to eradicate what the May Fourth activists perceived as "outworn cultural values." They recognized that national salvation could not depend on political revolution alone but required "a commitment to *jiuren*, the salvation of mankind," a kind of "critical-minded humanism."[5] May Fourth intellectuals saw "traditional culture" as the primary obstacle to a "modern orientation." This traditional culture not only included popular folk superstitions (of which Chinese elites had long been wary), but also the values of the classically educated Confucian scholar class from which most of these intellectuals came.[6] Enlightenment necessitated an iconoclastic rebellion against one's own heritage to liberate younger generations from Confucianism's "entrenched habits of self-repression" and its "ethic of subservience to patriarchal authority" as dictated by elite familial and educational structures.[7]

To "save" China, therefore, was to "integrate her into the modern world" by freeing her from a "cosmic anomaly of immobility and stagnation."[8] This mission represented what C. T. Hsia famously referred to as modern Chinese literature's "obsession with China" and its "moral burden."[9] What began as a political demonstration on May Fourth against the governments who orchestrated and agreed to the 1919 Treaty of Versailles blossomed into an expansive, energetic exploration and importation of "new thought" (*xin sixiang*) from a global array of sources, resulting in the emergence of diverse (and sometimes opposed) ideologies and literary camps. Though the authors of New Literature varied greatly, there is general consensus about their overall literary ambitions: defeating foreign imperial aggression could not begin from a revalorization of "the native past," but rather from the exposure and eradication of the "feudal tradition" that made China particularly vulnerable to external exploitation.[10]

To this end, New Literature relied on establishing a clear, inviolable temporal and geospatial dichotomy: a temporal rupture between an enlightened modernity and a crippled tradition, and a geospatial demarcation of the boundaries between "us," the Chinese nation (as a single territory and people) and "them," the foreigners (predominantly Western and Japanese aggressors). New Literature's prescribed content is deceptively simplistic, merely requiring the "realistic" depiction of the nation's victimization at the hands of foreign imperialism and native feudalism. Mainland Chinese historians further delimit the scope of New Literature as a Marxian project of class struggle. Though writers explored a vast array of subjects such as "peasants, women and intellectuals, as well as the urban problems of alienation and isolation," these themes get absorbed under the rubric of class-based oppression.[11] May Fourth activists distinguished their movement from previous political, cultural, and literary reforms through their articulation of and appeal to "the masses."[12] As opposed to the esoteric scholarly essay or the serialized sensational popular novel, authors of New Literature advocated fictional realism in an often figurative, allegorical, short-story mode adapted from Western literary trends: by distilling a complex, contemporary social crisis into a single anecdote, short fiction could poignantly agitate readers with a modern sense of immediacy. While fictional realism ranged from the subjective reality of the individual (provided by the often unreliable perspective of a first-person narrator) to an omniscient one, it was ultimately supposed to awaken readers to broader social truths.[13]

Adopting fictional realism and targeting the masses meant eschewing the classical literary script (*wenyan wen*)—the common written medium of the scholar-elite—to capture the vernaculars of the "nation's people" (*guomin*), particularly when rendering spoken dialogue. The impulse toward vernacular realism was actually one toward linguistic plurality—not unification—that shattered rather than consolidated the collective ideal of a "common script" (*tongwen*) among the Sinitic languages. Yet the vernacular movement (*baihua yundong*) intended to foster a unified—not pluralized—notion of national culture. The institutionalization of "standard Chinese" as a common vernacular script—literally "pure speech writing" (*baihua wen*)—was based on conformity to a monolingual standard: the grammatical patterns and vocabulary of spoken Mandarin and its northern Chinese variants. The vernacular movement naturalized the perception that standard Chinese reflected the social reality of a nationwide readership. As the "National Language" (Guoyu), it was imagined as the "Common Speech" (Putonghua) of the masses. As the medium of New Literature, standard Chinese was more the creation of a new social reality than it was its reflection.

Of course, the formal experimentation of New Literature was not a mere exercise in propagating a standard vernacular. Exposing an overemphasis on the vernacular script as modern Chinese literature's primary revolution in form and as its foundational "technology," scholars have revealed other novel tools and technologies heralding its arrival. These include the advent of visual media such as film and photography.[14] Modern Chinese literary histories characterize May Fourth writers as the pioneers of new forms who experimented with novel "tools" and "absorbed all the main trends in Western culture—romanticism, realism, naturalism, and symbolism."[15] These writers were well versed in Western literature, whether in its original languages or in Chinese or Japanese translation. Beyond that, they also spent at least some portion of their young adulthood studying abroad or sojourning in places such as Japan, Europe, and North America. The Western and/or Japanese education these authors received was a major contributor to the enlightenment ideal of May Fourth discourse: they saw experimentation with Western literary forms (sometimes patterned after similar Japanese experimentations) as necessary for Chinese literary, intellectual, and spiritual development.[16]

Given the scholarly emphasis on the lengthy periods that many canonical writers of New Literature spent studying, working, or traveling abroad in the West and Japan, advancements in steam-engine technology that revolutionized transoceanic travel in the late-nineteenth century should likewise be recognized as another profound technological influence on Chinese literary modernity, for these steamships made possible the writers' distant sojourns and returns.[17] Although travels to Japan and Western countries were no doubt integral to the creative impulses of Chinese literary modernity, these sites were not the only travel destinations of significance. Yet modern Chinese literary histories are generally bound by a tripartite China-West-Japan paradigm that masquerades as "the world."[18] This paradigm precludes broader readings of modern Chinese literary enlightenment and nationalism: namely, it pins these ideals to the deceptively clear-cut spatio-temporal dichotomies between a native feudalism and a foreign imperialism while reducing them to a literary blend of "Western form" and "Chinese content."

The China-West-Japan paradigm of New Literature fails to capture its truly global character, mainly by suppressing its transcolonial dimension. Consider the following story, which follows a fairly conventional May Fourth plot line: a young man aspires to receive a modern, Western education, but his more traditional father opposes, particularly because the Western imperial powers have disgraced his country. The young man falls in love with a childhood friend, but his father opposes the match because the couple's horoscopes do not align. The young pair allegedly commits suicide by drowning themselves in a lake—their ultimate tragedy drawing attention to the larger social forces (feudalism and imperialism) that control their fate. This is the plot to "Birds of a Feather" ("Mingming niao"; literally "birds of the same fate"), a short story first published in China's *Literary Monthly (Xiaoshuo yuebao)* in January 1921. The author, Xu Dishan, is one of New Literature's foundational authors. The plot in which two young people navigate a broadening sphere of progressive ideas and cultural influences, but are thwarted by their parents' adherence to feudalistic superstition, is actually the story's least fascinating and most clichéd feature. Rather, the appeal of "Birds of a Feather" is that it is considered New Literature's first work with a truly "exotic tone" (*yiyu qingdiao*).[19] The story takes place entirely outside China and none of the characters are Chinese.[20] Instead, they are Burmese, and the story is set in Rangoon.

Xu Dishan wrote the imaginative "Birds of a Feather" from personal experience: from 1913–15, he lived in Rangoon as a Chinese-language instructor at a local middle school. In the story, Xu frequently refers to Burmese sites and historical events from the British colonial era. For example, Jialing's father harbors long-standing resentments over the British construction of a military post on the grounds of the holy Shwedagon Pagoda in 1852. This outrage morally justifies his irate opposition to his son's desire to attend an Anglophone school established by Christian missionaries. After debating the matter, Jialing and his father reach a compromise, agreeing that he will attend the Rangoon School of Advanced Studies, since the institution apparently strives harder to "preserve Burmese customs."[21] Through the colonial Burmese setting (rather than the imperial centers of Japan or the West) and Burmese characters (non-Chinese subjectivities), Xu Dishan's discrepant overseas route of "enlightenment" challenges the "obsession with China" that permeates the origins of a Chinese literary modernity constituted from a China-West-Japan global paradigm.

Although he was the first author of New Literature to compose a work of "exoticism" on colonial Southeast Asia that reflected his travel biography and cultural interests, Xu Dishan was by no means an anomaly. Most of the authors who embarked on transoceanic voyages to Europe and North America passed through Southeast Asia on their way to study in the West. Travelers aboard steamships bound for England often made stops in the British colonial ports of Singapore, Penang, and Rangoon. Sojourners to France stopped over in the French colonial port of Saigon. Ships bound for the United States might temporarily dock in the American colonial port of Manila. For some writers, these cities were not stopovers but destinations: until the founding of the PRC in 1949, the southbound writer from China was a fixture in Southeast Asia, predominantly in the port cities of colonial Malaya (especially Penang and Singapore), but also in Burma (Rangoon), Siam (Bangkok), the East Indies (urban centers on Java and Sumatra), and Indochina (mainly Saigon). Regardless of the duration of their stay, most of these writers eventually returned to China. Yet the legacy of South Seas color in modern Chinese literary history should not be disregarded as a passing fancy. These authors' impressions of the Nanyang reconcile not only with China's traditional perceptions of the feminized "otherness" of the South but also with their introduction to Western Orientalism's gendered projection of the otherness of the East. This intersection of Chinese and Western knowledge of the Other—as a "Nanyang Orientalism"—surfaces in the representation of the "difference" embodied by Southeast Asian cultures and peoples, complicating the enlightenment of the modern Chinese (male) subjectivity.

NANYANG ORIENTALISM

Traveling by ship to and through Southeast Asia exposed the southbound writers to the modes by which Western imperial regimes classified and administered subject populations in racialized ways reflecting European knowledge production about the Orient. Versed in various Western literary trends and styles, many southbound writers, when they arrived in Southeast Asia, were already quite familiar with the modern West's imagination and projection of Asia within its own worldview. New Literature internalizes this othering worldview and transforms it into self-perception, accepting China's place in the continental construct of "Asia" (Yazhou) and Asia's place in a modern "world" (*shijie*) defined and ordered by the West with its stark civilizational dichotomies between "oriental" (*dongfang*) and "occidental" (*xifang*).[22]

The southbound writers were also well versed in Chinese literary traditions, from which they inherited a premodern Chinese ideology placing the "Middle Kingdom" (Zhongguo) at the heart of the civilized world (*tianxia*). The imperial Chinese worldview relegated various Southeast Asian populations to the status of "southern barbarians" (*fan*) who existed "beyond the realm of civilization" (*huawai*). Its North-South structure of reference shares some of the East-West civilizational dichotomies that Edward Said describes in *Orientalism*: the Western concept of the Orient and the imperial Chinese concept of the Nanyang both constitute a mode of retrieving and producing knowledge about, while ordering and exerting authority over, a primitive, exotic, and feminized civilizational Other.[23]

The Nanyang imagination of popular fiction from the Qing dynasty before its mid-nineteenth-century decline (which marked the decline of the imperial Chinese world order) propagates the tribute system while exaggerating the exotic and erotic qualities of Southeast Asians to legitimize their inferiority and subjugation. Several of the popular novels are sequels to classic Chinese novels, such as Cao Xueqin's eighteenth-century masterpiece, *Dream of the Red Chamber* (*Honglou meng*). *Revisiting the Silken Chambers* (*Qilou chongmeng*; composed 1797–1805 by the "Master of Langao") illustrates an imperial Chinese fantasy of the Nanyang, extending the sensual reverie of *Dream of the Red Chamber* into an absurdly pornographic realm. Although Cao Xueqin's original work indulges in the household affairs of an aristocratic Manchu estate in Beijing, a steady influx of exotic tributary gifts—many from Southeast Asian kingdoms—illustrates how officialdom and foreign diplomacy both nourish and contaminate this domestic enclosure.[24] The sequel takes the importation of exotic tribute items one step further: the Qing emperor invites Southeast Asians themselves to the court and the Jia household for "closer inspection" by the story's protagonist, Xiaoyu, who is not only the son of Jia Baoyu, the protagonist of the original work, but also his spirit reincarnate. Xiaoyu is determined to defend the strength of the Qing empire when a female warrior from Annam comes to Beijing as part of a tribute mission. Like the exotic tribute that accompanies her—including orangutans, baboons, and python gallbladders—the warrior appears as another item on the list in her resemblance to "an orangutan or a baboon." She challenges China's top fighters and disposes several Qing military strongmen, but the young Xiaoyu vanquishes her by exposing her "tender spot"—that is, her vagina. After the "friendly" battle, Xiaoyu invites the Annamese warrior to a banquet at the Jia estate, where she attempts to seduce him. Xiaoyu resists and again strips her naked, whereupon he ultimately humiliates her by inserting a plum in her vagina. The family then discovers the warrior's uncanny ability to shoot projectiles from her genitalia, a spectacle that makes all of the demure, "properly trained" Manchu women of the Jia household blush uncontrollably.[25]

Although the pornographic *Silken Chambers* spoofs "more high-minded sequels,"[26] its reference to the hypersexualized "southern barbarian" female warrior draws upon patriarchal Chinese anxieties over matrilineal social patterns among Southeast Asian neighbors, feeding the imagination of a mythological, Amazonian "kingdom of women" (*nüguo*).[27] The female warrior alludes to imperial China's historical project of "pacifying the South," which is the meaning of "Annam" (Annan, a name given to the area by imperial China), by invoking the rebellion of the Trưng sisters, who took control of areas in Annam and southern Guangdong during the Western Han dynasty. Despite leading armies against Chinese invasion, the Han military captured and executed the sisters by decapitation.[28] *Revisiting the Silken Chambers* recalls the Trưng sisters to confirm that Annam has always been "a capricious, barbaric and roguish place" on China's southern border,[29] whereas Vietnam has historically valorized and commemorated the sisters for their "matriarchal rebellion against China."[30] Stereotypes of female sexual deviancy and anecdotes of subduing matriarchal resistance affirm Confucian patriarchal orthodoxy while reinforcing tributary patronage, or in some cases direct imperial authority over, these less-than-human "southern barbarians."

The legacy of imperial Chinese perceptions of Southeast Asians as an exotic, primitive, feminized, and hypersexualized Other informed and inflected the modern rewriting of the South Seas in twentieth-century New Literature. This is evident in the southbound writers' impressions of differences in the cultural and sexual mores among Southeast Asian communities. The modern era in which the southbound authors traveled, however, presented a vastly reconfigured matrix of global powers: no longer was China able to vie for political and military supremacy in Southeast Asia. Since the end of the first Opium War in the mid-nineteenth century, inaugurating what the PRC would later officially dub as "a hundred years of national humiliation," China's relationship to the Nanyang was based on massive emigration to the region under conditions of famine, war, poverty, foreign incursion, and political instability in southeastern China, coupled with the Western imperial conquest of Southeast Asia. In this context, southbound writers were not simply tourists to the region indulging in fanciful imaginings about "southern barbarians" whom they longed to subjugate. Instead, they were students, intellectuals, and professionals that traveled to or through Southeast Asia on the heels of mass emigration and the Western imperial reordering of the globe.

In New Literature, South Seas color blends the genres of travelogue and fiction to reflect upon and critique the traveler's own subjectivity and values. As the intersection of Western- and China-centric modes of observing Southeast Asian "others," Nanyang Orientalism exposes the biases of the traveling subject. Rather than reaffirm Chinese patriarchy and cultural mores, the southbound writer's Nanyang Orientalism critiques the social constrictiveness of the dominant cultural codes in China. Yet this critique does not necessarily serve to espouse—or even correct perceptions of—the supposedly uninhibited "nature" of the female Southeast Asian Other, but instead reinforces the West's Orientalist gaze as a liberated and enlightened aesthetic.

This is particularly evident in the lone work of South Seas color by Xu Zhimo (1897–1931), in which the author's initiation into and aesthetic cultivation of the modern Orientalist gaze truly colors his perceptions of the female Southeast Asian Other. Xu Zhimo's short story is based on his brief stopover in Singapore during a return trip from Europe to China in 1928. Xu Zhimo only spent several days in transit, yet his literary interest in the South Seas was based on the assumption that the tropics were the last preserve of "primitive lust" (*yuanshi qingyu*), a sensation that permeates his story.[31] Xu derives his perception of "primitive lust" both from his education in European art and literature and from his elite Chinese background. A native of Zhejiang province (the incubator of generations of literati), Xu studied at Columbia and Cambridge, where he cultivated a poetic voice that transformed him into one of modern China's foremost poets.[32] Though canonized for his poetry, Xu also dabbled in fiction but belittled the outcome. His modernist style of fiction evokes the 1930s Shanghai New Sensationists (Xin Ganjue Pai), namely Shi Zhecun, Mu Shiying, and Liu Na'ou. Like those authors, Xu Zhimo plays with form, using a stream-of-consciousness style to capture the sensations of the modern city and the neuroses of the urban male subject, particularly in his treatment of heterosexual desire.

In Xu Zhimo's small collection of fiction, Singapore is but one site in a quartet of experimental short stories about four major cities of the world. His Singaporean narrative contributes to modern Chinese literature a novel adjective to describe a tropical sensation: "insolubly rich" (*nong de huabukai*).[33] Xu noted the multisensory ubiquity of richness in the tropics—from the brightness of its abundant greenery to the heavy dampness of its humid air to the fullness of its floral fragrances—that stuck to one like "tree resin."[34] This equatorial richness was "insoluble"—it would not dissolve or dissipate with changing weather patterns or the turning of the seasons, as there were no "seasons" to speak of here. Instead of resorting to a northerner's cliché—such as "eternal summer"—to describe a climate that does not experience the distinction of a "summer," Xu Zhimo's invention of "insolubly rich" reflects the experimental, open, and observant consciousness that the author cultivated in composing his narrative.

"Insolubly Rich (Singapore)" ("Nong de huabukai [Xingjiapo]," 1928) is the second in a quartet of short stories chronicling the travels of the protagonist, Lin Lianfeng. In addition to tracing the itinerary Xu Zhimo traveled in 1928, each story, as its title suggests, describes the sensation of a particular city: "A Seduction of the Flesh in Paris" ("Rouyan de Bali"); "Insolubly Rich (Singapore)"; "Insolubly Rich, Part ii (Hong Kong)" ("Nong de huabukai zhi er [Xianggang]");[35] and "Dead City (A Night in Beijing)" ("Sicheng [Beiping de yiwan]").[36] "A Seduction of the Flesh" depicts Lin Lianfeng's visit to a French bohemian painter's studio on a Paris rooftop. Lianfeng and the painter discuss how to capture the aesthetic beauty of the female form. Bashfully viewing the impressionist paintings of a multiethnic cast of voluptuous nude models on the studio walls, and incredulous that the impoverished artist has actually lured all these women here, Lianfeng learns of the artist's affliction: a "hunger of the eye." Lianfeng laments to the artist about his strict and prudish Confucian upbringing in China, where he never learned to fully appreciate the beauty and allure of the female physique. Yet the images produced by the Parisian artist's "hungry" gaze have sufficiently aroused Lianfeng's scopophilia.[37]

The narrative movement from France to colonial Singapore is similar to a physical penetration of one the "exotic" paintings in the Parisian studio: what started as visual desire here travels to the other senses of the male body and becomes all-consuming. Lianfeng experiences tropical sensations and gazes upon the Southeast Asian Other only after his initiation into Western modes of looking at and craving the female body. From his hotel room, Lianfeng watches a tropical rainstorm and becomes restless. He tries to capture his sensations in a poem, but he finds the available vocabulary in his vernacular repertoire insufficient to describe the tropical setting. His thoughts continually interject in the process of poetic composition:

> The downpour hits the banana trees like a clanging on a bronze dish. Strange—the "red-heart banana"—what beautiful words. So richly red. Perfect. It should be red, and it should be hot. It should be intense, and it must be rich, insolubly rich . . . rich like tree resin. "My heart is like that of a banana, red. . . ." No, that won't do. "It folds up tightly, my rich red banana heart . . ." That's even worse. I'd better stop writing such poetry before it gets too late.[38]

Lianfeng cannot absorb the "insoluble" tropical colors, scents, and textures into the poetic repertoire or signifiers at his disposal. Wanting to convey the reality of his subjective experience, his mind instinctively intrudes upon and rebuffs his attempts to bend syntax. Language breaks down, or is deformed, by his physical sensations and his surroundings, and it is on this level that Xu Zhimo initiates his tropical modernism.

Like works of Shanghai New Sensationism, "Insolubly Rich (Singapore)" is a subjective treatment of the modern city. Trying to escape the claustrophobic humidity of his hotel room and dissolve the richness of the sensations he feels, Lianfeng takes a nighttime taxi ride. He gazes upon Singapore at night, capturing the city in a montage of fragmented and fleeting images:

> Quickly, quickly, the giant, ghostly palm of the banana tree, the high coiffure of the coconut tree, the white protruding eye of the rubber tree, the big, furry leg of the palm tree. . . . Quickly, quickly, Malay pergolas, Chinese clay pots and lanterns, Western milk bottles, Muslim caps . . .[39]

In cinematic fashion, the proportions of these fragments get jumbled with respect to their proximity to the viewing eye. In this South Seas brand of urban modernism, the moving gaze does not juxtapose the fragmentary images of colonial multiculturalism with the modern city's magnificent skyscrapers and radiantly lit nightclubs (as Shanghai New Sensationism does),[40] but rather with nature imagery on the tropical island. Whereas Shanghai New Sensationism generally correlates the desire for the novel mechanical spectacles of the semicolonial cosmopolis to a parceled desire for the urban female body, Xu Zhimo's story eroticizes the "greater richness, greater savageness, and greater licentiousness" of primitive femininity in the colonial tropics.[41] Thus begins Lianfeng's erotic fantasy of departure from "civilization."

Unable to cool off in a bayside pavilion that he discovers already occupied by a pair of young lovers, Lianfeng returns insatiate to the dark security of his hotel room, where he is overcome with a sensation he likens to one evoked by gazing upon a Matisse painting, or the taste of "Nestle's chocolate saturated with cream." Lianfeng then attempts to satiate his lust by concocting his "dark" Nanyang fantasy: a sexual tryst with a Malay "chocolate girl" (*zhugulü guniang*) who sidles to the edge of his bed. He soon discovers she is not a beautiful woman who has come to seduce him, but rather a ferocious "Malayan tiger" that seeks to devour him. What began as tropical lust transforms into a horrid nightmare, and Lianfeng wakes up in a frightened sweat to find he has squeezed his "Dutch wife," or pillow, into a "little gourd."[42]

This exploration of primal sexuality demonstrates the ambivalent binaries of Nanyang Orientalism—the desire and horror, beauty and repulsion of the "darkness" perceived by the aesthetically "enlightened" gaze of the West (feminizing and dominating the East) and the aesthetically "repressed/repressive" gaze of China (feminizing and dominating the South). Here, these repressed primal desires are worthy of the curious artist's observation, experimentation, and description, but not total satiation (they are, after all, "insoluble"), because they constitute a dangerous "heart of darkness" in which the modern Chinese male subject might lose himself (his body and language) entirely.

Xu Zhimo's Nanyang Orientalism expresses a desire to shift the aesthetic lens through which his protagonist experiences the tropics and gazes at Southeast Asians from the repressed/repressive China-centered one to a presumably enlightened West-centered one. Yet Lin Lianfeng lacks the authority to make that shift possible, as both lenses occupy a position of superiority and dominance over observed "others" and their milieu. He is not only estranged from the locals, but also from both the (current) Western and (former) Chinese imperial positions of authority. Lianfeng's perception of colonial Southeast Asia, doubly mediated and contained by two epistemes whose authority he cannot claim, isolates him from his surroundings: he is unable to meaningfully connect or relate to those around him. He can only concoct a vague sensual fantasy and sexual nightmare over which he feels powerless. He remains mystified and disoriented by his impressionistic sensation of the "exotic," which he struggles to express in familiar language.

In New Literature, the exposure to and pursuit of modern Western knowledge typically engenders a deep crisis in the modern Chinese subject's relationship to his *own* culture and tradition. In "Insolubly Rich (Singapore)," this pursuit also brings about a crisis in the modern Chinese subject's relationship to another Other of the West. The narrative only scratches the surface of this crisis, as "South Seas color" is here but a transitory sensation experienced briefly in the author's experimental fiction. When considered within the context of his quartet—as a series of travelogues detailing the urban cultural and environmental sensations of Paris, Singapore, Hong Kong, and Beijing—Xu Zhimo's South Seas moment broadens the global framework of cultural comparison and inspiration in May Fourth enlightenment discourse. As a port of passage, the Nanyang is here a nodal point of North-South comparison that momentarily interjects in and disrupts a discourse predominantly thematized as East meets West. Though hastily and superficially depicted, this Nanyang itinerary—with the disorientation and disruption of cultural bearings it involves—adds a panoramic dimension to the cosmopolitanism of Chinese New Literature.

THE SOUTH SEAS ITINERARY: A DISCREPANT COSMOPOLITANISM

In accounting for New Literature's cosmopolitanism, the modern Chinese canon not only favors the West and Japan as the primary metropolitan sources of creative influence and interest, but also favors destination over itinerary. This focus by and large marginalizes the colonial world, such as South and Southeast Asia, as a potential contributor to this cosmopolitanism, as for many traveling writers, these regions only figured into the journey as part of the itinerary, a mere stopover on the way to or from another seemingly more important destination. Shifting the focus from destination to itinerary draws attention to the process of travel itself as an enlightening experience, thereby inviting all of the spaces in between origin and destination into the discourse of modern Chinese literary cosmopolitanism.

The South Seas itinerary, as one leg on a longer global tour that many writers of New Literature were inspired to describe in their fiction and prose, belongs to what anthropologist James Clifford calls the "trajectory of a different cosmopolitanism," a pattern of "discrepant movement" that diverges from a West-and-the-Rest or metropole-colony archetype. This trajectory brings into historical view previously unidentified modes of travel and "travelers," redefining and expanding the concept of "traveling cultures" to include the nonelite and non-Western "accomplices" of travel in the colonial world, such as translators, servants, cooks, companions, and local guides or "informants."[43] The southbound writers partook of a discrepant trajectory that followed the North-South itinerary of a non-Western, largely nonelite traveling culture: their "accomplices" were the hordes of Chinese migrants journeying to and from Southeast Asia, where they crossed paths with many other sojourners from around the world.

The southbound writers of the May Fourth era not only followed in the wake of the Chinese migration wave, which dated back to the mid-nineteenth century, but also accompanied it. The 1920s registered the "high point of emigration" to Southeast Asia, with 1927 as the peak year: nearly four million Chinese entered Southeast Asia from 1921–30, while nearly three million departed the region during the same period.[44] By this time, Chinese migration was a diverse world unto itself, structured by social networks (associations based on kinship, language or dialect, and native place), a class system (from poor coolies and petty traders to wealthy bankers, estate managers, and merchants), and the colonial economy of global capitalism. Though this migration took advantage of certain Western colonial networks—such as the British banking and shipping networks between Shanghai, Hong Kong, and Singapore—Chinese migration was, unlike Indian migrant labor at the time, "much more autonomous of the colonial state," with its labor primarily "destined for work in Chinese-owned enterprises."[45] The southbound writers were latecomers in this trans-colonial network, but it shaped their travel itineraries, largely determining what areas of Southeast Asia they would visit and what kinds of employment or educational opportunities they would enjoy there.

Of course, the southbound itinerary—including sites visited, length of stay, and purpose of travel—was not uniform among these authors. Sea voyages by passenger steamship from port to port were the norm. This itinerary generally limits the potential scope of South Seas color to images of Southeast Asia's urban seaports (in addition to the sea itself), and provides very few close encounters with its agrarian hinterlands and tropical jungles.[46] In New Literature, the maritime world of the passenger steamship and the sea it navigates are settings that are just as evocative of South Seas color as the territories visited. Here, this maritime world becomes an important symbol of modernity, enlightenment, and cosmopolitanism.

Perhaps no other southbound writer truly honored and cultivated the enlightenment ideal in his travels and his fiction as much as Xu Dishan (1893–1941), who wrote under the penname Luo Huasheng and was dubbed "Uncle Nanyang" (Nanyang Bo) by Hu Yuzhi, a southbound author of the 1930s and 1940s whom Xu inspired.[47] A globetrotter who studied at two top-tier Western universities—Columbia and Oxford—Xu Dishan engaged in the type of travel and educational pursuits typically ascribed to the originary impulses of modern Chinese literature—he "learned from the West." Yet his particular fields (anthropology, philosophy, and theology) and areas (South and Southeast Asia) of scholarly inquiry are rarely associated with the May Fourth enlightenment ideal. Literary histories portray Xu Dishan as somewhat of an eccentric Bohemian and renaissance figure: he donned "an unusual style of dress and grooming" with his long hair and goatee, and he was nicknamed "Shakespeare."[48] His interest in Theravada Buddhism, which forms the basis of his inaugural work of New Literature, "Birds of a Feather," originates with his experience teaching at a secondary school in Rangoon in 1913, a position his father—a Qing dynasty official in Taiwan with many Southeast Asian connections—helped him secure. In 1926, after finishing his studies at Oxford, Xu visited India on his return trip from England and spent a year studying Sanskrit, Buddhism, and Indian literature there. Fluent in Bengali, he later translated Lal Behari Dey's *Folk Tales of Bengal* and wrote China's first treatise on Indian literary history.[49]

Xu Dishan's long-term commitment to the serious study of South and Southeast Asian cultural, literary, and spiritual traditions represents the pinnacle of the enlightenment ideal in its South Seas trajectory. Unlike other southbound writers, Xu does not resort to Western- and China-centric stereotypes of a desired but feared feminized Other to grapple with the alienation of colonial modernity in Southeast Asia. Rather, he cultivates the exotic aesthetic to imagine the colonized subject's spiritual evolution and rebirth through a modern distillation of religious teachings that remains sufficiently enigmatic so as not to preclude open-ended interpretation. He calmly depicts the double suicide of the young lovers Minming and Jialing at the end of "Birds of a Feather," in which they drown themselves in Rangoon's Kandawgyi Lake, not just as the lamentable effect of an alienating modernity and oppressive feudalism hindering progress, but as a moment of reincarnation and potential enlightenment:

> Hand in hand, they walked into the water casually and unrestrained, like a pair of newlyweds entering their nuptial chamber, showing no signs of reluctance. Amidst the reflection of moonlight on water, Jialing could still be heard saying, "We are but passengers of life, and now we are headed to that new world. That gives me great joy."
>
> Now they are gone! The moonlight still illuminates the path they walked. The distant Shwedagon Pagoda sends them off with the sound of drumbeats and music. The wild animals in the zoo are all singing them a majestic parting tune. Only the water, which cannot comprehend human emotion, is unwilling to keep this journey a secret. It will find an opportunity to send the shells of their human form back once again.[50]

The omniscient narrative voice treats the suicide with elegant detachment, just as the characters detach and transcend their physical form. The illuminating "reflection of moonlight on water" is a motif of enlightenment: their lake burial symbolizes the return to water as the source and renewal of all life.

Among the New Literature pioneers, Xu Dishan was both the most knowledgeable about South and Southeast Asian cultures and spiritual traditions and also the most intimate with life at sea and seaside living.

In fact, "The Sea Realm" ("Hai shijian," 1923) is the subject, as well as the title, of one of Xu's odder short stories: in this very concise, conversational, non-action-oriented piece, the traveling narrator, who is on a transoceanic voyage, philosophically expounds upon the differences between the "sea realm" and the "terrestrial realm" (*lu shijian*).[51] Xu's attention to the epistemological differences of landscape and seascape is a subtle challenge to the continental supremacy of the Central Plains—and terrestrial rather than oceanic roots—in defining Chinese culture.

This interest in the "sea realm" is of course linked to Xu Dishan's background: born in Tainan, Taiwan, he took a keen interest in the maritime exploits of his Hokkien forebears and contemporaries. Xu made many trips across the South Seas during his lifetime, and his narratives often take place on passenger steamships and feature protagonists who are fellow travelers that the narrator encounters. Xu was initiated into this network of Chinese travelers from a young age, as his father lived for extended periods in Taiwan, Singapore, and Siam and died in Sumatra in 1917.[52]

The death and burial of his father in Sumatra was a source of intense contemplation for Xu Dishan: he alludes to this episode in another short story reflecting upon the sea realm entitled "Lone Star on the Cape" ("Haijiao di guxing," 1923). The narrator, on a steamship off the coast of Malaya, encounters a fellow traveler whom he met on a previous journey from China to Penang. The young man now appears sickly and emaciated, and moreover he is a widower, bereft of the young wife with whom he optimistically set out from China a decade earlier to eke out a living in a newly opened town at the edge of the jungle near Penang. On the night the narrator once again crosses paths with the young man at sea, the man later dies in his cabin, forcing the ship's crew to perform an impromptu funeral in which they burn paper money and then cast the corpse overboard. The narrator reflects upon the wife's burial in the deep "evergreen thicket" of the Nanyang jungle and the husband's burial in the deep "emerald green" sea. In the continental Chinese epistemology, which suggests that only return and burial under the earth of one's ancestral village constitutes a proper funeral, dying in such a faraway tropical and marine environment would give the couple's souls no rest, and they would eternally be "wandering ghosts," alone and forgotten. While Xu Dishan certainly acknowledges the tragedy of their deaths—they represent dashed dreams, not success stories, of migrant Chinese pioneers in Southeast Asia—the occasion still provokes a solemn sense of profound awe in the narrator: the reflection of light from an infinity of stars, as an archaeology of the cosmos, illuminates the ocean waters, the source of life to which the soul returns for its renewal.[53]

In Xu Dishan's narratives of South Seas color, contemplative reflections on the ocean (and the motif of water in general) as a source of renewal and rebirth are not only a way of reconciling with death but also the catalyst for more awakened lives. Xu Dishan's combined interests in world religions and migrant communities in Southeast Asia are important features of his narrative reflections on the sea. In "The Toiling, Web-Mending Spider" ("Zhuiwang laozhu," 1922), the protagonist Shangjie lives in a very small, tight-knit, and conservative Christian Chinese settler community in colonial Malaya near Penang, where she regularly attends an English missionary's church. After aiding a wounded burglar who attempted to rob her property, Shangjie's jealous husband stabs her in the shoulder. Although the virtues of forgiveness and compassion espoused by her faith compelled her to help the burglar, Shangjie's congregation expels her because they choose to believe the testimony of Shangjie's husband. According to their "righteous" logic, Shangjie's "infidelity" must have provoked her husband to take such extreme action. The small religious settler community is highly sensitive to corrosive gossip. Shangjie, disappointed to find out that her fellow churchgoers have misunderstood her as well as their own religious teachings, comments, "It may be the same water, but when the cow drinks it, it turns to milk; when the snake drinks it, it becomes poisonous venom."[54]

Shangjie is forced to leave her home and four-year-old daughter. Her longtime friends, who believe her innocence, secure her a place at their villa on Pulau Tuba, a small island in the Langkawi archipelago off the west coast of Kedah. The pearl industry sustains the island's local economy, and Shangjie, with nothing to do but sit on the beach in solitude and meditation, marvels at the Malay pearl divers who brave the depths of the sea, never sure if they will catch anything:

> Risking the dangers of the sea all day long, the pearl gatherers had not the slightest certainty about what and how much they would get. . . . Every day, when she saw those people groping around in the murky depths, she began to understand that her course in this world was like that of the pearl gatherers. . . . In the end she had to take her chances diving into the sea day in and day out, as this was her lot in life.[55]

Shangjie receives her own pearl of spiritual wisdom by watching the native islanders repeatedly brave the vast, unclear depths of the ocean with a kind of blind but boundless hope, like a spider slowly mending its broken web. As she opens her soul to the lessons of the seascape, she receives spiritual wisdom, not of a doctrinal or textual nature, but from her calm attention to and passive absorption of her surroundings: the surf of the ocean as wave after wave rolls upon the shore, and the persistence of the pearl divers as they seek their livelihood in the deep sea.

Xu Dishan's calm and contemplative reflections on the "sea realm," and his depiction of female travelers who awaken to the sea's spiritual pearls despite their bondage to a male-dominated transcolonial network, economy, and society, offer positive spiritual twists on an otherwise turbulent, often violent, and occasionally lethal South Seas itinerary. Drawing on his observations of transoceanic travel and the colonial economy in the South Seas, as well as his theological and anthropological knowledge, Xu Dishan's stories take a feminist approach to the subject of spiritual enlightenment and evolution. Religion in Xu's stories—whether Buddhism, Hinduism, Islam, or Christianity—appears as a heavily gendered institution: on the one hand, there are its dogmatic doctrines that are manipulated by male-centered claims to power and used to oppress women; on the other, there are its scattered pearls of wisdom, which provide strength for Xu's female protagonists to escape the abuse of their husbands, who treat them as their property. Eclectically gleaning positive kernels from multiple religions (rather than adhering to one), these female protagonists are the true cosmopolitans in Xu's stories.

In its depictions of the vibrant maritime world of the modern passenger steamship, of the spiritual development and release from bondage of a female traveler who navigates different religious teachings, and of the intersection of world cultures, religions, and languages in the Nanyang, Xu Dishan's canonical short story "The Merchant's Wife" ("Shangren fu," 1921) epitomizes the role of South Seas color in New Literature's cultivation of a cosmopolitan enlightenment. The title of Xu Dishan's story refers to the female protagonist, whom the young male narrator addresses throughout the story as Siok Gua (Xiguan, a Hokkien term of address for a woman who is of one's generation or slightly older). The opening scene sets the stage for the story by describing the noise and excitement of the mess hall one morning on a steamship traveling from India to China via Penang and Singapore. Passengers gather for tea and to discuss the latest news from the region, speculating as to whether it was the Indian Revolutionary

Party that instigated the 1915 Sepoy Mutiny in Singapore, or whether it was a wise decision for Yuan Shikai (China's president from 1912–15) to have proclaimed himself emperor: "The buzz and din nearly turned the mess hall into a marketplace."[56]

Seeking quieter environs to read in peace, the narrator goes out onto the ship's starboard. There, his attention is drawn to a visually intriguing female passenger and her young son, whom he had previously spotted the day before when the ship docked in Penang:

> I had seen this woman the previous day at the Pond for Releasing Life in the Temple of Supreme Joy. I had also seen her boarding the ship, and I often ran into her on the port and starboard, where she went to cool off. Seeing her immediately piqued my curiosity, because even though she wore Indian clothing, she carried herself in a way that didn't seem very Indian.[57]

Here, Xu Dishan challenges the young, sojourning Chinese intellectual's preconceptions about ethnic difference based on phenotype, costume, mannerism, and language. The narrator's perception of difference is a misreading and misrecognition of the Other, as the woman surprises the narrator by speaking Hokkien in his hometown accent: as it turns out, the two are originally from the same place in Fujian.

The initial moment of misrecognition serves as the catalyst for the story's central action: the narrator's interest is piqued by this Hokkien-speaking, Indian-attired woman. As Siok Gua begins to tell the narrator about her life, she, as "the merchant's wife," takes over as the main narrator and protagonist. The story's title draws attention to a type of sojourner (namely female, but also nonelite) and a set of travel conditions (Siok Gua's status as someone's "wife" determines her reason for traveling to Southeast Asia) quite distinct from those that describe the young male narrator.

Siok Gua's story begins in Fujian when her husband's gambling debt leaves the couple bankrupt. Desperate, he devises a plan to "travel overseas to [the land of the] southern barbarians" (*guo fan*), a Hokkien phrase that Xu Dishan explains in parentheses for his Chinese readership as meaning "traveling to the Nanyang." The merchant vows to send for his wife after he has established himself in Singapore. Siok Gua mulls over the idea with doubts, certain that "the majority of men who went to the Nanyang never missed home."[58] Indeed, ten years pass with little word from her husband. She then decides to *guo fan* herself, where she discovers that her husband, now the wealthy owner of a grocery store in Singapore's Tanjong Pagar district, has taken a Malay wife. Siok Gua recounts her initial encounter with the new wife:

> Her manners, from what I could tell, were very disrespectful, but I wasn't versed in the customs of the Nanyang, so I could only nod my head in apology. She wore diamonds and pearls in her hair, and underneath the gemstones, gold, and silver she wore, her swarthy face revealed its striking ugliness.[59]

Siok Gua's physical description of the Malay woman revels in her exotica: dark skin, excessive jewelry, and the habit of betel-nut chewing. Siok Gua's racial prejudice here is instigated by the threat to her status, identity, and livelihood that her husband's desire for the Southeast Asian "barbarian" woman represents.

In light of subsequent events that unfold in "The Merchant's Wife," Siok Gua's initial repulsion toward the Other becomes the author's self-reflexive critique of this racism, as Siok Gua herself is soon forced to adopt this very image that she perceives as ostentatious otherness. The merchant and the Malay woman conspire to sell Siok Gua into concubinage to an Indian merchant named Ahuja who forces her to convert to Islam:

> Since he made a fortune in Singapore, he wanted to take another wife back home to add to his happiness. My sorry fate had transformed me into his foreign curio. I hadn't even lived in Singapore a full month before he took me off to Madras. . . . Ahuja gave me the name Liya. He told me to unbind my feet and pierced a hole in my nose, in which he hung a diamond ring. He said that according to their customs, all married women had to wear nose rings, because it was the mark of a wife.[60]

Following Confucian tradition, Siok Gua contemplates suicide as an alternative to an "unchaste" second marriage to a "barbarian" and a total transformation of her outward cultural identity from a good Confucian and Buddhist Chinese wife with bound feet into an Indian Muslim wife with a nose ring and a *kurta* (Bengali: long blouse). However, rather than resorting to despair and self-loathing, she resolves to embrace her new identity as Liya to the best of her ability and "live out the rest of my life and see what fate would bring me."[61]

Liya subsequently befriends Akolima, another one of Ahuja's concubines who teaches her the Bengali language. The next few years of Liya's life are hastily recounted in the short story. First, she aids her neighbor, an abused Hindu widow. Fearing retribution from her husband for assisting a non-Muslim (reminiscent of the husband's jealousy in "The Toiling, Web-Mending Spider"), Liya flees with her young son, taking refuge in a Christian mission in northern India where she learns some English from a British nun named Elizabeth. Elizabeth sponsors Liya's attendance at a school in Madras while her son stays at the mission. After her schooling, Liya decides to return to Singapore with her son to see what had become of her former Chinese husband and if he might repent for his past sins. Even though much of her "traveling" has taken place in a condition of bondage—exchanged as "property" between two male merchants (one Chinese, one Indian) who derive their living from the colonial economies of Southeast Asia—her multiple spiritual rebirths have led her to assert her individual agency as a sojourner, a "female Robinson Crusoe."[62]

Here, the narrative returns to the present on the steamship, and the reins of narration are passed back to the young male traveler who has been listening with rapture to Siok Gua's background story. As the ship approaches Singapore, Siok Gua enlists the narrator's help to inquire about the whereabouts of her former husband. The next day, after the ship docks, the narrator picks up a clue at a local Cantonese teahouse:

> According to the shopkeeper I questioned, Lin Yinqiao had stirred up resentments among the Tang people in the area. At that time, some people had said it had been his decision to sell her [Siok Gua], while others said it was his southern barbarian wife, but in the end who was to blame remained uncertain. Yet his business suffered because of this, and, seeing that he couldn't stay on in Singapore, he closed up his shop and moved the entire family elsewhere.[63]

Without any real leads, "The Merchant's Wife" ends with a question over Siok Gua's future: Where will she go, and which society will welcome her?

The narrator suggests to Siok Gua that she return to China, but she outright refuses, anticipating the racial hostilities toward her as an "Indian woman" and toward her "brown-skinned," multiethnic child.[64] Through Siok Gua's initial encounter with the Malay wife and her subsequent transformation into an Indian woman with a mixed-race son who will not be welcomed back into her home village in China, Xu Dishan contributes to New Literature its earliest and most thoughtful interrogation of Chinese stereotypes and negative attitudes toward "yellow-brown amalgamation." According to Emma Teng, although Chinese nationalists of the late Qing and early Republican era generally opposed all forms of miscegenation (the ROC imposed bans on overseas student intermarriages after the 1911 revolution), cosmopolitan reformers who accepted social Darwinian discourses of racial survival, hybrid vigor, and to some extent Orientalist epistemology promoted "the particular amalgamation of yellow and white, or Chinese and European." Yet even these "progressive" reformers opposed mixing with "black, brown, and red races as the abject, colonized, and/or enslaved . . . 'darker races,'" with the "brown" category including South and Southeast Asians as well as Pacific Islanders.[65] Xu Dishan's South Seas color calls upon his Chinese readership to examine its own ethnocentrism by depicting categorically deplored models of miscegenation and creolization in the Nanyang, foregrounding an issue that otherwise took a backseat to questions of class and gender oppression in May Fourth enlightenment discourse. The problematic encounter between the young, privileged male intellectual and the subaltern woman in "The Merchant's Wife" evokes a typical plot of New Literature perhaps most familiar to readers in Lu Xun's "The New Years Sacrifice" ("Zhufu," 1924), in which a widow forced to remarry wonders if she will go to hell and be ripped in half by the ghosts of her dead husbands after she passes away. Like the male narrator of "The Merchant's Wife," Lu Xun's narrator is unable to give an assured answer and provide consolation to the woman.[66] However, Xu's South Seas color summons ethnicity and race to complicate the narrative of gender oppression, challenging prevailing Chinese attitudes toward "yellow-brown" miscegenation and creolization, both in China and in colonial Singapore.

Returning to Singapore, Siok Gua now views the colonial city with fresh eyes as Liya: she tells the narrator that she "never thought [she] would see this place again. The leaves on the coconut trees are still dancing, and the seagulls are still flying back and forth over the sea to welcome guests."[67] The depiction of Singapore as a settlement that "welcomes guests" suggests the possibility that Siok Gua may fit comfortably into the fabric of diasporic life here. Yet the fact that the Chinese Singaporean community drove Siok Gua's husband and his "southern barbarian wife" out of the area, not because the couple sold Siok Gua into bondage, but because they sold her to an Indian Muslim, hints at some of the deep-seated racial intolerance that lies beneath the surface of diasporic cosmopolitanism. While Siok Gua refuses to return to China, she is less certain about her and her son's prospects in Singapore, and although she plans to stay there a few days, she admits she most likely will have to go back to India.[68] Here, "The Merchant's Wife" subtly addresses the racialist dynamics of Singapore's colonial history: her identity now shaped by experiences traversing Chinese (Hokkien), Indian (Bengali), and English languages and cultures, Siok Gua/Liya fuses the disparate diasporic and colonial components of cosmopolitan Singapore. Yet like China, Singapore seems unwilling to welcome and tolerate the conditions of "yellow-brown" miscegenation and creolization that Siok Gua and her young son embody.

The South Seas color of New Literature, representing a quest for enlightenment, follows a discrepant cosmopolitan itinerary that challenges some basic assumptions about modern Chinese literary history. Despite the recognition of Xu Dishan as a pioneer of New Literature who answered the call for modern vernacular writing in standard Chinese, the author's literary pursuit of the enlightenment ideal via the South Seas itinerary does not exert such a consolidating and unifying force on language. Throughout his short fiction on the Nanyang, Xu brings multilingualism into play as part of the cosmopolitan aesthetic, mixing Hokkien, Malay, Bengali, Sanskrit, and English terms into his standard Chinese script. Additionally, the culturally and linguistically disorienting impressions of the South Seas evident in Xu Zhimo's short story (inspired by his short layover) in Singapore hint at the crisis in the modern Chinese subject's relationship to Southeast Asian "others" in the context of a new, Western-oriented colonial order. Xu Dishan, inspired by his lengthy exposure and research into theology and anthropology, explores this crisis in more depth: his South Seas itinerary draws out the discrepant cosmopolitanism of the forgotten or subaltern travelers of the Nanyang who distill the best of world spiritual teachings to navigate the crippling conditions of the colonial order. Xu Dishan's pursuit of the enlightenment ideal further leads him to question Chinese ethnocentrism, a "national trait" that must be overcome in the liberation of the modern nation. In this sense, his work brings into question the ideal of "national salvation" in New Literature.

CHAPTER 2

Transcolonial Challenges to Diasporic Ethno-Nationalism

As the second common theme of Chinese literary modernity, "national salvation" was both a major catalyst and desired outcome of the first theme, enlightenment. Though New Literature criticized and satirically lampooned those who clung to "feudalistic" expressions of Chinese civilizational superiority,[1] it nonetheless hoped to arouse a modern, more enlightened patriotism among readers. Like the enlightenment ideal, the promotion of nationalism in response to foreign imperial incursions dating back to the Opium Wars transformed the ways in which modern Chinese authors who traveled to Southeast Asia imagined the South Seas as a literary trope. Representations of the Nanyang in the imperial Chinese worldview as an uncivilized, matriarchal aberration reaffirming the superiority of Confucian patriarchy were not appropriate for expressing the new Chinese nationalism, for they highlighted the very feudalistic attitudes that New Literature attacked and that its authors saw as blinding China's ruling classes to the nation's vulnerability to foreign imperialism. Traveling abroad—particularly to the West and Japan—left many authors of New Literature disheartened and resentful toward their treatment as inferior, "second-class Chinese" in those societies. Many of the southbound writers who traveled to colonial Southeast Asia used the trope of the Nanyang to project their nationalist desires, not onto indigenous Southeast Asian "others" but rather onto the "Overseas Chinese" in the region—the Nanyang Huaqiao or "South Seas Chinese."

Though much of the South Seas Chinese population lived under Western colonial regimes, they were nationals of the Chinese republic, since most Western authorities classified local Chinese populations as temporary "foreign" subjects. As such, the Nanyang Huaqiao earned a reputation for being fervent long-distance nationalists who helped plan and finance the 1911 revolution that overthrew the Qing dynasty and gave birth to modern China. From what the southbound authors heard or read prior to their arrival in Southeast Asia, the Nanyang Huaqiao were fierce loyalists, desperately committed to China's modernization and extremely resentful of colonial incursion there. Furthermore, the 1920s and 1930s—precisely when southbound authors visited Southeast Asia—were an especially vibrant time for this diasporic nationalism. With the 1911 revolution and overseas reverberations of China's May Fourth movement, the Nanyang Huaqiao—particularly in colonial Malaya (Singapore and the peninsula)—began to identify as a cohesive (and increasingly intellectually active) unit overcoming divides of clan, language (or dialect), and ancestral region primarily by importing standard Chinese as the modern language of Sinophone education and print culture.[2] For the southbound writers who came to colonial Southeast Asia in the 1920s and 1930s, the Nanyang Huaqiao were the true pioneers of the region: they—not the Western empires—were the hands-on architects of its modernity and cultivators of its wealth. The vibrant nationalism and economic accomplishments that characterized the Nanyang Huaqiao inspired several Chinese writers to visit or extend their stopovers in Southeast Asia.

Despite projecting nationalist desires onto the South Seas Chinese, the Nanyang trope in New Literature does not affirm, but rather critiques, diasporic ethno-nationalism in Southeast Asia. The authors Lao She and Yu Dafu expose its major pitfall: it is too often ethnocentrism camouflaged as anticolonial gesture. In Southeast Asia, these authors observed the ways in which diasporic nationalism slipped into an ethnocentrism that reinforced the divide-and-rule strategies that Western colonizers used to legitimize their exploitative presence. In Lao She's fiction, the Nanyang trope "writes back" to China, providing a strong critique of the Han ethno-nationalism that was a key pillar of the republic's founding. Southbound writers like Yu Dafu also commented on and actively promoted the development of local Sinophone literature in colonial Malaya. Though Yu's relationship with the Sinophone intellectual and literary community was ambivalently marked by an unevenness of cultural capital, his commentary specifically acknowledged the need to transcend diasporic ethno-nationalism in order to evolve a broad-based (multicultural and multilingual) yet locally situated anticolonial Malayan literature distinct from modern Chinese literature. Through its critique of diasporic ethno-nationalism, the Nanyang trope gains a transcolonial signification that simultaneously addresses the emergent national contexts of China and Southeast Asia. This signification of the Nanyang challenges and undermines the logic of Chinese ethno-nationalism as an effective anticolonial strategy, whether back home in China or among Sinophone communities in Southeast Asia.

THE ETHNO-NATIONALIST PRINCIPLE: NEW LITERATURE AND DIASPORA

The canonical nationalism of New Literature derives from the "imagined China" of writers who traveled to the West and Japan, often for study, then reflected back in their literary works personal perceptions of China based on experiences of being Chinese abroad. This embodies a double consciousness: a self-view of the Chinese subjectivity through one's own eyes (with a critical distance in the metropole) and through the gaze of the colonizer. From this "superior" position, the writer observes a uniform, undifferentiated Chinese consciousness in need of national awakening. This is not only true of modern Chinese literature's "inaugural scene" in Lu Xun's preface to his collection, *A Call to Arms* (*Nahan*, 1922),[3] but also of other canonical texts such as Lao She's London-based novel *Mr. Ma and Son* (*Er Ma*, 1929) or Yu Dafu's Japan-based short story, "Sinking" ("Chenlun," 1921). The critical distance of the imperial metropole intensifies the authors' perceptions of China's uniformly victimized condition. This "imagined China" is a diasporic projection (from living abroad), but—premised primarily on travel to the West and Japan—it differs from that in narratives based on travel to colonial Southeast Asia, where China's first nationalist revolution found one of its largest bases of support.

Travel to colonial Southeast Asia and observations of the South Seas Chinese in New Literature complicate the idea of a singular "Chinese subjectivity," drawing the authors' attention to differences between ethnicity and nation to critique the ethno-nationalist vision of Chinese national culture inherited from the 1911 revolution. This vision originated in turn-of-the-century revolutionary efforts to overthrow the Qing dynasty, using the Qing's corrupt and outdated imperial structure, its "foreign" (non-Han) Manchu rulers, its granting of extraterritorial concessions along the eastern seaboard to Western imperial powers, and its cessation of Taiwan to Japan as primary rallying points. As the leading orchestrator of the 1911 revolution and modern China's "founding father," Sun Yat-sen (Sun Zhongshan) visited Southeast Asia many times, including eight trips to Singapore alone between 1900 and 1911, where he oversaw the establishment of local branches of the Chinese Revolutionary Society (Tongmenghui). Sun Yat-sen famously referred to the South Seas Chinese as the "mothers of the revolution" for the integral role they played in the successful overthrow of the Qing in 1911.[4]

The ethnic appeal to diasporic nationalism in Southeast Asia in the early twentieth century amplifies the Han ethnocentrism of mainstream modern Chinese nationalism. The conveniently ambiguous sense of the term *Zhong Hua minzu*, meaning the "Chinese nationality," can flexibly refer to all the ethnic groups of modern China as well as the Han majority. The Republic of China's official discourse following the 1911 revolution reflected this: in order to avoid "catastrophic territorial failure" on China's geopolitical borders, the Nationalist government tempered its revolutionary ethnic rhetoric with a more inclusive discourse of multiculturalism. Downplaying the Han ethnocentrism of the revolutionaries, the KMT proclaimed China a "Republic of Five Peoples" (*wuzu gonghe*, a concept ironically borrowed from the overthrown Qing), consisting of Han, Manchu, Tibetan, Mongolian, and Hui.[5] Bearing the legacy of late nineteenth-century reformers' proposal of a "Chinese race" (*Zhongguo renzhong*),[6] the notion of the *Zhong Hua minzu* was crucial to Sun Yat-sen's formulation of the "ethno-nationalist principle" (*minzu zhuyi*). As the first tenet of Sun Yat-sen's "Three People's Principles" and the only one "unanimously accepted by the revolutionaries," this principle pits the "Chinese nationality" not only against Western and Japanese imperial aggression, but also against the supposedly "foreign" Manchus.[7] Sun recognized that "for the most part, the Chinese people are of the Han or Chinese race with common blood, common language, common religion, and common customs—a single, pure race."[8] The designation of the Han ethnicity (Hanzu) was a construct of late Qing intellectuals to distinguish Han from Manchu and to offer a racialist rationale for delegitimizing Qing rule. The flexible ideological construct of the "people" or "citizenry" (*guomin*) conveniently shifted its discursive Other between foreign imperial powers (an abstract West and Japan) and the Manchus, a "domestic enemy" and ethnic

Other.[9] The conceptual slippage between statist-nationalism (*guojia zhuyi*) and ethno-nationalism (*minzu zhuyi*) suppressed ethnic and linguistic multiplicity in China and envisioned the emergent nation as a majority Han-centered one.[10] Conveniently flexible and ambiguous in its domestic connotations, the ethno-nationalism of the "Chinese nationality" is overt in the multiethnic context of colonial Southeast Asia, where it attempts to hail a "Hua people" (Huaren) by singling them out from their colonized brethren of different backgrounds.

Although most Western regimes already classified Chinese settler communities in Southeast Asia as a singular "Chinese race" prior to the twentieth century, the settlers' own sense of community was primarily based on language (Hokkien, Cantonese, Teochew, Hakka, Baba Malay), ancestral region, kinship, and generation of settlement, with native-place associations (*huiguan*) functioning as community centers and transitional networks that fostered continued links to ancestral villages.[11] Many South Seas Chinese were drawn to Sun Yat-sen's ethno-nationalist principle because they related to Sun's personal experiences of overseas migration and colonial racialization, from his Cantonese background to his years spent in US-occupied Hawai'i and British Hong Kong: Sun was the offspring of "maritime China," the "China of the coastal provinces and overseas communities."[12] These resonances highlight the diasporic, maritime origins of modern Chinese ethno-nationalism, despite its territorial orientation toward the continental mainland. After 1911, the ROC, with support from the Nanyang Huaqiao, began establishing Mandarin-medium "Chinese" (Zhong Hua) schools in Southeast Asia to expand loyalties to the new nation. The notion that these various groups were divided and needed Mandarin to bring them together is somewhat dubious, for other majority Sinitic languages already served as lingua franca of local communities, such as Hokkien in Malaya, Cantonese in Vietnam, Hakka in Borneo, and Teochew in Siam. Widely spoken non-Sinitic languages such as Baba Malay and Thai also facilitated inter- and intraethnic communication in their respective locales. The institutionalization of Mandarin ostensibly consolidated ethnic citizenship in the Chinese nationality, yet it also used racialist inculcation to transform creole societies into an "overseas" diaspora.

Although diasporic Chinese nationalism in Southeast Asia took various and sometimes competing forms throughout the first half of the twentieth century, with specific Nationalist (KMT) versus Communist Party (CCP) articulations, the ethno-nationalist principle was the dominant mode of organization. Some southbound writers participated in making these nationalist appeals. Others, such as Lao She, mention extending their stopover in Southeast Asia during this era simply to observe the legendary Nanyang Huaqiao, renowned for their loyalty to China and their pioneering tenacity and entrepreneurial ingenuity. The Nanyang trope of New Literature denotes the author's nationalist desire to extol the South Seas Chinese as a model citizenry for modern China's emulation.

However, travel to colonial Southeast Asia, whether to engage in propagandistic appeal to the diaspora or to applaud its accomplishments, often compels a revision of this desire. Departing from orthodox sentiments of anticolonial ethno-nationalism in which the implied target—or interlocutor—is the (Western or Japanese) colonizer, the Nanyang imagination reveals the primary interlocutor of diasporic Chinese nationalism in Southeast Asia (intended or not) to be other colonized ethnic groups because they are more physically present in one's daily life than the colonizer himself. The assertion of ethnic pride is not necessarily an anticolonial gesture here, since Western colonialism itself appears as more of a background power structure than the actual presence of European characters. Southbound writers from China, whose anticolonial reflexes were ingrained in their ideal of national salvation, become aware of the ethnocentrism of the idea of the "Chinese nationality" when applied to settlers in the creolized New World of the Nanyang. The southbound authors observe that such ethnocentrism in fact perpetuates the colonial condition and stunts the emergence of a truly inclusive national literature, whether in China or Southeast Asia.

VIEW FROM THE COLONY: WRITING BACK TO CHINA'S ETHNO-NATIONALISM

The Nanyang imagination of Lao She's *Little Po's Birthday* (*Xiao Po de shengri*, 1931), a novel critically dismissed as "fantasy for children,"[13] exemplifies the transcolonial critique of diasporic ethno-nationalism. Raised in Beijing and of Manchu background, Lao She (pseudonym of Shu Qingchun [his Manchu surname was Sumuru], 1899–1966) was a foundational author of New Literature. *Rickshaw Boy* (*Luotuo xiangzi*, 1936), Lao She's devastatingly ironic novel of a rickshaw puller in Republican-era Beijing, is arguably the most widely read and highly regarded novel in the modern Chinese canon.

A landmark achievement in Chinese vernacular realism, *Rickshaw Boy* was the culmination of a decade of eclectic experimentation in various literary genres and different foreign settings where Lao She lived in the 1920s before returning to China.

Lao She first stopped in Singapore on his way to England in 1924, yet this was an unremarkable layover. While teaching Mandarin at the School of Oriental Studies in London from 1924 to 1929, Lao She enjoyed reading Joseph Conrad's stories of the tropics. Narratives such as *Lord Jim*, a novel about a drifting British shipman who ends up stabilizing a troubled region of Malaya, left a visceral impression on the young Chinese author. When he later reminisced about reading Conrad, Lao She wrote that when he closed his eyes, he could still "see the ship in the stormy sea and the people of different races in Nanyang."[14] Conrad's influence stoked in Lao She a fascination with the South Seas and inspired his decision to write about the region upon his return journey through Singapore, which would involve a more extended stay, in 1929.[15]

Lao She's initiation into Western Orientalism did not inspire him to depict Southeast Asian "others" so much as much it stoked his desire to witness and extol the pioneering accomplishments of the Nanyang Chinese. This desire can be traced to Lao She's experience in London of the kind of anti-Sinitic racism depicted in his 1929 London-based novel, *Mr. Ma and Son*. When the novel's Chinese protagonist and his father arrive in London, they discover that "since China was a weak country," the British "accused hardworking Chinese, who were simply trying to make a living in this foreign land, of all sorts of things," claiming "they all smoked opium, smuggled weapons, hid the heads of those they killed under their beds, raped women young and old, and did all sorts of things for which they ought to be hacked to pieces."[16] Beyond such outrageous claims, this Western "Yellow Peril" ignores ethnic diversity within Asia or China itself, such as differences between Manchu and Han. Lao She responded by trying to recover his wounded national pride not only as an "Overseas Chinese" citizen but also as a member of the "Chinese race." This is evident in Lao She's lone critical remark on Conrad's work: Conrad was more interested in the pathos of his protagonists (exclusively white officers in the colonial regime), while Asian characters—especially Chinese migrants and settlers—only made rare, inconsequential appearances as "supporting cast" and "added color." Lao She was determined to write a South Seas historical epic in the vein of Conrad that would foreground the "greatness" of the Overseas Chinese, whose "achievements made the Nanyang what it was."[17]

The plan for a historical novel about Nanyang Chinese pioneers was a far cry from the project Lao She actually undertook in Singapore. After arriving in Singapore, Lao She took a position as instructor at the Nanyang Overseas Chinese Middle School.[18] Unlike southbound writers such as Yu Dafu who observed the colonial society through its Sinophone literary and intellectual developments, Lao She accessed it through the children he taught. His day-to-day teaching responsibilities kept him from obtaining three prerequisites for writing his planned South Seas epic: he did not have time to research the colony's economic situation; he did not have the opportunity to visit the Malayan heartland of merchants, rubber tappers, and tin miners to observe their lives and listen to their stories; and, as a North China native, he lacked a basic grasp of the primary Sinitic languages spoken in the colony—Hokkien and Cantonese—not to mention Malay. Lao She admits that he found it difficult to be a disciplined writer in Singapore: the daytime was too hot and humid, and during the evenings, while trying to "write with one hand and swat away mosquitoes with the other," sounds of scurrying geckoes in his building distracted him and street cafés beckoned him outside to relax.[19] Lao She's life in colonial Singapore did not corroborate the "historical reality" of the South Seas epic he initially planned to compose. In colonial Singapore, the ethno-national pride he sought to recuperate after observing anti-Sinitic racism in London took on a disturbing guise that would become the subject of satire in *Little Po's Birthday*.

Lao She based *Little Po's Birthday* on the "smallest slice" of Singapore he was able to observe: the multiethnic world of schoolchildren. A blend of satirical realism and children's fable, the novel was serialized in China's *Literary Monthly (Xiaoshuo yuebao)* in 1931. The first eleven chapters (of eighteen total), composed in Singapore, combine Lao She's observations of the colony with his characteristic flair for comedy and farce.[20] The author shows how Singaporeans internalize, adapt, or defy the racialist ideology and diasporic ethnocentrisms governing the island's social structure, satirizing them through the "naïve" child's perspective of a young Chinese Singaporean named Little Po (Xiao Po). The last seven chapters, written in Shanghai after Lao She left Singapore in February 1930, escape the realistic setting via an extended dream sequence into a fantastical realm: Little Po falls asleep at the cinema on his birthday and takes a fairy-tale journey to the "Shadowland" (Yingrguo), with "shadow" (*ying*) directly connecting the dream to the experience of watching a movie (*dianying*; literally "electric shadows"). Shadowland also forms a pun with "land of babies" (*ying'er guo*), enhancing its function (and that of the novel itself) as a realm of child's play removed from the surveillance of adult authorities.

Little Po, who comes from a family of Cantonese merchants, is fascinated by labels and titles. In the first chapter, he learns the origin of his name as well as well as that of his older brother, Big Po (Da Po), and his younger sister, Xianpo (or "Sagely Po"). All three siblings share the character *po* ("slope") in their names, which appears in the Sinophone transliteration of "Singapore" (Xinjiapo).[21] Little Po learns that he and his brother are named after colloquial terms for streets (whose official names are Anglophone ones) in and around Singapore's Chinatown. An immigrant from Guangdong, Little Po's father first opened up a shop selling Chinese imports on Big Po Street (where Big Po was born), but later moved operations to Little Po Street (where Little Po was born). Little Po learns that his younger sister was given her name because, as a baby, she was delivered to the family "wrapped in a banana leaf" by "an old sage with a white beard in the middle of the night."[22]

With the more grandiloquent name, Big Po is the eldest son who gladly obeys his parents' wishes. Carrying the torch of the immigrant culture, he represents the diasporic orthodoxy of colonial Singapore. This orthodoxy is traceable to Sir Stamford Raffles's founding vision of the colony as a potential trading port in 1819, which included plans to carve up the area around the Singapore River into separate, exclusive quarters for different ethnic groups.[23] The British view of themselves as the indispensable arbiters of a "plural society" depended entirely on "preserving the distinctions between the separate communities."[24] They believed that by allowing various settler communities (predominantly Chinese, Malay, and Indian) to observe their customs unmolested, with each community providing its own schools, they would face few challenges to their rule.[25] Big Po, who "went to school in order to study and make his parents happy," is somewhat emblematic of this vision. He attends a Cantonese school, where he also takes lessons in Mandarin, his "national language" as a Chinese citizen, and English, the "foreign devil's language" (*guizi hua*) of colonial administration. Whenever Big Po sees Little Po "playing with Hokkien, Malay, or Indian children," he goes to "report it to their father, prompting their father to remark that Little Po had no future prospects."[26] Dutifully attending his community's school, preparing to inherit the family business, and associating primarily with members of his own race, Big Po represents both a consummate member of the Chinese diaspora and ideal colonial subject.

By contrast, Little Po's mischievous antics antagonize his parents and teachers. Calling his father the least tolerant of his insatiable curiosity, Little Po avoids asking him difficult questions about the world, as his father always responds: "Seal your lips!" When Little Po's father "asked you something, if you shook your head and refused, you would be in danger of having your ear whacked."[27] Little Po recalls an incident when

> his stern-faced father intently whacked, with a loud smack, the ear of the Indian gatekeeper who stood outside his shop. In Little Po's eyes, the Indian gatekeeper was a "great man." If even a "great man" had his ears whacked by his father, then should news of Little Po feigning an illness in order to miss school reach his father's ears, Little Po's ears would be whacked at least four or eight times, or even more![28]

To escape his father's punishment, Little Po realizes that he does not have to obey his father's commands, but instead simply avoid the surveillance of his older brother. Lao She describes the authorial pecking order in the family structure:

> The members of the family were like a little pagoda, with one level managing the next. As long as the lowest level remained sufficiently concealed, then the highest level was like an idiot who didn't know anything. Think about it! His father, sitting at the tip of the pagoda, was like an idiot—how hilarious![29]

By avoiding the surveillance of his older brother, the middle rung in the structure, Little Po undermines his father's "administration." The pagoda's symbolism extends beyond the family to the colony at large. As the concealed "little man" in the familial and social hierarchy, Little Po embodies minor Singapore and its quotidian transgressions of authority. These transgressions make possible Little Po's small acts of kind chivalry: while skipping school, he helps an elderly woman carry her groceries and a Malay man carry baskets of rambutans and bananas.[30] At school, Little Po is inattentive, preferring to be the class policeman by mediating disputes and defending weaker students against bullies. A capable fighter, he has no interest in becoming a merchant when he grows up, even though his father tells him this is his obligation.

Little Po's innocent twist on the institutionalized correlation between ethnicity and occupation, or the racial division of labor, is a crucial component of Lao She's colonial satire. Early in the novel, Little Po confides in his sister his dream for the future:

> Little Po had two ambitions that only his younger sister knew about: to be an Indian gatekeeper (all the big stores in Singapore had Indians guard the gates throughout the night) and a Malay traffic officer.
>
> In Little Po's view, the Indian gatekeeper who kept night-watch was so dignified and handsome! . . . From morning till night, he had no need to fret over his affairs. He just sat in front of the gate, observing the hustle and bustle outside. . . .
>
> The Malay traffic officer carried a slender baton on his shoulders. . . . As soon as he turned to face east, all the east-west traffic came to a halt, while the north-south traffic rushed past. What power and control—now that was exciting! If Little Po were a traffic officer with that baton on his shoulder . . . he might turn in circles in the middle of the street, causing the traffic from all directions to crash—that would add to the excitement![31]

On the streets of Singapore, Little Po discovers the professions that will allow him to wield power and mete out justice—like he does in the classroom—while spending all his time outside. Although he has internalized Singapore's racialized division of labor, he has not yet internalized the immutable biologic of European racialism: if Indian Sikhs make excellent gatekeepers and Malays make superb policemen, then he certainly must be Indian and Malay as well, since he too is drawn to developing those skills.

Lao She interrogates the "race question" (*zhongzu de wenti*) in chapter 2, as Little Po ventures to determine whether he is "Hokkien, Cantonese, Indian, Malay, white, or Japanese." His mother tells him that "she and his father came from China" and that "the gatekeeper at the shop was from India," but Little Po wonders whether this is merely "rubbish talk," because he can find "no China or India on the map of Singapore."[32] When Little Po's father scolds him for playing with Hokkien, Indian, and Malay children, he learns that his father despises people who are not Cantonese. His sister tells him:

> "The kids on the east end of the street all have Malay fathers—our father must also be Malay."
>
> Shaking his head, Little Po said, "I've got it! The Malays must be from Shanghai—our father looks down on the Shanghainese, and that must be why he also despises the Malays. . . ."

> "Dad is from Guangdong. Mom told me that Guangdong is the nicest and richest place on earth!" Xianpo now acted as if she were Little Po's wiser older sister.
>
> "Guangdong must be India!"
>
> Xianpo thought for a while. "That's right!"[33]

Despite their misunderstanding of world geography, Little Po and his sister expose the absurdity of ethnic and region-based prejudice, especially among communities that now share the same settlement.

The two siblings "resolve the race question" by reasoning that one chooses her race just as she chooses her future profession. Xianpo tells her brother that if she ever has a child, the child will be Indian. She anticipates her mother's negative reaction:

> I'll tell Mom that when Indian children grow up, they can become Chinese too. Just look at our two, little yellow chicks: aren't their feathers slowly turning black and red? Children can also change colors in this way.[34]

The siblings see no reason why Little Po cannot play with children of other ethnic groups and grow up to be an "Indian gatekeeper" or a "Malay traffic officer," or why Xianpo cannot have an Indian child. For them, one's race is a matter of voluntary (not predetermined) affiliation. This thinking, which rejects both the colonial authority's interpellation and diasporic cultural conservatism, is later mirrored in Little Po's "minor defiance" of his father's orders on his birthday: although Little Po performs a mandatory demonstration of filial piety by kowtowing to his father, he negates its Confucian symbolism by performing the same gesture for his younger sister (when he was supposed to do so for his older brother) because he wants to demonstrate the genuine gratitude he feels toward her. Though Little Po's parents reprimand him, they laugh in amusement because the disarmingly innocent Xianpo is the common object of the family's love. Lao She bookends the novel with statements about how much Little Po loves his younger sister and highlights his gentle conscientiousness toward her throughout: every night, Little Po "helped her set up her mosquito net, covered her with her blanket, and only then was he himself able to go to sleep."[35] As the banana leaf-wrapped baby delivered from the heavens, Xianpo symbolizes the unadulterated nature of the tropics and the innocent, playful wisdom of children not yet inculcated in colonial knowledge and ethnocentrism.

In addition to the family, Lao She satirizes Little Po's school as another allegorical structure of colonial and diasporic authority.

Little Po attends a Cantonese school (though he also takes a Mandarin class there) where he finds the daily lessons boring and pointless. Rather than reading a chapter in a textbook about steamships, he prefers to go observe all the different ferries in the harbor: he even skips school to go down to the pier, where he surreptitiously enters an overseas passenger steamship and tours it before a guard eventually escorts him off. He is frustrated that the more he advances in school, the fewer illustrations he finds in his textbooks. Lao She elaborates his conflict with the system: "Little Po loved his teachers, but they never saw eye to eye. He loved the number eight, but his teachers asked about seven. When he wanted to sing, his teachers insisted on teaching Mandarin. No one could resolve their differences for them."[36] Despite his aversion to school, Little Po is thankful not to be in his friend's position: Sanduo is home-schooled by a strict old Hokkien tutor who makes him recite phrases all day long, forcing him to stand outside the door under the hot sun as punishment for failing to memorize characters. Though Sanduo "recognized more Chinese characters than anyone," Little Po sees his education as useless, because Sanduo "only knew the words in books" and found himself "at a loss" when asked to read advertisements or street signs in Singapore. Little Po is jealous of his two Malay friends, a pair of sisters whose school begins later in the morning and offers more play time. He knows his father, who "despises the Malays," will not let him attend a Malay school. Little Po also envies the Indian brothers: they rotate turns attending an Anglophone school where their Anglo-American teachers cannot distinguish between them, allowing their parents to pay only one student's tuition and giving each child a holiday every other day.[37]

Lao She contrasts Singapore's ethno-linguistically divided social institutions—home, work, and school—with the colony's tropical "green" spaces of biodiversity and integration: the playground, the park, and the botanic gardens. Here, Little Po and his Malay, Indian, and Hokkien friends invent games and sing songs in many languages:

> Some sang Malay songs, some sang Indian songs, some sang Chinese songs, some sang Cantonese opera, and those who couldn't sing just stretched their necks and hummed.[38]

Although they sing in many languages (and nonlanguages), and although the novel itself is composed in standard Chinese, the Singaporean children, regardless of ethnic or regional background, speak to each other in Malay, which Lao She calls the unofficial Esperanto or "world language" (*shijie yu*) of the Nanyang: "All the children you meet on the streets, whether brown or yellow, speak Malay (even Xiao Po and his younger sister always spoke to each other in Malay)."[39] Not only do Little Po and his sister choose not to speak Cantonese to each other (the "mother tongue" their parents deem superior), they also avoid communicating in Mandarin. Bearing in mind that the school where Lao She taught was a Mandarin-medium Chinese school designed to strengthen the community's ethno-nationalism, the fact that Lao She underscores the siblings' choice of Malay (and their rejection of Mandarin and English) implicates the Singaporean schoolchildren as neither "loyal" Chinese nor "properly" colonized subjects. By speaking Malay—or more likely (had Lao She acknowledged this distinction) Baba Malay, the creole language (with Hokkien and English influences) associated with the Peranakan community—Little Po and his friends use the colony's unofficial lingua franca, a language symbolic of a creolization transcending diasporic ethnocentrism. Playing under the green canopy of Singapore's parks and gardens, away from the watchful eye of parents and colonial authorities, the children communicate in the language (or nonlanguage) of their choosing.

Lao She takes these green spaces of creativity a step further in the final third of the novel, which the author wrote after he returned to China. On his birthday, Little Po's parents take him to the botanic gardens and then the cinema to see a foreign picture. The show lulls Little Po to sleep and on a fantastical journey into the "Shadowland," a wild, fairy-tale jungle dreamscape of animal allegory: Little Po witnesses a "World War" between monkeys and wolves, transforms into a cat to brave the dangers of "Tiger Mountain," and then free-falls into the sea before finally waking up. Even though the animals Little Po encounters (or becomes) embody various aspects of warlike human behavior,[40] the author claims that Little Po has left human society and its structures, such as colonialism and capitalism, behind: "Only when sleeping does one truly possess a measure of freedom. . . . Only when you are asleep are you finally your own master, with your little bed as your palace." In contrast to Singapore, Shadowland is an uncolonized frontier, with no surnames, currencies, or police to tame or circumscribe one's sense of adventure.[41]

Although Little Po leaves Singapore behind in his extended reverie, Lao She acknowledges that the Shadowland is "still at times a light parody of Nanyang affairs,"[42] an uncolonized counterpart to

Singapore's orderly colonial structure and a reflection of the lush, wild, tropical Nanyang setting. Yet the dream sequence enhanced the reception of *Little Po's Birthday* as mere children's fantasy: though notable as a landmark work of New Literature in the underrepresented genre of children's vernacular fiction, its social significance is underappreciated. Scholarly debate on *Little Po's Birthday* centers on whether readers should value the novel more for its content—as a poignant satire of colonial Singapore—or its form—as one of the first children's stories written in the standard vernacular, filling an area of dearth in modern Chinese fiction at the time of its composition.[43] May Fourth proposals for a new indigenous "children's literature" (*ertong wenxue*) in standard Chinese tended to conflate notions of a literature written for children and one written about children (but primarily for mature readers), in which children appear as a romantic "symbol of light, hope, and progress."[44] This conflation undergirds the dichotomous interpretations of *Little Po's Birthday*: whereas Singaporean scholars emphasize the novel's irreverent satire through its realistic relationship to past and present Singapore,[45] literary critics in China espouse *Little Po's Birthday* for its innovative use of the standard vernacular and nursery rhyme, with select phrases from the novel even modeled in modern dictionaries of Beijing slang.[46] In his own reflections, Lao She claimed the novel's real achievement was its language, as his goal was to keep the diction as simple, lucid, and childlike as possible, which helped him distill the power of *baihua wen* ("pure speech writing").[47] The narrative offers few details regarding the Singaporean setting and does not use local Sinophone terms—Mandarin, Hokkien, Cantonese, or otherwise—that vary from northern Chinese vocabulary.[48] The author avoids common local phrasings such as *mada* (from the Malay *mata-mata*) for policeman and *Jining ren* (from the Hokkien "Kling") for Indians, terms commonly found in the local Sinophone literature from this period.[49] Even if Lao She was familiar with such terms, he likely did not want to alienate the China-based readership for whom the novel was intended.

This intended readership is evident in Lao She's diction, narrative voice, and use of colloquialisms more familiar to readers from North China. In chapter 3, for example, Little Po sends Lunar New Year's greetings to his imaginary friends around the world. Here, the omniscient third-person narrator intrudes to address the readers, suggesting that if they would like to send a gift to Little Po, the best present would be snow, since Little Po has never seen snow and imagines that it is red. In return, the narrator promises, Little Po would gratefully send some giant green banana leaves or huge snails to those who have never been to the southern tropics.[50] The interface between setting/subject (Singapore) and implied reader (China) brings forth the transcolonial context of *Little Po's Birthday*: for a primarily China-based readership, what are the implications of writing a social satire set in colonial Singapore and told through a child's perspective? This satire does not revel in exotic "South Seas color," wallow in morose sentiments of Chinese victimization abroad (like *Mr. Ma and Son*), or valorize diasporic nationalism through the figure of the Nanyang Huaqiao (Lao She's original intent). Throughout this "children's fantasy," ethnic pride (expressed mainly by Little Po's father) appears as chauvinism and essentialism targeting not the colonizers (British characters are entirely absent) but other colonized ethnic groups, thereby reinforcing the divide-and-rule strategy of British imperialism. The resolution of the narrative in a fantastical dream realm where only jungle animals roam signifies the ultimate departure from Lao She's initial desire to write a South Seas epic based in human history and reality. In Singapore, Lao She discovered uncolonized frontiers in the naïveté of the colony's children—in their unmonitored spaces, "irrational" logic, impromptu games, improvised songs and languages, and imaginative dreams. All of these minor frontiers expose the irrelevance of the institutional, racialist knowledge inculcating the children. While not impervious to ethno-linguistic prejudice and segregation, most of the children in *Little Po's Birthday* have no use for them.

Recognizable here is the familiar May Fourth refrain that hope for national salvation lies with children, a message conventionally understood in narratives of antifeudalism and class struggle, as in Lu Xun's "Diary of a Madman" ("Kuangren riji," 1918) and "My Old Home" ("Guxiang," 1921).[51] In contrast to Lu Xun, Lao She uses the children of a multiethnic Southeast Asian colony to express hope for overcoming ethnic-based prejudice and racial oppression in a future free from colonization. Lao She admitted in his memoirs that his Singaporean students surprised him with their perceptive views, even if he found them rather immature. They discussed sociopolitical issues in remarkably more progressive ways than Lao She's students in London, where he found even the most politically "impassioned speeches" could not compare to the observations of Singaporean middle-school students.[52] While not overidealizing the multiethnic environs of the colony, where proximity does not equal integration or mutual tolerance, Lao

She draws insight from the children of a colonial society who reject imperialist logic and the ethnocentrisms of their immigrant parents.

The transcolonial observations in *Little Po's Birthday* reconcile Lao She's differentially minoritized identities: his (sometimes self-effaced) ethnic background as a Manchu in China and his Overseas Chinese identity in London. Just as he was not immune to anti-Sinitic racism in Britain, Lao She was not ignorant of the anti-Manchu sentiments in the Han-centric formulation of Chinese nationalism, expressed most notably in his final, incomplete novel *Beneath the Red Banner* (*Zhenghong qi xia*; published posthumously in 1980).[53] Even though Lao She's Beijing vernacular is inflected by his Manchu heritage, the historical record of the New Literature movement subsumes such elements under the larger linguistic purification process of the vernacular movement, just as it subsumes his portrayals of ethnocentrism under the common motif of antifeudalism. In this literary history, Lao She's depictions of overinflated ethnic pride are merely another exposé of China's "corrupt society" and "foolish, old-fashioned characters,"[54] rather than a critique of an emergent Chinese ethno-nationalism.

Writing back to China, the trope of the South Seas in *Little Po's Birthday* plays an important transcolonial role. In Singapore, Lao She found himself—a Manchu author from North China—in a multiethnic colony ruled by a British minority elite yet largely inhabited by a heterogeneous Sinophone majority experiencing the rise of diasporic nationalism. If *Little Po's Birthday* critiques China's ethno-nationalist principle through its portrayal of ethnocentric immigrant parents in colonial Singapore, it also uses Singaporean schoolchildren to imagine a postimperial future for a China (in addition to a Singapore) free from ethno-linguistic biases. Through children, the novel envisions a nation that recognizes and values multiplicity (not uniformity or homogeneity), integration/interaction (not segregation), and equality (not hierarchy or rule by either ethno-linguistic majority or minority). This is the "imagined China" that emerges in the novel's transcolonial context of writing the South Seas.

A NEW WORLD VISION: FROM OVERSEAS CHINESE TO SINOPHONE MALAYAN LITERATURE

The transcolonial critique of ethno-nationalism by southbound writers in Southeast Asia not only "writes back" to China, reflecting on the discourse of national salvation there, but also engages the local Sinophone literary scene, especially in Malaya.[55] With the largest settler populations, the Straits Settlements of Singapore and Penang were regional centers of Sinophone literary production and diasporic Chinese nationalism in Southeast Asia. Here, a modern "Sinophone Malayan New Literature" emerged under the influence of the New Literature movement in China. The degree to which southbound writers shaped local attitudes about and set trends for this literature as an anticolonial project reflects the privilege and esteem that the settler communities granted them as intellectuals who came as ambassadors from the motherland in the "cultural wilderness" of the Nanyang. Southbound writers offered their perspectives about what should be the anticolonial causes of Sinophone literature, what role diasporic Chinese nationalism and "local color" (*difang secai*) should play in expressing those causes, and how such features might or might not articulate a relationship to the anticolonial nationalism of Chinese New Literature.

The southbound experiences of Yu Dafu (1896–1945) best illustrate the historical importance of this literary interrelationship and the debates it involved.[56] Not only was Yu already more of a modern Chinese literary celebrity than all other southbound authors by the time he came to Singapore in late 1938, but his relatively late arrival on the local Sinophone literary scene—after it had already absorbed (and debated) the influence of China's New Literature movement for nearly two decades—gave Yu a unique vantage point to assess and comment on this process. Whereas for Chinese New Literature, "South Seas color" denoted impressions of an exotic colonial space that reflected back on China's own modernity and emergent nationhood, it became for Sinophone Malayan New Literature a trope of the familiar, a mode to express one's cultural difference and affiliation to a tropical homeland. While Yu Dafu did not write any remarkable works of South Seas color before he was forced to take refuge in Sumatra following the Japanese invasion of Singapore in early 1942,[57] his newspaper editorials, sponsorship of literary forums, and dialogues with local authors testify to this historical shift in Nanyang signification. Yet the Nanyang never became its own geopolitical entity or category of literary production. Rather, in the debates and activities in which Yu Dafu took part, the Nanyang was a "New World" vision facilitating the ideological transition from one conceptual category—an Overseas Chinese literature bound to China by ethno-national obligation and use of standard Chinese—to another: a modern Sinophone Malayan literature inspired by anticolonial commitments and multicultural nationalist aspirations in the space of settlement.

Yu Dafu's presence in colonial Malaya is largely due to the Japanese invasion of China in 1937: helping to mobilize anti-Japanese resistance around Chinese nationalist sentiments preoccupied him while he was there. Yet his role in building a conceptual bridge between Chinese and Sinophone Malayan New Literature stems from the ongoing ideological reverberations of China's May Fourth movement (namely its language and cultural politics) among Chinese settler communities in Southeast Asia, where Mandarin (and standard Chinese writing) became the language of Sinophone print media, education, and diasporic nationalism. Although local Sinophone literatures not written in the standard vernacular predated (and coexisted alongside) these developments,[58] vernacular newspapers and their literary supplements were initially the domain (and creation) of southbound authors and first-generation immigrants fluent in Mandarin and adept at standard Chinese writing.

The first phase of Sinophone Malayan New Literature in the early 1920s was characterized by an "overseas Chinese consciousness" (*qiaomin yishi*) focusing on themes of dislocation and emigration: family financial crises back home, corruption of warlords and government officials in southeastern China, the lure of economic opportunity in the South Seas, and longing to return to the motherland.[59] Zhang Shunai, as editor of the Singapore-based *South Seas Commercial News* (*Nanyang shangbao*, better known as *Nanyang Siang Pau*) in 1919, expresses this "overseas consciousness"—imbued with Chinese ethno-nationalism—in his exhortation to readers in Malaya and the East Indies:

> We may reside overseas in the Nanyang, but our roots are after all located in China, because we are of the Han ethnicity and ultimately we are citizens of the Republic of China. Although we are now in territory belonging to England and the Netherlands, we are but sojourning guests. The ancients put it best: though the tree grows to great heights, its fallen leaves still return to the roots; if a tree is such, why not a person?[60]

Orienting the political and sentimental attachments of his readers in Malaya and the East Indies toward China—encouraging their ethnic affiliation as Han—Zhang's view reflects the dominant position of first-generation writers in the early phase of Sinophone Malayan New Literature.

As more local-born Chinese Malayans were educated in Mandarin and inculcated with loyalties to a distant Chinese nation, and as émigré writers came to terms with the unlikelihood of return to China, they began to resist the overseas consciousness. Not long after the first appearance of Nanyang exoticism in China's New Literature,[61] local authors introduced "South Seas color" (*Nanyang secai*) to Sinophone Malayan literature: this motif dominated local literary debates from 1925–33.[62]

One of the primary literary supplements advocating South Seas color was "Coconut Grove" ("Yelin") in the newspaper *Straits Gazette* (*Le bao*), which published the following statement by Huang Zhengfu—a direct rebuttal to Zhang Shunai—in July 1929:

> The perpetual assumption that those of us who reside abroad in the South Seas are but guests is to misinterpret the facts. . . . Most people foolishly hope that the situation in the motherland will change—they do not know there is no way the Overseas Chinese can leave the Nanyang. . . . Their creation of Overseas Chinese literature is based on this misconception. . . . Therefore we must awaken them to recognize the Nanyang as their homeland![63]

Along with his good friend Chen Lianqing (the editor of "Coconut Grove"), Huang encouraged readers to look to North America as the Nanyang's New World model, comparing Chinese migration to the South Seas to English settlement in North America.[64] The same month Huang published his statement, Chen reiterated Huang's advocacy for South Seas color in a "Coconut Grove" editorial, underscoring the Anglophone North American settler colonial analogy:

> Let us observe North America: its colonial history is as long as that of us Overseas Chinese, yet they have already created a kind of unique American culture. I want all those hoping that a Nanyang culture can sprout here to diligently hasten its germination and foliation, so that its flowers can blossom.[65]

For Chen and Huang, South Seas color entailed depicting ways that Chinese settlers had adapted, acclimated, and localized in Southeast Asia, producing their own creole culture like European settlers in the Americas.

The Anglophone North American analogy only went so far: not only was North America a continental landmass while the Nanyang referred to an archipelago, but also the Southeast Asian territories were administered by many different authorities (none of them Sinophone), including Western colonial powers, which made the integration and liberation of a single Sinophone settler colony called "Nanyang" impossible. More an abstract idea than a specific place, the Nanyang had no "exclusive geographical meaning."[66] The earliest promoters of a "Nanyang literature" in 1922 preferred a broad definition of the term that essentially included anywhere in Southeast Asia with pockets of Sinophone communities.[67] This definition failed to recognize the diversity of creole Sinophone cultures that emerged from interactions with different indigenous peoples, settlers, environments, and colonial authorities. By the 1930s, Sinophone Malayan authors acknowledged this issue: in a *Singapore Daily* (*Xingzhou ribao,* better known as *Sin Chew Jit Poh*) editorial from 1935, Peng Yuhe noted that the Nanyang—as a term that the imperial Qing's Ministry of Foreign Affairs had used to cover an area "spanning 170 million square kilometers" and "a population of over 100 million"—should be replaced by individual local terms, just as the "Eastern Seas" (Dongyang) became Japan and the "Western Seas" (Xiyang) was replaced by Europe and the Americas.[68] For Peng, the Nanyang was an outdated Sinocentric concept, unsuitable for the modern world.

By the mid-1930s, the meaning of "Nanyang literature" was specifically narrowed to cover Sinophone literature produced in British colonial Malaya. The narrowing of the Nanyang's scope hastened its decline as a descriptive name for this literature: if its geography was limited to Malaya (a peninsula as opposed to an archipelago), why not use the latter term? By the mid-1930s, Malaya replaced the Nanyang, just as "Sinophone Malayan" and "Chinese Malayan" (Ma Hua) replaced "South Seas Chinese" to describe the community as well as the literary and cultural endeavors of local writers and intellectuals.[69] In Sinophone Malayan New Literature, South Seas color did not disappear as a motif, but was resignified as "local color," a politicized term intended to depict and express outrage at the hellish reality of living under colonialism, such as the lives of not only Chinese coolies "sold as piglets" (*mai zhuzai*) to their employers, but also Indian coolies and Malay peasants working in the shipyards, mines, and plantations.[70] Like the 1930s left-wing literature (*zuoyi wenxue*) in China, Sinophone Malayan New Literature moved toward anticolonial socialism, yet it advocated a different, specifically Malayan nationalism, with some authors promoting cross-ethnic alliances with Malays and Indians. Some modern writers from China who played leading roles in Sinophone literary circles were supportive of this move on the part of Malayan writers to assert their literary, cultural, and political autonomy. Yu Dafu, as editor of several literary supplements for *Singapore Daily*, oversaw publication of many of the young authors who championed Sinophone Malayan leftist realism and local color.[71]

The tenor of the movement shifted with the outbreak of the Pacific War in 1937, as the Japanese invasion and occupation of eastern China stimulated the largest migration of Chinese intellectuals and writers to Southeast Asia. "Anti-Japanese Resistance" became the primary propaganda tool that they used to reenergize diasporic Chinese nationalism in the region. Southbound writers brought news of atrocities from the motherland, igniting a common rallying point among all factions of the Sinophone Malayan intellectual scene and subsuming all literary activity under the banner of Resistance and "responsibility to China." During the War of Resistance period from 1937 until 1941, when the Japanese launched their "southward advance" (*nanshin*) into Southeast Asia, the political agendas and ideas of prominent southbound writers became the foci of Sinophone Malayan literature.

Sinophone newspaper editors awarded southbound writers like Yu Dafu key positions in the Sinophone Malayan intellectual arena, not merely because of their status as highly acclaimed writers from China but also because they were more familiar with the situation there and the prospects for the Anti-Japanese Resistance. Advocates of Sinophone Malayan literary autonomy reconciled this reorientation toward China with their general practice of supporting anticolonial movements near or far.[72] Considering the pressures on Malayan authors to prioritize China's crises and conform to Resistance literary models in terms of language, form, and content, the transcolonial observations of Yu Dafu's critical but sympathetic editorials about the struggles of Sinophone Malayan literature, as well as his sponsorship of independent literary forums for local Malayan authors, are all the more remarkable. These editorials provide a complex view of Yu Dafu as a writer who supported the development of an autonomous Sinophone Malayan literature, even though his privileged position problematized his authority to cast judgment, as it was premised on the fact that, for the settler community he addressed, Yu *embodied* modern Chinese literature and culture.

When Yu Dafu arrived in Singapore at the end of 1938, he immediately became chief editor of three literary supplements for *Singapore Daily*, whose editors reasoned that Yu Dafu's stature would boost the credibility of their enterprise, injecting it with new energy and creativity.[73] Many Sinophone Malayan intellectuals regarded Yu as a literary ambassador and expert on contemporary trends not only in Chinese but also Japanese and Western literature: Yu had studied in Japan between 1914 and 1922 and wrote widely acclaimed fiction there, joining with other Chinese authors to form the influential Creation Society. Several Malayan writers, however, felt that immediately awarding Yu Dafu such a prestigious position was unfair and unwarranted. Regardless of Yu's fame and stature, they saw someone completely unfamiliar with local history charged with the task of developing the local literary scene. These writers felt that Yu's associations with newspaper bigwigs and business magnates, who lavished the writer with large banquets, regaling him with expensive delicacies and wine and commanding him to compose effusive poetry to mark the occasion, was a betrayal of the writer's own progressive May Fourth spirit. In their opinion, a onetime iconoclast was now a decadent literatus who simply "flaunted his social status" and Chinese cultural capital.[74]

Those critical of Yu Dafu were most irked by his negative assessments of Sinophone Malayan literature in an article entitled "Some Questions" ("Ji ge wenti") in the "Morning Star" ("Chen xing") supplement on January 21, 1939, published not even a full month after Yu's arrival. To Yu's defense, his commentary simply consisted of responses to questions posed by another southbound writer. In the interview, Yu Dafu admitted that since his arrival in Singapore and recent trip to Penang, where Yu was sent on assignment to meet writers and familiarize himself with the social and natural landscape of Malaya, requests for his assessments of "Nanyang literature" were the most common, even though he felt unqualified to give them. Asked his opinion of local writers who borrow issues from mainland China as the subject of their own works, Yu responded that there was no reason to prevent local writers from addressing such issues. According to Yu, what truly mattered was how writers addressed them: with sincerity and from personal experience, or through exaggeration and repetition of stock phrases simply to tow the popular line? Asked how writers could enhance and better demonstrate "local color" in Sinophone literature, Yu again reframed the question: it was not a matter of whether "local color" per se was important—naturally, any author writing from experience brought a local flavor to the work—but rather the depth and detail of that color, which should reveal an honest power of "expression, observation, and absorption."[75]

Despite his rather deflective responses, Yu Dafu chose a non-Chinese writer—the "national hero" and "master" (*da zuojia*) of Philippine literature, José Rizal—as his model for Malayan writers. Through Rizal, readers across the world, many of whom like Yu knew nothing about the Philippines, were able to enter its landscape and become aware of colonial oppression there, even though it was never Rizal's stated intention to express "local color." He simply wrote from experience and the desire to expose and reform society's ills, not from a superficial thematic mandate.[76] Yu's responses implied a particular judgment of Sinophone Malayan literature: since its inception, its writers had misdirected their energies toward issues unworthy of prioritization. This position obviously offended some: on January 30, 1939, an article in *New Citizens Daily* (*Xin guomin ribao*) criticized Yu Dafu for being "only a passively resistant intellectual unable to keep in lock-step with the pace of the War of Resistance era."[77]

Yu did not respond in kind to individual attacks, reserving his critiques for the literature it was his job to assess. As he familiarized himself with the Sinophone literary scene in Malaya, Yu Dafu's observations of colonial society became more poignant: following local trends, he shifted his term of address from "Nanyang literature" to "Sinophone Malayan literature." Approximately one month after "Some Questions," Yu wrote an editorial entitled "Upon Reading Submissions" ("Kan gao de jieguo") in the Penang edition of *Singapore Daily.* The author complained that most of the submissions he received suffered from cliché, blandness, and monotony, invoking the same one-dimensional characters such as "Han traitors" (Hanjian) and wartime "profiteers."[78] He called for Malayan writers to bravely develop more depth and roundness to their protagonists and antagonists.

A year after his arrival, Yu Dafu proffered further suggestions in a "Morning Star" editorial entitled "Advancements in the Sinophone Malayan Drama Movement" ("Ma Hua juyun de jinzhan"). Having attended several performances by modern spoken drama troupes from China in Singapore, Yu recognized this genre as an outstanding forum for the work of wartime propaganda. The author assessed the prospects for spoken drama's grassroots development in Malaya, recognizing the difficulty local audiences had relating to the themes, particularly the satire, in the Chinese performances. Yu envisioned the creation of spoken dramas that would satirize the Nanyang by employing language more familiar to the locals. As a potential target for this satire, he suggested Overseas Chinese who still obsessed over "Chinese traditions." Yu Dafu perceived "Chinese custom" in Malaya as frozen in the past, stagnated by colonial policies relegating it to apolitical performances deemed nonthreatening. He considered those who stubbornly ignored contemporary China's progressiveness by sternly insisting upon the preservation of cultural traditions simply because of their "Chineseness" as suffering from a psychology of colonization and as suitable subjects in a satirical spoken drama relevant to Malayan audiences.[79] Yu criticized blind worship of the "superiority" of Chinese civilization, not simply when expressed as strict adherence to an ossified notion of traditional Chinese culture but also when favoring new, progressive literary trends simply because they came from China.

Yu Dafu's frank critique of Sinophone Malayan literature was balanced by his continual willingness to lend his eyes and ears to aspiring local writers. His residence in Singapore's Tiong Bahru district became a popular destination for young writers like Miao Xiu, who in 1961 recalled Yu Dafu fondly as warm, receptive, unpretentious, and sincere in his ambition to help budding writers.[80] While Yu Dafu reproved certain generic trends in Malayan literature, he felt that its more glaring shortcomings were its lack of capital and forums for publication. Yu helped writers develop their craft and also sought to draw voices outside intellectual circles into the literary arena by sponsoring amateur publications.

As editor, Yu Dafu pored through past issues of literary supplements from before his tenure. In the summer of 1941, he found an announcement calling upon readers to submit a creative journal entry capturing one day in their lives to a compilation to be entitled *A Day in Malaya* (*Malaiya de yiri*). Apparently, the idea was shelved due to lack of publication funds, editorial promotion, and reader interest. On July 14, Yu posted an announcement in "Morning Star" stating his intention to revive and oversee the abandoned project, inviting readers from "all walks of life" to try their hand at "engaging in introspection during this tense time of war."[81] In a subsequent announcement, Yu set August 15, 1941, as the "one day" that all submissions should document, reassuring readers that if funding became a problem, he would use his connections in Hong Kong to ensure the collection's publication. He reminded readers that he preferred quantity and diversity to quality: he hoped to see creative progress, if "only measured in inches," and widespread participation so that the publication would capture a diverse picture of wartime Malaya.[82]

A Day in Malaya never reached publication. In late 1941, as Japanese invasion appeared inevitable, Sinophone presses that sponsored Resistance propaganda ceased printing, as their staff members had to consider their individual survival. Up until then, the newspapers sponsoring the *A Day in Malaya* project received more than two thousand submissions, which the "Morning Star" supplement continued to publish almost daily through the end of September 1941. This surge in enthusiastic response to a previously failed project attests to Yu Dafu's prestige as a celebrity catalyst. Submissions arrived from people in a vast range of industries, including a cook, a hospital orderly, a student, a barber, a road construction worker, a server in a local café, and a prostitute. The dominant themes are wartime inflation and the toils of daily labor: writers lament long hours of intense work with little remuneration and wonder how they will survive the war with rising costs of food and other staples. Other common themes are nostalgia for China, as many of the writers were immigrants, as well as the difficulties of adapting to a new environment and communicating in other languages such as Malay. For example, a road construction worker described his job laying cement on mountain roads in upcountry Malaya. A recent immigrant, he wrote of his homesickness, his problems affording dental care for his tooth disease, and his attempts to learn English and Malay from his Malay and Indian coworkers and dorm mates.[83] The submission includes Malay, English, and Cantonese terms in transliteration with explanatory footnotes provided by Yu Dafu.

There is no way to verify the authenticity of the submissions to *A Day in Malaya*, as many of them were written under aliases. "A Day and Night in the Life of an Unlicensed Prostitute" ("Sichang de yiri ye"), written by Bi Xia or "Jade Hues," is more a sensationalized account of the author's life history leading up to her present circumstances than a single day's journal entry. She writes that she was sold off by her family in Guangzhou to a landlord who promised to find her work in Singapore, yet who turned out to be the madam of a brothel there that forces Bi Xia into prostitution in order to repay the debt for her South Seas passage. The remainder of the narrative discusses Bi Xia's "daily activities" on August 15, 1941, including the private lessons in English the author is forced to take because her madam hopes she can broaden her potential clientele.[84]

Regardless of their authenticity, the submissions to *A Day in Malaya* demonstrate the collaborative development of Sinophone Malayan New Literature in newspaper forums initiated by southbound writers that broadened literary participation among a working-class community traditionally stereotyped as illiterate or not interested in high cultural pursuits. The example of Yu Dafu as critic and sponsor of forums like *A Day in Malaya* suggests that modern writers from China did not bring consensus to local literary debates about what subjects, styles, and ethnic, national, regional, or local affiliations were worthy of literary evocation and approbation, even at the moment these writers were most unified around the Anti-Japanese Resistance. *A Day in Malaya* also marks the beginning of the end of this intimate collaboration in literary activity between the southbound writer (as a key figure of modern Chinese literary history) and the local Sinophone scene,[85] as war and postwar politics indelibly altered the historical trajectory of Malayan—and then Malaysian—literature.

Whether framing an allegory of colonial society (Lao She's *Little Po's Birthday*) or commenting on local literary production (Yu Dafu's critique and sponsorship of Sinophone Malayan literature), the trope of the Nanyang challenges historical consensus regarding the ethno-nationalist principle in the New Literature movements of both China and Malaya, revealing ethnic, cultural, and national identities as sites of debate, contestation, and (re)negotiation for the settler communities to determine for themselves. In Chinese New Literature, Lao She imagined the Nanyang to reflect back to Chinese readers the divisiveness of the ethno-nationalist principle, dooming its effectiveness as anticolonial strategy. For Sinophone Malayan New Literature, Yu Dafu offered his transcolonial perspective as a southbound writer to assist in the local resignification of the Nanyang as a New World concept through which creole settlers might explore, articulate, and proclaim affiliations of language, place, culture, and nation (like Malaya) distinct from those imposed by the ancestral homeland.

CHAPTER 3

Creolizing the Sinophone from Malaysia to Taiwan

Postcolonial Sinophone Malaysian literature inherits a long tradition of reterritorializing the South Seas trope from a Southeast Asian subject position. This tradition began with Sinophone writers from colonial Malaya in the early twentieth century who cultivated local "South Seas color" in their narratives and resisted an "overseas consciousness" that sought recognition and cultural capital from the ancestral homeland. Throughout the last decades of British rule (bridging Japanese occupation from 1942–45), Sinophone writers contended with an imperial authority that recognized them only as Chinese nationals and temporary residents. Malayan authors also grappled with their subordination to first-generation "southbound" (*nanlai*) writers from China who dominated Sinophone publications and often propagated diasporic nationalism while designating "Nanyang literature" a "tributary" (*zhiliu*) tradition that survived only through continual replenishment from the "motherland."[1] Situating their nationalism locally against colonial rule (British and Japanese), many Sinophone authors championed the Nanyang as the birthplace of an emergent Malayan creole culture created by interactions between settlers and their surroundings, rather than a cultural wilderness merely to be "opened up" by Overseas Chinese pioneers. Although favoring the leftist social realism of Chinese New Literature—focusing on lower, working-class, or exploited characters and preferring short stories and novellas with a lot of dialogue and spoken language (*kouyu* or *koutou hua*)—Sinophone Malayan authors also revealed how standard Chinese writing based on Mandarin (now the measure of one's "literacy") handicapped their literary and cultural pursuits. They developed their own strategies of multilingualism and creolization: primarily through transliteration, they allowed nonstandard Sinitic languages such as Hokkien and Cantonese—as well as the English, Malay, and Tamil vocabulary their local spoken varieties absorbed—to penetrate their standard Chinese, particularly when capturing dialogue. These code-switching experimentations of Sinophone Malayan realism intensified throughout the 1940s and 1950s, continuing past the end of the colonial period.[2]

However, the emergence of the postcolonial nation changed the landscape of Sinophone literature in Malaya. Cold War politics and national liberation movements throughout the 1950s and 1960s brought to an end the transcolonial network between south coastal China and Southeast Asia. Cut off (or freed) from mainland Chinese support and cultural patronage, Sinophone communities were no longer subjects of Western empires or overseas nationals (Huaqiao) of the Republic of China (ROC), but found themselves (potential) citizens of emergent Southeast Asian nations, though they frequently struggled for amicable inclusion and proportionate representation in the new national imagination. Since Malaysian independence (first as Malaya in 1957 and then as an enlarged Malaysia in 1963), Sinophone writers have grappled with their marginality, witnessing the colonial-era status of their literature as tributary to the national mainstream of modern Chinese literature transform into that of a "minor literature" peripheral to Malaysia's national mainstream.[3] Born and raised in an environment of intensified ethnic polarization, postcolonial Sinophone authors reflect upon their experiences as Malaysians and confront the racialized, nativist definitions of "Malaysianness" that exclude them.

Concurrent with its postcolonial minoritization, Sinophone Malaysian literature has transcended its national crisis by going transnational. The exclusionary, hierarchical multiculturalism in postcolonial Malaysia compelled the emergence of a transnational Sinophone Malaysian literature sustained and replenished through economic, educational, and cultural ties initially forged with Taiwan during the Cold War. The postwar trajectory of Taiwan as the island refuge of the ROC in exile after the "loss of the mainland" in 1949 helped foster this transnational Sinophone literary network. This network does not simply entail the physical relocation of Chinese Malaysian authors to Taiwan, but also their expanded access to

Sinophone publishers there. The literary link between Malaysia and Taiwan was first forged by Chinese Malaysian students who initially conceived of their travel to the exiled island republic for higher education as a "cultural return" to a metropolitan center that was the rightful claimant to continental Chinese traditions. Rather than continue the local-oriented nationalist and creolization tactics of Sinophone Malayan realism, their alienation from Malaysia compelled a desire for cultural belonging elsewhere: their move to Taiwan was often an extension of their ambition to embrace and cultivate Chineseness. The first crop of émigré Malaysian writers arrived in Taiwan in the 1960s amidst a burgeoning modernist movement, spurred on by the (physical and psychological) loss of mainland China, anticommunist authoritarianism under the Nationalist Party (Kuomintang, KMT), and US neocolonial patronage. The formation of poet societies such as Constellation (Xingzuo) and Divine Land (Shenzhou) encouraged Sinophone Malaysian creative escapism into the embrace of an imagined, mythical China through modernist poetry.

The course of Taiwan's history eventually shattered the myth of cultural return. By the end of the Cold War, the KMT had lost the legitimacy of its claim to China, both internationally (in terms of diplomatic recognition) and domestically (with the growing visibility of a Taiwanese nativist movement). The belated "loss of China" left Taiwan to confront a complex history of serial colonization from fifty years under Japanese rule to a Sinophone settler colony whose raison d'être was continental recovery. Taiwan's political and cultural sea-change around the lifting of martial law in 1987 reconfigures Sinophone Malaysian literature's link to the island: once perceived as a vertical bloodline of cultural return to the ancestral land, it transforms into an archipelagic network between two small maritime countries that circumvents the exclusive dissemination channels of indigenized Malaysianness and continental Chineseness. For more recent Malaysian arrivals, an uncanny sense of perpetual or "secondary" diaspora (as opposed to cultural return) informs their modernist literary reflections on their cultural upbringing as well as their critique of Sinophone Malaysian literary history.[4] Moving inadvertently from a "Chinese diaspora" in Malaysia to a "Nanyang diaspora" in Taiwan, this new wave of transplants, including authors such as Ng Kim Chew, Choong Yee Voon, and Chan Tah Wei, embodies not only the physical journey from postcolonial Malaysia to Taiwan, but also a literary journey from a self-understanding as diasporic Chinese subjects to the belated recognition of creolized Malaysianness.[5] While on the one hand the Nanyang trope symbolizes the sense of nationless status and repetitious displacement for these authors, on the other hand, it comes to define their specific connection to Taiwan, one that facilitates a temporally and spatially distanced renegotiation with their Malaysian experiences and subjectivities. Here, creolization is not simply the realist representation of culture as an ongoing process of localization, acclimation, and intermixing in the present. Magnified by the experience of Taiwan, creolization also becomes an imaginatively recuperated, retrospective, retroactive, revisionist, and metacognitive *acting on the past.*

Among the post–martial law generation of Sinophone Malaysian authors in Taiwan, Ng Kim Chew stands out for his distinctively metafictional rewriting of the Nanyang. Ng's short fiction details how creolization occurs under (and therefore belies) the conditions of its suppression and elision in postcolonial Malaysia.[6] In the histories Ng recuperates, creolization is not a harmonious blending and syncretism but a frictional transgression and messy desecration of ethnic, religious, and linguistic sanctity, blasphemous to Malaysia's official multiculturalism while satirically undermining the centripetal allure of diasporic Chineseness. Ng's narrative aesthetic is not to simply reflect reality, but to suggest possibility through exaggerated, farcical parody. Rather than bridging the rupture between spoken and written language, Ng reopens it to make Sinophone writing itself a point of interrogation. For Ng, the Sinophone is not simply the transformation of standard Chinese writing by the realistic inflections of a multilingual Malaysian acoustics, but a material artifact of forgotten cross-cultural traumas—forcible racialization, identity erasure, and incomplete assimilation—which can only be partially recuperated and incorrectly or unfaithfully mimicked, thereby requiring new embellishments and inventive possibilities. Ng Kim Chew's stories expose the fiction of cultural return by revealing persistent misreadings of diasporic origins. His short stories satirize certain clichés of the Nanyang imagination to critique the diasporic consciousness, locating its origins not in dislocation from the ancestral homeland but in colonial racializations and postcolonial nationalisms that assign identities while eradicating, assimilating, or "converting" others.

Through this transnational recuperation of creolization, the South Seas trope provides important contributions to both Taiwanese and Malaysian literatures. It reverberates with the potential to reframe

Taiwanese literary history not as the binary polemics of mainlanders versus Taiwanese or modernism versus nativism, but as beginning from cross-cultural contacts and creolization between settler, colonizer, and native, between Sinophone and non-Sinophone, and between archipelagic and continental orientations. The South Seas imagination of Ng Kim Chew also challenges Malaysia's paradigm of national literature, refusing to abandon the claim to Malaysianness and not simply embrace ethnic minority status. It also encourages Sinophone Malaysian writers to not just summon the Chinese literary canon as their creative inspiration, but to engage the discursive terrain and history they share—not always harmoniously—with non-Sinophone Malaysian literature and culture.

POSTCOLONIAL MULTICULTURALISM AND SINOPHONE LITERARY TRANSNATIONALISM

Ng Kim Chew situates his intellectual and creative practice within the context of Sinophone Malaysian literary history, against the backdrop of postcolonial nationhood and the legacies of British colonialism in Malaya that shaped Malaysia's political rhetoric of multiculturalism. British colonialism in Malaya operated on a regime of racialized management, tailoring different policies for communities identified as *bumiputera* or native "sons of the soil" (namely the Malays) and those identified as non-*bumiputera* (namely Chinese and Indians). Though census figures fluctuate, Malays compose nearly half of Malaysia's total population, while other groups designated as *bumiputera*, located mostly in Malaysian Borneo, account for an additional 11 percent. Among non-*bumiputera*, Chinese Malaysians form the largest minority at 24 percent and Indian Malaysians at 7 percent. In Peninsular Malaysia, these non-*bumiputera* percentages are substantially higher.[7] Encouraged by the British, the intense influx of Chinese immigrants to colonial Malaya between 1882 and 1932 made them the dominant ethnic group in the western coastal states of Peninsular Malaysia: this produced the demographic majorities Chinese Malaysians currently hold in urban centers such as Penang, Taiping, and Ipoh.[8] Their significant presence has long supplied fodder to Malay politicians disseminating nativist fears of being overwhelmed by "immigrants."

Beyond majority-minority and indigenous-settler demographics, racialized divisions of political authority (which Malays enjoy) and economic clout (which Chinese Malaysians enjoy) shape Malaysia's official multiculturalism. Challenging the Chinese Malaysian share of the national economy, Malay politicians have emphasized how the collaborative role of Chinese merchants in British colonialism made this share possible. In the colonial era, Chinese Malayans dominated most of the rubber and tin industries, as well as commerce. The employers and supervisors of mines and plantations were mostly Chinese settlers, many of whom amassed substantial wealth.[9] Indentured Chinese coolies—hardly likely to partake of that wealth—constituted much of the exploited labor force. With a divide-and-rule strategy, the British purposefully instilled among Malays a stereotype of Chinese settlers as greedy and unscrupulous, whereas among Chinese Malayans they perpetuated their own stereotype of Malays as lazy and indolent.[10] As new immigrants poured into Malaya throughout the late colonial period, the Malay elite successfully petitioned British colonial policy to defend against the "alien" usurpation of Malay authority.[11] Even though Malays descended from a commercial seafaring tradition, the British affirmed their status as the true *bumiputera* of the Malayan peninsula, redefined in the early twentieth century as the *tanah Melayu* ("Malay land").[12] Viewing Chinese settlers as "exclusively a transient labor force,"[13] the British imparted to the Malays the notion that the "Chinese" were loyal to China and had only a temporary interest in the *tanah Melayu* as a means to enrich themselves.

In the decade following Japanese occupation, prior to the British-backed and -brokered independence (*merdeka*), the United Malays National Organization (UMNO) organized broad support for a "Malay-rights" program that did little more than exaggerate colonial British policies claiming to protect Malays.[14] The coalition multicultural government known as the Alliance Party, formed from the more moderate factions of UMNO, the Malayan Chinese Association (MCA), and the Malayan Indian Congress (MIC), endorsed the position of Malays as *bumiputera* and approved a four-to-one ratio of Malays to non-Malays in the Civil Service.[15] In exchange, the MCA was granted few concessions to safeguard Sinophone education, media, and cultural institutions from the incursion of pro-Malay policies, yet privately funded schools and student-run literary magazines continued operating.[16] Significant numbers of Sinophone-educated students began seeking higher education abroad: many chose Taiwan as their destination, especially those seeking "cultural roots." While travel to China was out of the question, these students saw Taiwan as a place where they would fit in with the majority. Taiwan's KMT government encouraged this by claiming to be the "true heir to the Chinese cultural tradition," espousing a "Greater China" diasporic consciousness, and offering generous university scholarships to Overseas Chinese students (*qiaosheng*).[17]

The influx of Malaysian students to Taiwan was stimulated by the 1969 Kuala Lumpur ethnic riots (the May Thirteenth incident) and their political aftermath. Following Singapore's expulsion from Malaysia in 1965, many UMNO politicians felt the Alliance government was too soft on "agitators" who challenged Malay authority. At the same time, Chinese Malaysian voters in the largely urban constituencies were increasingly disenchanted with the MCA's failure to leverage their position. Malay dissatisfaction over the outcome of the 1969 general election, in which with the UMNO-led Alliance lost several parliamentary seats to opposition parties, touched off a volatile period of ethnic violence that led to the suspension of the constitution, parliament, and the press.[18] UMNO used the riots and threats of further violence as a basis for a reactionary national platform affirming a "more assertive Malay supremacy." Malay became the national language (and primary language of instruction in all public secondary schools), Islam the official religion, and "Islamic culture" the "norm of the Malaysian nation."[19] In 1970, the government began implementing stronger preferential measures and quotas to enhance the economic standing of the *bumiputera*. The New Economic Policy (NEP) became the defining terms of Malaysia's postcolonial multiculturalism under the UMNO-dominated Barisan Nasional (National Front)—which succeeded the dismantled Alliance Party in 1973—and the leadership of Mohamed bin Mahathir (PM 1981–2003).[20]

In 1971, the Malaysian government instituted a National Cultural Policy (Dasar Kebudayaan Kebangsaan), proclaiming Malay-language literature the only "national literature," seriously undercutting publication outlets for Sinophone literature.[21] Malaysia's Institute of Language and Literature (Dewan Bahasa dan Pustaka) officially designated Sinophone literature an "ethnic literature" (*sastera etnik*) and "sectional literature" (*sastera sukuan*), categories defined by language of composition, thereby conflating ethnicity and language.[22] In Malay parlance, ethnic/sectional literature is somehow diametrically opposed to "national literature" (*sastera negara* or *sastera kebangsaan*), as the rules of the National Literary Prize (Anugera Sastera Negara) define "national literature" as works written in Malay.[23]

Only works eligible for this prize receive publicly sponsored publication. Like Sinophone education, Sinophone publishers had to privately finance publication in an era when many Chinese Malaysians felt their economic base was under attack, thus rendering literature an extraneous expenditure. Such crises catalyzed the exodus of many Chinese Malaysian students, mainly to Taiwan but also to Hong Kong and the West, for higher education.[24]

Sinophone Malaysian literature's prominence in Taiwan,[25] where it has garnered much praise and critical attention in the post–martial law period, revolves around the formation of an increasingly active and visible *qiaosheng* community from Malaysia throughout the 1970s and 1980s.[26] Designated nonnative Chinese (Orang Cina) by Malays, and often internalizing self-perceptions as Overseas Chinese, many of these students sentimentally viewed their sojourn to Taiwan as a re-Sinicization process of "cultural return" (*wenhua huigui*) to an ethnic homeland.[27] Throughout the martial law period (1947–87), the KMT government, buffered by US military support and economic investment, complemented its claim to authentic Chineseness by officially sponsoring Westernization: these developments contributed to the emergence of a modernist movement in Taiwan's Sinophone literature. Several of the movement's forerunners studied at US institutions and were influenced by the ideals of American New Criticism.[28] These authors mostly came from Taiwan's "mainlander" (*waishengren*) population that relocated to the island with the KMT following the loss of mainland China. Their aesthetic experimentation with language and form, fascination with interiority and the human psyche, and cultivation of exile all influenced the Chinese Malaysian students who became renowned writers in Taiwan.

As relations between the United States and the PRC thawed throughout the 1970s and Taiwan eventually forfeited its international diplomatic standing, shattering the KMT myth of mainland recovery, the modernist movement faced new challenges. The changing political atmosphere presented a new discursive space and visibility to individuals who saw Taiwan as homeland rather than temporary exile and who felt oppressed under KMT policies. A new nativist (*xiangtu*) movement emerged as, according to Sung-sheng Chang, left-leaning Taiwanese intellectuals, "feeling indignant on behalf of Taiwan's farmers and workers who paid a high price in the process of urban expansion," attacked "the government's economic dependence on Western countries (especially the United States)."[29] Featuring peasant and working-class protagonists, rural landscapes, folk traditions, and the oral culture of Taiwan, nativist authors depicted the island amid a difficult transition in which technological modernization, foreign influence, and urbanization threatened village life.[30] Though an oversimplification, the modernist-nativist dichotomy is the overarching narrative of Sinophone literary history in Taiwan.

For many students from Malaysia, coming of age in this environment ended their re-Sinicization, creating dissonance between the imagined "cultural China" they sought and the reality of their Taiwan experiences.[31] Lumped in with "mainlander modernism" (despite not coming from China), Malaysian authors were left with little maneuverability within the modernist-nativist polemics. This disillusionment informs their transnational resignification of the South Seas trope: reconfigured as a journey between two margins (Malaysia and Taiwan), their cultural return becomes a creative literary "return" not to an imagined China, but to the Malaysia of their childhood upbringing. Upon this rerouted trajectory, they recuperate alternative visions of Malaysianness as creolized transgressions of both Malaysia's multicultural rhetoric and the diasporic pursuit of uncontaminated Chineseness.

Based in Taiwan, several Sinophone Malaysian literary critics, including Ng Kim Chew, Tee Kim Tong (Zhang Jinzhong), and Lim Kien Ket (Lin Jianguo), have challenged prevailing accounts of Sinophone Malaysian literary history, insisting that the view of this literature as rooted in the influence of Chinese New Literature and limited to works in standard Chinese is myopic. They deepen the literary history to include works written in the classical Chinese literary script (*wenyan wen*) by southbound writers such as Huang Zunxian (1848–1905) and Khoo Seok Wan (Qiu Shuyuan, 1874–1941) who came to Malaya during the late Qing, prior to China's national revolution. Ng, Tee, and Lim also broaden the category to include works written in Baba Malay creole by Peranakan, or "Straits Chinese," authors in the colonial Straits Settlements: these works predate the influences of the New Literature movement, diasporic Chinese nationalism, and the ethnic polarization of Malaya in the twentieth century.[32] For Ng Kim Chew, the elision of Baba Malay literature as a paradigmatic example of Sinophone creolization in colonial Malaya disregards its potential as a source of inspiration for postcolonial writers. The narrow understanding of Sinophone Malaysian literature as solely bound to the historical appropriation of China's New Literature model compels a reactionary stance against Malaysian nationalism's demand for "unconditional unification" based on assimilation to Malay standards: it assumes the polarized position of ethnic chauvinism, fosters feelings of "indebtedness" to the modern Chinese literary tradition, and recognizes only superficially the influence of the "native literary tradition."[33]

Despite acknowledging underappreciated traditions that challenge the ideological hegemony of the New Literature model, these critics recognize the historical reality that an overwhelming majority of Sinophone Malaysian literature, at least since the 1920s, has been written in the standard Chinese based on spoken Mandarin. As for the Sinitic languages native to South China historically spoken in Malaysia—Hokkien, Cantonese, Teochew, and Hakka—their vocabulary and grammatical patterns, unlike Mandarin, lack widely recognizable, standardized written forms. Acknowledging that standard Chinese comprises the linguistic base of Sinophone Malaysian literature, Ng Kim Chew and Tee Kim Tong underscore how the version of this script used by writers in the South Seas—who call this language Huawen—differs from the Zhongwen (the script of the "center") used by writers in China. Unlike Zhongwen, Huawen is *inflected* and *accented* by the multilingual environment of Southeast Asia, including the vocabulary and speech patterns of nonstandard Sinitic languages (such as Hokkien and Cantonese) and non-Sinitic languages such as Malay, English, Tamil, Thai, Burmese, Dutch, Javanese, Arabic, Tagalog, Sanskrit, and so on depending on a writer's location and education.[34] To replicate the acoustics of multilingualism, authors often transliterate by appropriating a written character—typically a monosyllabic combination of two components (one phonetic, one semantic)—based solely on its pronunciation in order to denote the sound of a word (or part of a word). The transliteration process nullifies—or to borrow a visual metaphor from Ng Kim Chew, "hollows out"—the semantic component of the character that indicates some aspect of its meaning.[35] Although this may read as a deficient and "broken" Huawen that is "difficult to consume,"[36] such transliteration practices have long been identified as the "unique features" (*dute xing*) of Sinophone Malayan/Malaysian literature that give it its exotic South Seas flavor.[37]

In reconceptualizing Sinophone Malaysian literary history, Ng Kim Chew expresses skepticism regarding the conventional techniques of creolization in Sinophone realism, claiming that the transliteration of select phrases and vocabulary creates a form of "bazaar Huawen" and is merely the "vulgarization" of standard Chinese.[38] Superficially and haphazardly transliterating a few words to ensure an exotic effect for a transnational readership does not, for Ng, reflect an honest absorption of the other languages, cultures, and literatures of Malaysia. At the same time, Ng criticizes the highly refined Sinophone modernist techniques among many of his Malaysian peers in Taiwan because its diasporic obsession with pursuing the "spiritual mystique" of Chineseness perpetuates ethnic chauvinism and is a limiting aesthetic practice. Ng does not call upon Sinophone Malaysian writers to transcend ethnicity (a demand of the Malay literary establishment that Ng lampoons), but rather encourages them to cultivate more fruitfully and articulate more precisely the Sinophone's historical relationship to Malay culture and literature specifically, as Ng feels this is rarely claimed as a source of influence or point of comparison.[39]

These sentiments inform Ng Kim Chew's own intertextual experimentations in his modernist short fiction, in which he engages these issues through an imaginative, ironic, and incisive parody of Malaysia's political, historical, and multicultural realities. Leaving no institution untouched—whether the Malay literary establishment, the Malaysian government, Malaysia's religious orthodoxy, Sinophone Malaysian literary trends (such as South Seas color), Taiwan's Sinophone literary circles, or Taiwanese politics—Ng's fiction, from its transnational vantage point between Malaysia and Taiwan, exposes the messy, duplicitous, frictional, unmentionable, even violent aspects of creolization. These come from the incomplete processes of forced assimilation and the impossible task of simultaneously embodying/performing yet keeping separate/concealing two presumably irreconcilable cultures.

BLASPHEMOUS CREOLIZATION: SATIRIZING DIASPORA AND INCOMPLETE ASSIMILATION

A professor of Chinese literature at National Chinan University in Puli, Taiwan, Ng Kim Chew (Huang Jinshu, 1967-) is originally from Johor, which, located opposite Singapore on the southern tip of Peninsular Malaysia, is the nation's largest rubber-producing state. The Johor rubber forests and kampongs—precisely the type of rural environment in which Ng grew up—are the "primal" settings to which Ng's narratives repeatedly return.[40] After arriving in Taipei as a student at National Taiwan University in 1989, Ng broke onto the literary scene in 1990 with the short story "The Disappearance of M" ("M de shizong"), in which the author not only satirizes the ethnolinguistic politics of national literature in Malaysia but also lampoons the major figures and concerns of Sinophone Malaysian literature. With "The Disappearance of M," Ng Kim Chew established himself as a maverick willing to offend the literary establishment in both Taiwan and Malaysia. The work later appeared as the opening story in his first collection of short fiction, *Dream, Swine, and Aurora* (*Meng yu zhu yu liming*, 1994). Besides *Dark Nights* (*Wu'an ming*, 1997) and *Memoirs of the People's Republic of the South Seas* (*Nanyang renmin gongheguo beiwanglu*, 2013), Ng's volumes of short fiction are notable for having Malay as well as Sinophone titles: *From Island to Island / Back Inscriptions* (*You dao zhi dao / Ke bei*, 2001) is also *Dari pulau ke pulau* (From Island to Island); and *Land and Fire* (*Tu yu huo*, 2005) is also *Tanah Melayu* (Malay Land). Ng's language play is particularly on display in *From Island to Island*, as the volume has a different title on the spine—*Back Inscriptions*—from its cover and the story titles listed in the table of contents differ from those given on each story's first page.

"The Disappearance of M" revolves around the appearance of a mysterious novel entitled *Kristmas* by an anonymous author known only as "M." Both the identity of M and the title of M's novel allude to a 1939 essay that the southbound author Yu Dafu wrote in Singapore: commenting on the prospects of "Nanyang literature," Yu argued that it could only gain international prestige with the appearance of a literary "master" and masterworks akin to the anticolonial Filipino writer José Rizal and his novel from the Spanish colonial era, *Noli me Tángere* (Touch me not, 1887). Yu notes that he learned of Rizal while stopping over to spend Christmas in Manila en route to Singapore in late 1938.[41] This allusion suggests that M and *Kristmas* are postcolonial Malaysia's literary master and masterwork and the direct though belated counterparts to Rizal and *Noli me Tángere* in the Philippines.

Though *Kristmas* is a Malay transliteration of the English "Christmas," it also alludes to the Malay novelist Keris Mas (meaning "golden *kris*," or sword, this is the penname of Kamaluddin Muhamad, 1922–92), Malaysia's first National Laureate in 1981. *Kristmas*, however, is not a Malay novel, but an Anglophone composition steeped in the former colonial language, much like Rizal's Hispanophone masterwork.

Kristmas is hyperbolically multilingual, inflected with vocabulary from "not only English but modern and classical Malay, Jawi, Arabic, Pali, German, French, Latin, Sanskrit, and even ancient Chinese oracle bone inscriptions!" *Kristmas* therefore belongs to a "unique genre" of multilingualism deemed "untranslatable."[42] Despite its esoteric nature, the fictional *Kristmas* is, like Rizal's *Noli* for the Philippines, the first work of Malaysian literature to put the country on the map for international, particularly Western, audiences. The Nobel Committee even considers the novel for its prize in literature.[43] The sudden arrival of a multilingual, multicultural, and distinctly Malaysian literary masterpiece incites an uproar in Malaysia's ethnolinguistically segregated literary circles, prompting them to convene emergency meetings to determine the identity (and ethnicity) of the mysterious maestro, M.

The narrator (who, based on his surname, is a fictional personification of Ng Kim Chew) is a reporter for the Sinophone newspaper *South Seas Commercial News* (*Nanyang shangbao*). On assignment to determine the identity of M, he first attends the National Writers Symposium convened by the Malaysian Writers Association, made up of "exclusively Malay-language authors," at the Hilton Hotel in Kuala Lumpur. Their main concern is to determine M's ethnicity, praying that he or she is not an Orang Cina. They also discuss whether to categorize an Anglophone work like *Kristmas* as "national literature," since it was not formally written in Malay. Their discussion then shifts to the rather mundane question of how to improve Malay literature's international stature and ensure that the world also understands "Malaysian literature" as literature in Malay. This preoccupation bores the reporters in attendance, so the narrator proceeds to the Selangor Chinese Assembly Hall where the Malaysian Chinese Writers Association is simultaneously convening its Sinophone Malaysian Literature Symposium.[44]

Ng Kim Chew's portrayal of the discussion of *Kristmas* among the Sinophone writers is equally comical: speculating that the novel is actually an Anglophone translation of a work originally written in Chinese, they ultimately determine that none of the authors in attendance possesses the requisite linguistic adeptness to compose such a complex work. Influenced by their speculation that it may have been written by a writer based in Taiwan, the narrator, under the guise of "an Overseas Chinese returning to the motherland," tags along with a group of old women to Taiwan to meet with Li Yongping and

Chang Kuei-hsing, two renowned Malaysian authors originally from Borneo.[45] "Based on the nativist, Americanized, or Sinicized trends of the Taiwan writers," the reporter determines it was impossible that M was Taiwanese. Essentially lampooning the entirety of Sinophone Malaysian and Taiwanese literary history in a few short pages, Ng Kim Chew critiques how each of its major writers, trends, and trajectories is insufficient to have produced M's masterpiece.[46]

The narrator then embarks on a lengthy investigation to produce his own supplementary report to *Kristmas* called "The Disappearance of M." As he follows clues into the heart of Johor's rubber forests, the story becomes more surreal and metafictional. The discovery of several scraps of writing in a hut in the forest prompts the narrator to briefly suspect the old man living there is actually Yu Dafu, and Yu is M. He asks: What if Yu Dafu's mysterious disappearance in 1945 did not end in his execution, but instead he eked out a living in the rubber forest writing and submitting literary works to local newspapers, "pirating the name of every Sinophone Malaysian author" in the process?[47] Here, Ng satirizes the ways in which the colonial specter of Yu Dafu has become its own form of "South Seas color" that continues to haunt the creative imaginary of Sinophone Malaysian literature.[48]

Amid an investigation in which he finds that "every scrap of writing suggested a different possibility" and that "all the possibilities contradicted one another,"[49] the narrator is surprised to read an article in *South Seas Commercial News* entitled "The Disappearance of M" (knowing that he has not yet submitted the piece), written by M:

> He felt intensely that he had written it himself, yet it was clear that it mocked his voice considerably. How could there be such an author penetrating all his thoughts and predicting his future while forcibly edging him out of his own position as "author"? This seemingly impossible situation presented a formidable "existential" challenge, suggesting that the "I" could be displaced entirely. . . . Yet who was doing this? Who was using the guise of M to displace his narrative on the disappearance of M?[50]

Here, Ng Kim Chew shifts from lampooning other Malaysian writers, trends, and techniques to parodying his own anxiety over his authority, authorship, imagination, and tenuous position within the multilingual landscape of Malaysian literature. The narrator finally determines that *Kristmas* must be a "collective work" (maybe an unfinished one?) and that M can only be a "composite function," of which even the narrator himself (and by extension the author) forms an "insufficient" part.[51] As Ng's inaugural short story, "The Disappearance of M" suggests the impossibility of an all-encompassing syncretic, multicultural Malaysian literature embodied by a single master or masterwork. Instead, there is only the unfinished business of creolization emerging from the composite portrait of the multiple literary discourses and traditions (native and settler alike), which, in the postcolonial present, attempt to edge one another out, vying absurdly for a space they can never legitimately reserve only for themselves.

If the single, consummate, syncretic author or work of literature truly encompassing all of Malaysia's languages, cultures, and textual traditions is a farcical impossibility, then the reality of creolized aesthetics is that they must begin with those processes conceived pejoratively: vulgarization, bastardization, and desecration become the base conditions of creolization in Ng Kim Chew's fiction. His depictions of seemingly noble, sacrosanct cultural pursuits—whether full cross-cultural conversion as a sacrifice for the Malaysian nation or the diasporic pursuit of one's authentic Chinese cultural origins—repeatedly turn ugly, scatological, carnivalesque, horrifically fetishistic, even violent.

In Ng's "Back Inscriptions" ("Ke bei," 2001), the diasporic journey to find the elusive origins of a mysterious, seemingly ancient practice of Chinese written inscription only leads to the historical traumas of British colonialism and Orientalist knowledge production in Malaya in the early twentieth century. The story is set at the turn of the twenty-first century against the backdrop of a fictive war between Taiwan and mainland China that breaks out after the Democratic People's Party (DPP, or Minjindang) declares Taiwan an independent republic. This creates a new wave of refugees from Taiwan in the South Seas, particularly in Singapore. The female narrator is a Taiwanese graduate student of Professor Yu, a Singaporean "expert on coolies" who has spent his career researching nineteenth-century overseas Chinese emigration. In conducting his research, Professor Yu has discovered several old Chinese Singaporean and Malaysian men—all former coolies—who have strange Chinese characters (most of them derivations of the character *hai*, meaning "sea") tattooed across their backsides. He inquires with his relative, a doctor who previously practiced traditional Chinese medicine in the former Straits Settlements, who has also discovered this phenomenon among his patients. Knowing that most of these former coolies were illiterate and could not even sign their own names, the doctor speculates that the tattoos came from "a system of classifying those coolies when they were 'sold as piglets' by their agents, just like the popular practice among Chinese Malaysians of branding their farm logo on the backs of the pigs they raise."[52]

After Professor Yu falls into a coma following a car accident, the Taiwanese narrator takes over his "illicit" coolie research (as his university refused to endorse it). She follows an old coolie home from the pier, where he goes every afternoon to stare silently out at the sea. At his home, she meets a regal, aristocratic old woman who mysteriously seems to have anticipated the narrator's arrival. The old woman launches into a story of her deceased husband, an Englishman and midlevel colonial bureaucrat who brought her from Shanghai to Singapore, where he abandoned his official post to open a wine house/brothel called Southern Sky (Nantian). Believing that a brothel offered the most ideal environment for a creative writer, and wanting to distance himself from other Europeans by "going native" as a modernist author in the colony, the Englishman set up shop in Chinatown and catered to local Sinophone and southbound Chinese literati, intellectuals, and political reformers, including Kang Youwei (who provided the calligraphy for his storefront sign) and Yu Dafu.[53]

As the Englishman "fell hopelessly in love" and became "frighteningly infatuated" with Chinese writing, particularly in its most archaic, pictographic form of oracle bone inscription, he abandoned English in order to devise the most "extraordinarily revolutionary and modernist scheme for writing Chinese"—carving characters, transcribed from ancient texts, onto the backs of Chinese coolies. He lured the coolies surreptitiously through the back door into his wine house (since it was supposed to be an elite establishment), where he wined and dined them, solicited opium and prostitutes to them, and allowed them to gamble. Once they accrued a debt they could not repay, he proposed to them his research plan: they could repay him with their backs. Insisting on using only Chinese coolies (since he discovered that the skin of Indian coolies at the pier was "too dark"), he felt he had "finally captured the most profound and esoteric essence of Chinese writing" by "using bodily pain as his textual medium." His widow tells the narrator that the coolies said they felt like they were "sodomized." She believes that in addition to tattooing them, he also sexually molested them when he was especially "aroused" by his project. In order to obtain enough "textual bodies" to compose an epic masterpiece, the Englishman tried to purchase a plot of jungle in central Johor and a horde of coolies to convert it into a rubber plantation, but his plans were interrupted by the Pacific War, and he was presumed to have been killed in his interrogations by the Japanese. According to his widow, the delusional Englishman's writing never advanced beyond "a primary school level," and his characters—as evidenced by the extant "texts"—always contained a few mistaken (or invented) strokes.[54]

Despite his death, the Englishman's masterwork takes on a postcolonial afterlife, not only in the traumatized bodies and minds of the former coolies but also in the idolatry of local-born Chinese Malaysians who still approach his widow to admire and imitate his craft. The widow tells the narrator about a "Peranakan man with a thin moustache" who "insanely worshipped" the Englishman:

> As you know, these Peranakans don't understand written Chinese, and they worship foreigners like it is no one's business. Since many of them have Indian nannies at home, they often speak Tamil as their mother tongue. He was just like those other Peranakans who, since they don't understand Chinese writing, are even more enchanted by it, and they treat written characters as if they are Taoist talismans.[55]

Adding this postscript to the Englishman's story, Ng Kim Chew satirizes the diasporic psyche of Chinese Malaysians: feeling distant from their ancestral heritage, their desire to recover lost origins and possess the mystical knowledge of an ancient language prompts a postcolonial misreading of a historical trauma in colonial Malaya as talismanic Chineseness, an act that mimics the Orientalism of the Western colonizer. The "original inscription" (the object of attraction) is a marker not of Chinese cultural authenticity, as the miswritten characters and invented strokes mark this writing not as "Chinese" but rather as the "bastardized" language produced under colonial violence. Branded like pigs, the backs of the coolies become the desecrated historical texts not of "Chinese culture" but of a racialized colonial burden.[56] The pursuit of Chineseness, particularly through fetishizing the Chinese script, becomes a symbolic legacy of the torturous colonial transformation into human "livestock." The back inscriptions speak not of the ancestral continent, but—written in a blue ink that "shimmers like ocean waves"—of the torture of the indentured coolie's transoceanic passage into the New World of the Nanyang. These textual bodies reveal the fraught creolizing process of colonialism and the hardships of overseas passage (and survival) that form the base conditions for Sinophone literature and its creolized Malaysianness.

In the postcolonial South Seas imagination of Ng's fiction, the diasporic desire to recuperate cultural origins is also produced by the contradictions between the political assignation of a minoritized identity (or second-class citizenship) and the demand for unconditional assimilation as a "holy rite" in the nation-building process. Ng treats these contradictions in his short story, "The Will of Allah" ("Ala de zhiyi," 1998). Framed by a Koranic passage on "infidels" and an opening caveat that the subsequent text is a Sinophone translation of the "original Malay," the narrative begins around the time of Malayan independence in 1957, when the narrator, Liu Cai (whose name puns on the phrase "to leave behind wealth/materials"), is arrested for conspiring with the Malayan Communist Party (MCP) to launch a revolutionary insurrection. Prior to his scheduled execution, he is visited by his "royal friend," a Malay official and member of the aristocracy who grew up with Liu Cai in the same kampong:

> Originally no one knew that he had royal blood. Perhaps he was the son of a concubine. From a young age, he was sent to our kampong, where he lived, fished, climbed trees, trapped birds, picked rambutans, and swam in the streams with the other village children. Maybe it was fate, but we got along so well, sharing the harvest we reaped with one another. . . .
>
> My royal friend and I slowly parted ways after being childhood playmates. He fervently held on to his language and ethnicity, and I mine.[57]

It is difficult not to read their interethnic childhood friendship during the late colonial era when the two children partake of the same natural resources, contrasted by their adolescent parting around the time of liberation when they confine themselves to their own ethnolinguistic circles, as a metaphor for postcolonial ethnic polarization. Now, Liu Cai's royal friend treats him as someone who has betrayed their friendship, the young and fragile nation, the special rights of the Malay race, and his own aristocratic entitlement.[58]

As the firing squad prepares to execute him, Liu Cai faints. He wakes up on a small boat. Even though he is not dead, the remainder of the story details a type of "afterlife," as his royal friend stipulates several conditions for his pardon: Liu Cai must live in eternal exile on a small Malaysian island in the South China Sea called Pulau Jelaga (meaning "black smoke island") inhabited by Orang Laut (literally "sea people"), assume a new identity and name as Musyi Abdullah, convert to Islam and undergo circumcision, open up the island's wetlands and arable soil for cultivating rice, vegetables, and fruits, raise livestock (except pigs), marry an indigenous Muslim woman on the island (the daughter of the local chief) and bear children, teach the islanders farming techniques and the Malay language, and serve as a religious leader. Speaking and writing Chinese (even to himself), contacting friends and family from his "former life," and leaving the island (even to attend the graduations or weddings of his children and grandchildren on the peninsula) are all strictly prohibited.[59]

Agreeing to the conditions, the narrator recalls a childhood conversation with his royal friend, who asked him what gift he would like to be granted in the future when the royal friend became a raja. Liu Cai requested a small island:

> "Why?" He was a little surprised. "Don't you Chinese all like vast plots of land and old-growth forests you can chop down to expand your wealth? What use is a small island?"
>
> I shook my head, struggling to find an explanation: "My parents come from a small island off the coast of southern China."
>
> . . . His expression suddenly soured and became serious. He was rather angry: "That can't be possible. . . . How is that possible?"[60]

The royal friend's reaction to the young Liu Cai's request has two connotations: first, since there are certain regulations against non-*bumiputera* land ownership, a small island is an impossible request for him to fulfill. Second, it suggests his disbelief that someone of Chinese descent could have an islander lineage. Here, Ng Kim Chew challenges misconstrued stereotypes of an archipelagic Malay and continental Chinese civilization as mutually irreconcilable, instead revealing the historical affinities between them as the longtime migrant seafarers of the South Seas. Ng's allusion to Taiwan as the island off the southern Chinese coast further draws a South Seas connection between the insular cultures of Taiwan and Malaysia. Ironically, the adult Liu Cai/Musyi Abdullah receives his childhood wish for a small island, but it is now premised upon subjecting himself to his royal friend's "cruel experiment"—a "cultural blood transfusion."[61]

One may read "The Will of Allah" solely through the lens of the narrator's passive assimilation requiring total erasure of his Chineseness, yet Musyi Abdullah's responsibility is not merely to become one of the indigenous islanders. Based on the government's stereotype of the diligent, pioneer Chinese agrarian settler, Musyi Abdullah becomes an unwitting agent of the postcolonial government's Land Reclamation Project, part of its New Economic Policy. He is tasked with transforming the Orang Laut's "multigenerational habits of living off the sea," which he describes:

> Before, during the rainy season or when there was a shortage of fish, the islanders took up the chance to become pirates, marauding hapless merchant vessels that came nearby to avoid thunderstorms. For them, this was like the fisherman's catch, "a heavenly gift (the will of Allah)." As for my exile (heavens, I can still remember this melancholic word!), it was also, according to them, "the will of Allah."[62]

There is a direct connection between Musyi Abdullah's passive exile/conversion and his active complicity in the modernization/conversion of the Orang Laut to meet the national agenda. The state's manipulation of what it considers the essential strengths of the Chinese is reminiscent of the mutually beneficial elite business partnerships between Malay government officials and Chinese Malaysian business leaders.

Yet Musyi Abdullah is a halfhearted participant in this scheme: despite the benefits he receives over the decades, such as the seventeen children his wife bears who receive government scholarships to study on the peninsula, he feels they are "children of the state," not his own. Although he must act as if he is and has always been Malay, his royal friend continues to unconsciously racialize him as "you Chinamen," and even the islanders seem aware of his cultural "strangeness." No matter how valiant his efforts, Musyi Abdullah will always remain an "infidel," his conversion incomplete. Wondering why he cannot become "thoroughly Malay," Musyi Abdullah recalls a concept "instilled" in him by his parents at a young age: "Chinese cannot become barbarians, and barbarians cannot become Chinese." Haunted by his Chineseness from both his parents' diasporic ethnocentrism and the interpellation of the state, Liu Cai/Musyi Abdullah finds himself trapped in an island exile between two identities.[63]

Musyi's Abdullah's psychological response to this predicament highlights Ng Kim Chew's creative illustration of creolization. While preparing soil for cultivation, Musyi Abdullah discovers some archaeological remnants of a previous, but now seemingly vanished, Chinese presence on the island, such as shards of a Tang porcelain bowl and a stone tablet with ancient Chinese writing on it. Illicitly taking a small boat to a deserted neighboring island, Liu Cai/Musyi Abdullah decides to leave behind a record of his own presence there for posterity by inscribing replicas of pictographic Chinese characters on some stones. Knowing "it would be too obvious" to the authorities if he inscribed standard Chinese characters (a breach of his agreement), yet also untrained in ancient calligraphy, he has to rely on his imagination to visualize archaic pictographs.[64] Like the Englishman's coolie experiments in "Back Inscriptions," the narrator's stone carvings in "The Will of Allah" are not a "pure" replication of an ancient Chinese artifact: with their miswritten and invented strokes, they do not even constitute Chinese writing. Under the dual conditions of an incomplete assimilation of Malayness and the sanctions against his Chinese linguistic expression, the archaeological "recovery" and "preservation" of his Chineseness is actually the invention of a new script: a type of hieroglyphic creole attesting to his own history of localization, one fraught with friction, contradiction, and struggle. This creole autobiography is a repressed one that, as the narrator explains at the beginning of the story, must be concealed because of the disastrous repercussions it might have for Malaysia's postcolonial multiculturalism and the maintenance of interethnic harmony.[65] An "experimental" cultural bridge between Malays and Chinese Malaysians, the figure of Musyi Abdullah is also sacrilegious, a profane blemish upon the integrity of both groups.

Ng Kim Chew satirically takes the blasphemous creole figure of incomplete conversion a step further in "My Friend, Abdullah" ("Wo de pengyou Yadula," 2002). Inspired by the short story "Never Mention It Again" ("Bie zai tiqi," 2002) by fellow Sinophone Malaysian author Ho Sok Fong (He Shufang, 1970-), in which a Chinese Malaysian businessman's funeral becomes the desecrated battleground for burial rites between his first (Chinese) and second (Malay) wives,[66] "My Friend, Abdullah" is a prelude to Ho's story that details the businessman's life prior to this moment. His secret conversion to Islam, name change, and polygamy were strategic assimilations designed to gain him *bumiputera* advantages under Malaysia's New Economic Policy, which also helps him establish preferential trade relations with other Muslim countries.

Abdullah's audaciousness to convert and marry "outside his clan" impresses the narrator, who is one of his drinking buddies, because intermarriage is generally stigmatized among Chinese Malaysians and because religious conversion cannot guarantee wholehearted acceptance into Malay society. Abdullah's buddies teasingly refer to his intermarriage as his "sacrifice to the nation." Yet Abdullah continues to reserve "basic human rights" for himself: eating pork, drinking alcohol, and visiting prostitutes. The narrator describes Abdullah's covert lifestyle:

> After converting to Islam (or, in the words of my buddies, "after snipping off that precious foreskin"), if he was accompanied by his Muslim wife when meeting some friends, they would only eat Indian, Malay, or fast food. Only when his "black gold" was not present beside him, he would eat everything from pork rib soup to steamed pork buns as compensation for his past deprivation. Half earnestly, he would complain, "You don't know how much I suffer eating at home." Yet you couldn't tell by looking at his face and body, which showed no symptoms of suffering. Only during the month of Ramadan did he appear to suffer a bit, but as long as he could find a place to sneak away to and eat, he was the most adept at stuffing himself until he had violent diarrhea, even during Ramadan.[67]

With this blasphemous satire, Ng Kim Chew reveals Abdullah's self-sacrificing conversion to Islam and noble pursuit of a harmonious Malaysian multiculturalism as merely selfish, hedonistic indulgences: his Malay wife, and the Middle Eastern oil money to which she gives him access, is his "black gold," while his "deflowering" of a young Indian prostitute is his means of "promoting friendly relations with the barbarians." Abdullah tells his buddies that his ultimate "diplomatic" aspiration is to have four wives: one Chinese, one Malay, one Indian, and one Orang Asli from Kedah.[68]

In addition to Abdullah's religious conversion and promotion of multicultural harmony, Ng Kim Chew parodies his "passionate patronage" of Chinese culture in Malaysia and his desire to be a great Sinophone writer. Attending a community event in which a local Sinophone newspaper hosts a renowned author from Taiwan, Abdullah asks:

> "My dear maestro, I have a question for you that has troubled me greatly. I have published over a dozen books, and none of them sell well at all. Even more pathetic is the criticism I get from my friends in the literary world. Since I only write about Chinese people in my fiction, they call me ethnocentric and ask why I don't write about Malays, Indians, or Kadazan people. Another critic is even more absurd, asking why I don't write about space aliens. Since I like to write about politics, the economy, and education—as these are major issues of concern to the Chinese community—they criticize me for not writing about highway toll increases, the nipah virus, dengue fever, droughts, or other social issues that more directly impact the lives of the general public. . . ."
>
> The maestro's reply was also memorable: "You can write about orangutans."
>
> "Huh?"
>
> "Aren't your Malaysian jungles full of red-haired orangutans?"[69]

As in "The Disappearance of M," Ng offers a scathing parody of Malaysian literary politics, including high-minded Sinophone realism and demands for multiethnic representation by the Malay establishment. In the irony of the Taiwanese author's dismissive response, Ng further satirizes tropical Nanyang exoticism as an implicit expectation of Taiwan's literary establishment and its tokenizing gesture toward Sinophone Malaysian authors.

Stunted in his literary and economic pursuits, Abdullah becomes haunted by a creole specter of the colonial past whose compromised position in a racialized administration as an intermediary between settler and indigenous cultures uncannily resembles his own. After 9/11 (2001), the American military bombs Abdullah's mineral-water plant in Afghanistan and he is blacklisted as an "Asian Osama." Not long before Abdullah's death, the narrator finds him taking refuge in a Confucian temple: in a state of delirium and babbling in a mixture of Malay, Hokkien, Tamil, and Arabic, he is possessed by the spirit of Munsyi Abdullah, better known as Abdullah bin Abdul Kadir (1797–1854). Munsyi Abdullah was a Malay-language author, interpreter, scribe, and teacher of Arab and Tamil descent employed by the British during its early years of colonization in Malaya. Paraphrasing from his *The Story of Abdullah* (*Hikayat Abdullah*, 1848), a Malay literary classic, the possessed present-day Abdullah tells how his father Abdul Kadir, a midlevel official under the Dutch in Malacca before it transferred authority over the port to the British in 1824, was sent as an emissary to the Malayan interior, including the states of Pahang, Terengganu, and Kelantan, to negotiate with the local sultans and collect Malay texts. The possessed Abdullah also tells of his own close working relationship with the British administrator Stamford Raffles, whose ideas of civil structure and social order Abdullah admired. Transcribing ancient Malay manuscripts for Raffles, Abdullah describes the Englishman as an avid "naturalist."[70] With his allusion to *The Story of Abdullah*, Ng Kim Chew shows the multicultural landscape of Malaysian literature and society as haunted by the officially suppressed and unmentionable creole past of colonial Malaya: Munsyi Abdullah, the "forefather" of modern Malay literature, was, as Sanjay Krishnan puts it, not Malay "in the ethnic and racial senses that determine usage in the postcolonial period," but was actually a product of "the polyglot and creolized colonial ports in which Chinese, Arabs, Malays, and Indians were familiar presences."[71]

Beyond "My Friend, Abdullah," Ng Kim Chew's frequent intertextual allusions to Munsyi Abdullah and his Malay literary classics serve not only as a challenge to the *bumiputera* politics of indigeneity governing Malaysian national literature, but also as a transnational rewriting of the Nanyang trope that bends the diasporic homeward journey to the ancestral land back towards the creole origins of postcolonial Sinophone Malaysian culture. In "Slow Boat to China" ("Kaiwang Zhongguo de manchuan," 2001), Ng Kim Chew frames the short story with a short quotation (in the original Malay) from Munsyi Abdullah's *The Voyage of Abdullah to Kelantan* (*Kisah pelayaran Abdullah ke Kelantan*, 1838),[72] an allusion to which the author does not return until the end of the narrative. "Slow Boat to China" summons a laughable parade of iconic South Seas clichés—deserted islands, the rubber forest, the durian fruit, the white tiger, and Zheng He as the heroic naval explorer who "discovered" the New World of the Nanyang for imperial China—parodying them as mandatory referents for Sinophone publishers and readers in Taiwan. Ng cleverly packages his Nanyang exoticism in a diasporic fantasy of China—a tale of old "Mount Tang" (Tangshan, the settler's name for China)—spun by an elderly, nameless Chinese Malaysian language teacher who ekes out a living outside the "official state census" of Malaysia:

> The stories he told most often were about the "Three-Jeweled Palace Eunuch" Zheng He's voyages upon the Western Seas. It is not worth mentioning his familiar anecdotes such as the one about how the origins of the durian as the "king of fruits" came from Zheng He's nice habit of squatting down to shit on trees: from the variable consistency of his feces (runny or hard) came different varieties of durian. The old man also frequently spun a tale about how Zheng He actually left behind a treasure ship in a hidden harbor in the north, and how every year on the eve of the Dragonboat Festival, it would set sail at an extremely slow pace toward Mount Tang. Between three and five years later, it would arrive, docking in Beijing. Later, it would return to its original port to await new passengers.[73]

For spinning his tall tales, the old teacher is dealt tragicomic justice: one day, a durian falls on the old man's head and kills him. Yet a young kampong boy named Tieniu gullibly believes the legend of the "slow boat to China," which, according to the old teacher, "only carried children under the age of thirteen." Since Tieniu's mother euphemized his father's death by saying that he had "returned to Mount Tang," Tieniu assumes that if he catches

Zheng He's ship before his thirteenth birthday, he will be reunited with his father.[74]

The remainder of Ng's narrative is devoted to Tieniu's journey to find Zheng He's ship. Riding his water buffalo, Tieniu leaves his home in the rubber forest and sets off through the jungle. In contrast to the interethnic friction that characterizes Ng's other stories, the author here details many acts of kindness and generosity toward Tieniu as he passes through Malay, Indian, and Orang Asli villages in the peninsular hinterlands. He stays with an Orang Asli man who gives him roasted sweet potatoes and an Indian family with only daughters that share their delicious ripe papayas with him, tempting him to abandon his quest and "stay there for good to enjoy a life helping them pick papayas."[75]

Continuing on, Tieniu loses his way and stumbles upon a street lined with dead bodies, a postmassacre scene of the 1969 ethnic riots. Here, the May Thirteenth incident becomes a metaphor for the nation's (and Tieniu's) figurative "thirteenth birthday." It represents the disillusionment of childhood innocence and the ideal of multicultural equality, as well as the start of a new trajectory for an exclusionary and assimilatory Malaysianness. For Tieniu, it is a rerouting of his diasporic homeward journey: he is adopted by a Malay truck driver and his wife that welcome him as a gift from Allah. His new parents convert him to Islam and change his name to Abdullah (obviously a recurrent motif in Ng's fiction). In the harbor of the new village where he lives, Abdullah discovers the wreckage of an old treasure ship and a white tiger lurking near it that mysteriously embodies the ancient spirit of Zheng He. It seems Abdullah has arrived too late: in its plans to develop the harbor, the government removes the wreckage.[76]

Tieniu never returns home to his mother on the rubber plantation, nor does he ever reach Mount Tang to see his father: the diasporic homeward journey to the ancestral land actually becomes a tale of the boy's multiple interethnic interactions and incomplete rite of passage into the native Malay culture. This incompleteness leaves Tieniu/Abdullah, after he leaves home, in a state of limbo, adrift at sea working as a deckhand:

> Many years later, he found himself wandering from island to island like a tramp. One day on some small island, suffering from excessive thirst, he ate a rambutan too quickly and accidentally choked. He then passed out and was left there, lying hapless among the withered trees and weeds. He didn't know how much time passed,

> but when he awoke, all his experiences, feelings, and thoughts suddenly converged on one evening in the distant past, with the many interim years negated in an instant. He only sensed a foggy, unclear universe around him. He didn't know where he was, and he couldn't recall who he was.
>
> He struggled to open his eyes. Amid the sound of water lapping around him, he heard someone speaking Hokkien: "He's finally awake." Standing there were three very short, middle-aged Chinese men and a thin, swarthy man wearing a bright Malay outfit, a *songkok*, and brandishing a shiny, golden *kris*. His eyes were open wide, and between his mouth and nose was a thick, lustrous moustache. He looked Indian. Huffing through his flat, duck-like lips, he appeared disinterested in the others. One of the Chinese crew introduced him: "This is our captain, the famous Mr. Munsyi Abdullah. We just finished our voyage to Kelantan, and we are now heading back to Singapore."[77]

In the end, Tieniu finds himself not on Zheng He's treasure ship to imperial China, but rather back in the colonial past on the slow boat of Munsyi Abdullah. From a literary standpoint, "Slow Boat to China" invokes the exotic Nanyang imagination of Chinese literature, but it concludes by referencing the Malay literary tradition, underscoring not its indigenous difference with Sinophone literature, but rather its shared creolized roots with Sinophone literature as emerging from settler-indigenous encounters under colonial conditions. Emphasizing Munsyi Abdullah's Indian appearance underneath Malay attire (as opposed to his Malayness), Ng Kim Chew envisions a lateral creolization between Indian and Chinese Malaysian traditions as two settler cultures minoritized in the postcolonial era. Ng creolizes a more China-centric South Seas imagination with the India-centric concept of the Suvarnadvipa, the "Golden Islands" of ancient Sanskrit lore, as they both "migrate" into Malaysian literary history. With the multiple allusions to Munsyi Abdullah in his fiction, Ng Kim Chew has responded to his own call for Sinophone Malaysian authors, particularly those in Taiwan, to cultivate a literary aesthetics that goes beyond the diasporic obsession with Chineseness by creatively engaging Malaysia's multiple literary traditions.

Ng's creolized aesthetics of Malaysianness and his transnational rewriting of the Nanyang imagination offer insights into how Sinophone Malaysian literature also functions as a Taiwan-based practice. The success of Ng and other Sinophone Malaysian authors in Taiwan who invoke the Nanyang in the literary return to their Malaysian pasts cannot be dismissed as merely attributable to a desire for exotic escapism among Taiwanese readers. In contributing to a post–martial law environment of cultural pluralism in Taiwan, Sinophone Malaysian literature and the Taiwanese literary world play symbiotic roles. Taiwanese publishing companies such as Rye Field (Maitian) and their literary anthologies have vitally helped canonize Sinophone Malaysian literature, enhancing its visibility. As a center of transnational Sinophone literary publication, Taipei functions much like London and New York for Anglophone literature and Paris and Brussels for Francophone literature. Rather than a site of cultural return, Taiwan is a "special zone" for Sinophone Malaysian literature. The transnational context of Sinophone Malaysian literature has further provided opportunities to writers who have not migrated to or studied in Taiwan, but who have nevertheless accessed its publication outlets. The Taiwan connection has even revitalized Sinophone literary activity and private outlets for publication in Malaysia, such as Got One (Youren) Publishers in Petaling Jaya, just outside Kuala Lumpur.[78] By delineating the limits of diaspora and the fiction of cultural return, the Taiwan experience of Sinophone Malaysian authors has encouraged their creative rediscovery and modernist reevaluation of creolization in all its historical messiness and reconciliatory possibility.

For Taiwan, Sinophone Malaysian literature has reciprocally helped propel the local literary establishment beyond the entrapping dichotomy of "mainlander modernism" (both China-centric and Westernized) and "Taiwanese nativism" frequently deployed to narrate Taiwan's literary history. Sinophone Malaysian recuperations of creolization reverberate in analogous post–martial law treatments of Taiwan's complex history of colonialism, multiculturalism, multilingualism, and settler-indigenous politics. Narratives on the legacies of British colonial traumas in Malaya, including racialized labor exploitation and political suppression, intersect with literary treatments of the violent imperial Japanese regime of multicultural management in Taiwan. Interrogations of anticommunist repression and the 1969 Kuala Lumpur ethnic riots in Malaysia, which prompted the national culture policies of the NEP era, find intriguing parallels in assessments of the February 28 incident (2/28) of 1947, which led to the KMT's institution of martial law in Taiwan and a regime of "White Terror" waged against suspected communists.[79] Malaysian and Taiwanese authors similarly grapple with modes of creolizing Sinophone writing by introducing nonstandard

Sinitic and indigenous languages into the standard Chinese script. Finally, the move from the dialectic between a continental ancestral homeland (China) and maritime space of settlement (Malaysia and Taiwan) to the reinvigoration of archipelagic ties that bypass the continent represents a resignification of the South Seas trope that draws contemporary Taiwan into its parameters.

CHAPTER 4

An Ecopoetics of the Borneo Rainforest

An "ecopoetic" mode of Sinophone Malaysian writing from Taiwan specifically addresses the historical and cultural, but more critically the ecological, context of Malaysian Borneo (East Malaysia), where the incredible biodiversity of the island's tropical rainforest has faced the continual plunder of generations of multiple colonial and postcolonial powers. This "rainforest modernism" transforms the trope of the South Seas into a primal, archaic symbol of cross-cultural superimposition and biogenesis that dissolves monolithic tropes of continental Chineseness into the (pre)history of settler-indigenous relations within Borneo's actively evolving equatorial ecosystem. While Borneo's history of settler-indigenous encounter, ethno-cultural intermixture, and linguistic creolization serves as a counterpoint to the rigidly racialized history of Peninsular Malaysia in postcolonial Sinophone Malaysian literature, the ecocritical writing of Borneo foregrounds the island's captivating forestscape, its environmental history, and its ongoing ecological crises.[1]

Of all the Sinophone modernist writers from Malaysian Borneo who publish in Taiwan, Li Yongping (1947-), who hails from Kuching in Sarawak, is arguably the best known and most critically acclaimed. As witness to the final decade of British colonialism (following Japanese occupation) in Sarawak and the state's volatile 1963 merger (along with neighboring Sabah) into postcolonial Malaysia during his childhood, Li has intermittently—throughout his long writing career in Taiwan after moving there to attend university in 1967—made Borneo the setting and historical backdrop to his semiautobiographical fiction and creative memoirs, namely *Son of Borneo* (*Poluozhou zhi zi*, 1968), *The Snow Falls in Clouds: Recollections of a Borneo Childhood* (*Yuxue feifei: Poluozhou tongnian jishi*, 2002), and his massive two-volume novel *River's End* (*Dahe jintou*, 2008 and 2010).[2] Certainly no discussion of the Borneo imagination in Sinophone Malaysian modernism from Taiwan should exclude Li's groundbreaking contributions, yet not only have his diasporic aesthetics of perpetual homecoming and displacement received substantial critical assessment elsewhere, the "virgin rainforest" of Borneo mainly figures in Li's work as a support structure for a more anthropocentric inquiry—concerned primarily with human history and psychological crises—into questions of cultural identity.[3] By comparison, in the Borneo writings of Pan Yutong and Chang Kuei-hsing, the experience of ethno-cultural and linguistic marginality that has led other Sinophone Malaysian authors to aesthetically cultivate diasporic Chineseness or recuperate creolized Malaysianness, while still important, becomes secondary to an environmental crisis that demands its own literary response.

In the rainforest modernism of Pan and Chang, the shift in aesthetic priority—from ethnicity to ecology—marks a revaluation of indigeneity: rather than negatively connoting a politicized *bumiputera* rhetoric of ethno-linguistic and religious favoritism that marginalizes Sinophone cultures in Malaysia, indigeneity here highlights a Sinophone settler desire to approach (without claiming to fully know) an indigenous Dayak rainforest-centric epistemology that provides a salient response to the ecological exploitation of Borneo as a marginalized colonial-cum-national frontier.[4] This literature prioritizes the island's historical, cultural, and ecological uniqueness in the face of serial and overlapping exploitation by Western colonizers, Chinese settlers, the Malaysian state, and multinational corporations that objectify the territory and its indigenous inhabitants. Pan and Chang use the tropical rainforest ecology to cultivate a formal modernist poetics that demands rethinking the epistemological relations between language/culture and environment/landscape. They endow the Borneo rainforest with a cyclical, opaque, umbilical, maternal, life- and language-giving and sustaining narrative subjectivity that de-links Sinophone writing—as an artifact of migration and settler colonial epistemology—from its chronological, patrilineal, consanguine "descent" from the continental ancestral homeland to the north. Striving to undo the colonizing epistemology that seeks to reduce, tame, and commodify the landscape in order to give critical agency to the local ecology, Pan and Chang make the rainforest a significant protagonist that acts, moves, and speaks potently, elusively, and enchantingly.

Like Li Yongping, Pan Yutong and Chang Kuei-hsing cultivate their modernist aesthetics against the backdrop of their transnational access to the academic and literary capital as well as the publication outlets offered by Taiwan as a Sinophone cultural and metropolitan center. Just as Sinophone Malaysian literature's recuperation of creolization indirectly addresses and contributes to Taiwan's literary recognition of its own historical creolization and ethno-linguistic diversity,[5] so too do the Borneo writings' place-based aesthetics of narrative and language present models for analogous literary treatment of Taiwan's own island ecology. As the authors traverse the South Seas—both physically and figuratively—from metropolitan Taiwan back to the embrace of the Borneo rainforest as their motherland, rustic heartland, and "hometown" (*guxiang*), the archipelagic orientation between the two islands (rather than ancestral bonds to the continent) becomes the primary network of affiliation that is the Nanyang.

POSTCOLONIAL ECOCRITICISM AND MODERNIST POETICS

The term "ecopoetics" captures how Sinophone literature on Borneo combines the political activism of a transnationally informed but Borneo-situated postcolonial ecocriticism with modernist literary aesthetics cultivated in the context of US Cold War neoliberalism and post–martial law cultural pluralism in Taiwan. Since the beginning of the new millennium, the coupling of ecocriticism and postcolonial theory has broadened subjects of study in both fields, leading to the development of neologisms such as ecological imperialism, biocolonization, and environmental racism or "speciesism."[6] Postcolonial ecocriticism departs from conventional postcolonial theory focusing on sociocultural exchange/domination and identity politics to examine the legacy of colonialism in the radical transformation of occupied landscapes, environments, and ecologies through industrialized capitalism. Drawing upon the impact of colonialism and neoimperialism in shaping the global climate crisis, postcolonial ecocriticism examines the disruption and displacement of postcolonial communities not by ethnic strife or sectarian violence but by environmental catastrophe and lack or loss of access to endangered natural resources, issues that overlap with and exacerbate disparities of ethnicity, class, and gender. Furthermore, postcolonial ecocriticism self-reflexively problematizes the relationship between elite environmentalist discourses associated with the "advanced" developed states of former imperial metropoles and those of "indigenous" resistance movements in (post) colonial societies.

Interrogating colonial methods of environmental exploitation, postcolonial ecocriticism generally lumps "classic colonial" occupation or "blue water colonialism" (here referred to as maritime imperialism) together with settler colonialism.[7] Postcolonial ecocritics such as Graham Huggan and Helen Tiffin observe both colonialisms as Western modes of relating to and cultivating the land of settlement, suggesting that

> ideas of animal treatment and land use initially formed in Europe predisposed colonial administrators and settlers to a facile belief in the apparently limitless resources of the settler colonies. Such places, after all, were apparently untamed, unowned and, above all, *unused*; and, accordingly, settlers set about rendering them productive and profitable through imported methods rather than by accommodating them to local circumstances.[8]

This dynamic produces confrontations over methods of land tenure between colonists and indigenous populations, with little distinction between the nonindigenous populations: whether the colonists are colonial administrators managing the production of plantation crops for export to the distant metropole using imported slave, indentured, or hired labor, or they are settlers cultivating the land to enrich themselves in the New World, the systems they impose and the capitalist markets they serve are often identical.

Yet there are important distinctions between settler colonialism and maritime imperialism in terms of their motivations and processes. Whereas imperialism is premised on the indispensability of indigenous populations as colonized subjects and exploitable labor for deriving power, settler colonialism, according to Lorenzo Veracini, promotes "the *dispensability* of the indigenous person."[9] Settler colonization is a process that numerically overwhelms, displaces, and/or replaces the indigenous population. References to the land as vast and empty, as if there were little or no indigenous population present, are a typical narrative strategy of the settler colonial imagination that seeks to lay claim to the new territory.[10] In this imaginary, the indigenous person simultaneously constitutes a shadowy threat (compelling the settler to organize a mercenary defense against indigenous "raids"), a vanishing and tragic "noble savage," and an appropriable symbol for the settler's own "indigenization."[11]

Besides maritime imperialism, settler colonialism is also a distinct process from migration and diaspora: whereas settlers become the founders of political orders in the new homeland—migrating "to *their* country"—diasporas are formed through migration "to *another* country" with an already formed political order.[12] These discrepancies are important when considering the ecocriticism deployed in the fiction on Borneo, as Sinophone Malaysian literature inherits a history of Chinese migration and settlement prior to and alongside Western (Dutch and British) maritime imperialism. In Borneo, pioneer Chinese settlers (mostly Hakka) initially occupied positions apart from the imperial regime, as they—defying Qing prohibition—began migrating there during the eighteenth century (with "direct immigration from China" established by the 1760s), before the political authority of the Malay sultans was consolidated under the Dutch. In addition to becoming smallholders of homesteads on which they cultivated pepper and other cash crops, these mostly male Hakka settlers—accustomed to a rugged life as frontiersmen and miners in southeastern China—organized mining and jungle-clearing operations and even established their own, self-governing mini-republic in what is now West Kalimantan. Historian Philip Kuhn describes the "Lanfang Republic" as a Hakka settler society (pejoratively called a "secret society" by the Dutch, who eventually defeated and disbanded it in 1884) based in Pontianak in West Kalimantan that represented an "independent confederation of mining communities." The "management committee"—or *kongsi* (*gongsi*)—of the confederation organized private militias for protection against the harsh jungle environment and their "chief antagonists," who in the early years of the settler republic were not Dutch colonists but indigenous Dayaks, as the settler republic's relationship with Dayak communities was "complicated by the fact that many Hakka pioneers took Dayak wives."[13] The charismatic founder of the republic, Lo Fang Pok (Luo Fangbo), further stipulated that only Hakkas (from a particular county in China no less) could hold positions of leadership or participate in elections.[14]

Reflecting on the long and complex history of Chinese settlement, development, and interethnic relations in Borneo, Sinophone Malaysian literature demonstrates how the three systems (and attendant desires) of maritime imperialism, settler colonialism, and migration/diaspora converge on the island, implicating one another in the displacement of indigenous Dayak livelihoods and in the exploitation of the rainforest. With an historical imagination traversing experiences of Chinese migration/diaspora and settler colonialism, Sinophone Malaysian writers often evoke and celebrate pioneering Hakka forebears who "opened up and cultivated the wilderness" (*tuohuang* or *kenhuang*) of rural Borneo.[15] The ecopoetics of Pan Yutong and Chang Kuei-hsing involves a more critical approach to this history: their central focus on the rainforest ecology spans historical regimes of Western imperialism, Chinese migration and settlement, and Malaysian state formation, registering their effects on indigenous Dayak communities and the environment. Occupying a moral position that combines historical reality with a formal aesthetic of environmental writing, their ecopoetics illuminates how "postcolonial ecocriticism preserves the aesthetic function of the literary text while drawing attention to its social and political usefulness, its capacity to set out symbolic guidelines for the material transformation of the world."[16] The environmental imagination of Pan and Chang showcases their meticulous research and intimacy with the setting, yet it also revels in the mystery and inexhaustibility, or opacity,[17] of the rainforest ecology and indigenous cultures. For Pan and Chang, this blending of knowledge and mystery, familiarity and distance recognizes "nature and natural elements (landscape, flora and fauna, etc.) as self-standing agents, rather than support structures for human action, in the world."[18]

It is not only the authors' environmental agenda and knowledge of Borneo's ecology and history, but also their respective initiations into literary modernism in Cold War–era Taiwan and the atmosphere of cultural pluralism following the end to martial law there that inflect their modernist ecopoetics. Under the influence of the Sinophone modernism (associated primarily with post-1945 settlers from mainland China) and nativism that dominated the literary scene when Chinese Malaysian students first came to Taiwan for higher education and began publishing there, Sinophone Malaysian literature from Taiwan largely adopted the modernist movement's aesthetics of language and form, as well as its themes of exile and psychological separation. Of course, in terms of articulating a sense of place (or placelessness) and an imagination of a (lost) homeland, China is consistently the dominant topos associated with modernist literature from Taiwan.

The main figures of the modernist scene in 1960s Taiwan used their formal literary initiation into Western modernism (primarily through cultural and educational ties to US institutions) to bring about an "aesthetic transformation" of the China motif, reinventing the signifier as a "potent aesthetic trope" in order to depoliticize and dissociate it from its anticommunist, propagandistic usage by KMT-sponsored writers.[19] For example, the poet, essayist, and mainland exile Yu Kwang-chung (Yu Guangzhong)—one of the forerunners of the modernist movement—recasts the China trope as a mother figure in his 1966 poem "When I Am Dead" ("Dang wo si shi"):

> When I am dead, lay me down between the Yangtze / And the Yellow River and pillow my head / On China, white hair against black soil, / Most beautiful O most maternal of lands, / And I will sleep my soundest taking / The whole mainland for my cradle. . . .[20]

Yu's physical and psychological separation from China manifests as a generalized, abstracted poetic landscape in which the geographical body of the nation takes on a maternal, nurturing image that caresses and nurtures the author's dreams.

Though cast as a nurturing environment and invoking the images of the Yangzi and Yellow Rivers, which provide historical sustenance for the agrarian civilization of continental China, the China trope of the Taiwan modernists is not typically associated with an ecocritical agenda, but more predominantly the fanciful, melancholic longing for lost ties of kinship and consanguinity. In fact, scholars note that Taiwanese nativism—which rose to challenge the modernist trend in the 1970s—registers more of an ecocritical impulse, as the nativists saw the chimeric escapism (detachment from local reality) and Western literary style and syntax of Taiwan's modernists as complicit byproducts of the US neoliberal order that radically transformed the Taiwanese landscape throughout the Cold War.[21]

Since the end to martial law in 1987, an environment of cultural pluralism and literary "vocationalism" in Taiwan has blurred the stylistic conventions of the heretofore starkly drawn boundaries between "mainlander modernism" and "Taiwanese nativism."[22] Publishing in this environment, the Sinophone Malaysian authors Pan Yutong and Chang Kuei-hsing evoke Borneo as an island trope of the South Seas in a way that blends the abstract, melancholic longing and psychological distance of the China trope in Taiwan modernism with the engaged cultural, political, and ecocritical agenda of Taiwanese nativist writing. As these authors supplant iconic, continental referents of Chineseness such as the Yangzi and Yellow Rivers with Borneo's major waterways such as the Sungai Kinabatangan in Sabah and the Batang Rajang in Sarawak, the measure of affinity to place becomes less about ethnic ancestry and more about the cross-cultural collection and combination of stories and myths that detail modes of being in and relating to Borneo. Here, the modernist projection and longing for the landscape as a maternal figure is not simply an expression of psychological exile or the desire to recover or return to a lost birthplace, but a moral supplication for the ecological preservation of the planet's tropical rainforests (to which Borneo is a center rather than periphery), as they constitute humanity's umbilical lifeline to "mother earth." Casting the rainforest in dreamlike imagery, this ecopoetic modernism is not a mode of escapism from present realities but the recognition of global ecological interdependency, imaginatively linked through the authors' allusions to the archipelagic network of the South Seas.

A CONCENTRIC RAINFOREST NARRATOLOGY

Pan Yutong (penname of Pan Guichang, 1937-) is a "pioneer of rainforest prose."[23] Though nearly all of his short stories are set in Borneo, Pan himself originally hails from rural Negeri Sembilan in West Malaysia. He left Malaysia to study agriculture at National Chung Hsing University in Taichung, Taiwan, where he was initiated into Sinophone literary modernism while writing for and editing a journal for "overseas students." Like many of Taiwan's prominent modernist authors of the 1960s, Pan Yutong opted to continue postgraduate study in the United States, but instead of attending the Iowa Writers MFA Program more popular among Taiwan's renowned modernists, Pan chose to continue his research in the natural sciences. He received a PhD in plant breeding and genetics from Oklahoma State University, an important center of innovation and experimentation in American agro-engineering during the Cold War era. He later returned to Malaysia to work in the agricultural sector as a reporter, often traveling to East Malaysia to report on the environment. A retired estate manager in Johor, Pan sees himself as a farmer, not a writer. With critically acclaimed works such as his short-fiction collection, *Riverbank Legends* (*He'an chuanshuo*, 2002), Pan has continued to access the Taiwanese publishing platform, connecting him to a broader transnational arena of Sinophone literary modernism.

Pan Yutong bases much of his short fiction about the East Malaysian state of Sabah on news reports he both read and wrote there. His fiction draws attention to how Borneo remains a marginalized national frontier and contested political frontline among Malaysia, Indonesia, and the Philippines.[24] Though the abundant, valuable natural resources of Sarawak and Sabah (namely timber and oil) generate much of the funds funneled into Kuala Lumpur's "Vision 2020" (Wawasan 2020) for the development of the nation's globalizing economy, very little of the revenues generated return to the two East Malaysian states, where poverty and unemployment rates are higher than in West Malaysia.[25] In evoking these disparities, Pan details the exploitation of undocumented migrant workers in Sabah who come from the southern Philippines and Indonesian Kalimantan. Pan's "The Country Shop" ("Ye dian," 1998) is essentially an allegory of how West Malaysia's development and globalization occurs at the expense of the environment and economy of Sabah, plunging the people of the state into deeper poverty and subservience.

Susima, the protagonist of "The Country Shop," migrates to the town of Semporna from the Philippine island of Sibutu. She initially earns a meager living selling cigarettes on the street, but then meets Ah Cheng, a Hakka entrepreneur from West Malaysia who owns a dried seafood shop in town. Ah Cheng manufactures and sells items that fetch a higher price on the peninsula, where he already has a shop, a home, a wife, and children. Needing someone to watch over the Semporna shop during his frequent return trips to West Malaysia, Ah Cheng hires Susima as his shop assistant. He soon makes Susima his mistress and she gives birth to a son, Ah Ka. Eventually, Susima discovers she is unhappy with the arrangement and begins arguing with Ah Cheng, who looks down on her and calls her stupid. Susima and Ah Ka complain that Ah Cheng brings all the valuable commodities to West Malaysia and privileges his family there. Susima feels that Ah Cheng has exploited her and their son simply so that he can extract goods from Sabah to be turned into wealth in West Malaysia. Furthermore, Ah Cheng refuses to pay for Ah Ka's education, telling him that he is better off "rinsing sea cucumber" than going to school. Susima laments that Ah Ka's West Malaysian siblings "all go to secondary school and will be attending university in the future. We earn the money, but they get to enjoy it."[26] The dynamic between Susima and Ah Cheng allegorizes the disparities between East and West Malaysia. Since both characters are technically "migrant workers" in Sabah, the author does not configure these disparities as a settler-indigenous conflict (though the differences of ethnicity, gender, and citizenship between Susima and Ah Cheng do play a role in the economic exploitation), but predominantly as an effect of West Malaysia's economic colonization of Borneo for its globalizing market demands.

Although regional economic inequity in Borneo is an important concern for Pan Yutong, the most critical issue in his fiction is the postcolonial destruction of the rainforest at the hands of global capitalism. In his ecopoetic writing of the Borneo rainforest, Pan adopts a consistent modernist structure of storytelling best described—or visually illustrated (see Figure 4.1)—as a "concentric narratology." This structure is certainly evident throughout the short stories in his critically acclaimed volume published in Taiwan, *Riverbank Legends*—in which each story is set along the Sungai Kinabatangan in Sabah—but is also evidenced in earlier stories such as "Tropical Rainforests" ("Redai yulin," 1996). Pan's narratology places the various actors and agents in the stories on different concentric circles in terms of the directness regarding their portrayal and development within the narrative: the more indirectly they are portrayed (meaning the more they exist on the story's periphery), the more power they in fact wield as plot catalysts. The outer circle consists of both rainforests and multinational corporations (or the system of global capitalism more generally), as these two opposed structures possess the greatest potency, power, and mystique: though they are all-encompassing as the main catalysts in the stories, they are also portrayed indirectly, elusively, and abstractly as generalized backdrops.

The second circle of indigenous Dayak women and Western (or Western-trained) scientists denotes sometimes intersecting, sometimes competing environmental epistemologies. In the stories, these figures appear at sites of deforestation and development as both intermediaries/messengers of the rainforest and as by-products of multinational capitalism. As prostitutes, cooks, and maids working at the construction sites, the Dayak women—usually of the Kadazan-Dusun or Bajau tribes of Sabah—typically embody native legends or oral literature about the Borneo rainforest: they are water sprites whose presence warns that "the destruction of the rainforest will infuriate the mountain spirits."[27] Cataloguing rainforest biodiversity and endangered species, the scientists propagate a modern, cause-and-effect discourse of environmentalism. Like the Dayak women,

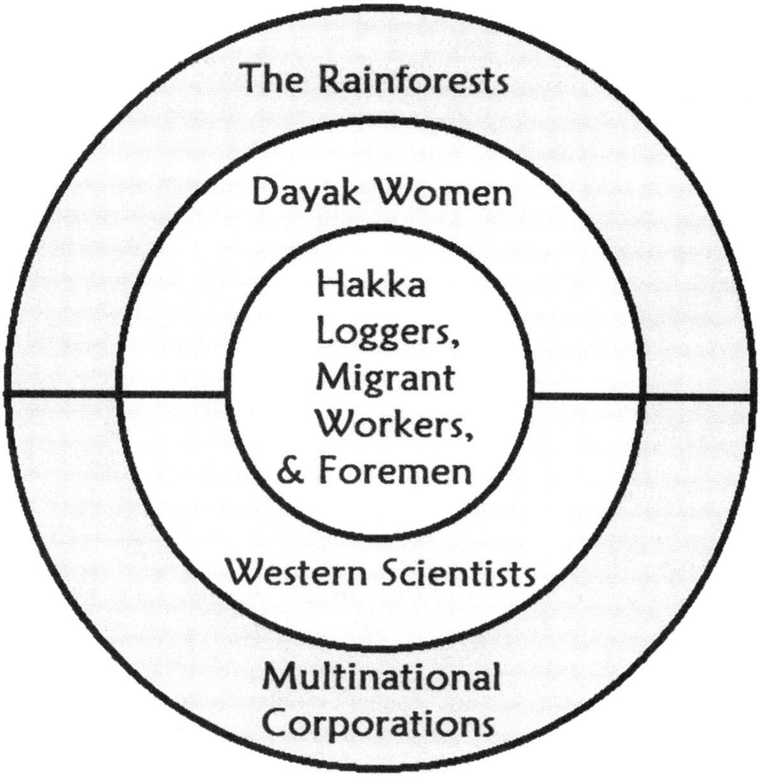

Figure 4.1 Pan Yutong Concentric Narratology

they receive direct portrayal, but little development or resolution in the narratives, thus remaining to a certain degree on the periphery.

The inner circle of Pan's narratology typically consists of migrant Hakka construction workers, loggers, planters, commercial fishermen, and foremen in Sabah, who as protagonists receive the most direct portrayal and development in the plot line. Through the perspectives of migrant workers, Pan shows how environmental exploitation gives rise to conflicts between industries (such as fishing, timber, and oil), or between small-scale farmers or fishermen and the larger commercial industries they serve. In Pan's "River Mouth" ("He kou," 2002), Taro Lin, a poor, lonely old Hakka fisherman who struggles to make a living by catching crabs at the mouth of the Sungai Kinabatangan, captures crabs that have developed extra legs in the polluted river. Forest depletion on the riverbank has eroded the crabs' natural habitat, with plantation runoff contaminating their waters. Taro can no longer catch the profitable white pomfret because of commercial fishing just beyond the river mouth. His adopted son, Frankie, now an adult living in the city, rarely visits Taro because he is ashamed of the environment his father lives in. Frankie describes the conditions as "unsanitary" and insinuates that it is the responsibility of the inhabitants—the destitute "river mouth people" such as Taro—to clean up the mess. Taro claims to know nothing about "environmental sanitation" but implies that it is the trash of urbanites that has degraded the place: "We may be dirty, but you eat the fish and shrimp we catch. Now there is almost none left. The fish and shrimp in the sea have all swum away."[28] Here, environmental sanitation is a paradoxical discourse: the urbanites want the environment cleaned up, blaming the fishermen and loggers for the unsanitary conditions that are simply a by-product of manufacturing the commodities that enable a more "sanitary" urban lifestyle.

Having worked on an oil palm plantation himself, Pan Yutong is empathetic to the plight of his migrant-worker protagonists, as they have few alternatives to the relatively meager living they make in subservience to distant markets beyond their reach. Pan carefully and lengthily depicts the techniques of planting and logging as well as the mundane details of their daily lives. He also draws attention to the loggers' own beliefs about the rainforest environment, showing that they do not simply consider their personal survival but also the greater consequences of their labor. In "Drought Demon" ("Han ba," 2002), the loggers at a rainforest construction site along the Sungai Kinabatangan refuse to cut down an old-growth tree, or "old uncle tree" (*bogong shu*) sacred to Hakka legend. This stalls the entire construction project, infuriating their employer. A project supervisor promises the story's protagonist, a nameless Hakka logger referred to only as "the man," that he will receive an increase in his rice rations if he cuts down the tree.

Before carrying out the order, the protagonist thinks of the warning issued by his Dayak girlfriend, Wasida, who works at the construction site as a maid. She has recently returned to the site after serving as a temporary worker at a nearby environmental research station, where she became exposed to "modern scientific knowledge" about the adverse impact of deforestation. She warns the protagonist that the forest spirits will exact retribution for the loggers' work:

> Ever since she had returned from working at that research station, she had changed. She was going around saying that when the drought

> demon came to the riverside to drink in the misty mornings, he would drink all the water in the river. . . . Who did she think she was, helping the people at the research station by saying that we should not cut down trees, kill apes, trap large-headed birds, or catch sharks in the river? It was best to let the river sharks eat her, the deranged woman![29]

Dismissing Wasida's warning, the logger finally decides to cut down the old-growth tree, but its branches inexplicably fall on him from the forest canopy above. The sky spins and he collapses as his chainsaw is transformed into a "blood-red wildflower."[30]

Whereas the Dayak women function as omens to impending retribution in Pan Yutong's short stories, the environmental researchers tie Borneo's ecological plight to that of other critical rainforest habitat in the postcolonial world that is also threatened by globalization. In Pan Yutong's short story "Tropical Rainforests," the protagonist, Ye Yuntao, is a scientist who is also the son of a logging company manager working in the river basin of the Sungai Segama in eastern Sabah. Conflicted about the livelihood that has supported his privileged, modern education, he frequently accompanies the loggers to the zones slated for deforestation and attempts to chart and collect samples of the biodiversity there before it vanishes. One day, he opens a map of the entire rain-forested area of the equatorial world and draws a red line from Gunung Palung National Park in Kalimantan to Monteverde Cloud Forest Reserve in Costa Rica:

> From Kalimantan in the south, the [rainforest's] mountain range stretched out majestically and enchantingly. It emerged from the center at the equator, expanding to latitudes of 20 degrees north and south. To the east, it reached New Guinea, and to the west it ran through Sri Lanka, Uganda, Cameroon, French Guyana, Brazil, Panama, Costa Rica, Colombia, Ecuador, and Peru.[31]

As Ye Yuntao's map spans the equator, the author puts the global destruction of rainforests in apocalyptic terms:

> What sound do the tropical rainforests make when they cry out in unison? Most of the million-plus named life forms on the planet can be found there. Amazingly, more than 700 different species of tree can be found on a twenty-acre parcel of forested land in Malaysia. The same goes for animals. More than a thousand species of butterfly can be found in the Amazon Basin. Life here is so densely complex. But the sad thing is that these tropical rainforests are disappearing: every year, a huge area covering 55,000 square miles vanishes. . . .
>
> As a wall of rainforest ten million miles long disintegrates, it neither wails nor bleeds; it simply sacrifices. From the buzzing scriptures

> of the chainsaw, we can read the sky and earth; we can read the interdependency of everything in the world. After reading the buzzing scripture, we must await a ceremony, a fire ceremony igniting chaos in the sky and on the ground as everything is returned to its primal state. Then, in no systematic order, the glorious earth manifests itself before our eyes, beginning with the equator and quickly expanding north and south in latitude. Asia, Africa, and South America are peeled away layer by layer.[32]

Like the rainforests in the South American Amazon, the biodiversity of the Borneo rainforest is astounding, with countless species of mammals, birds, amphibians, fish, trees, and flowering plants. Yet this rainforest, which used to cover the entire island, is depleting rapidly: according to the World Wildlife Foundation, more than half of Borneo's forest cover was logged by 2005.[33] Pan Yutong situates his modernist poetics within a transnational ecocritical discourse, tying Borneo's plight to other rainforest habitat around the world threatened by globalization. As an interdependent Planet Earth depends upon the life-giving sustenance of its rainforests, their destruction becomes a funeral pyre for all.

Pan Yutong's ecocritical concern for the global destruction of the rainforests looms larger than his empathy toward the migrant workers, who become implicated in the logging for timber export and conversion to plantations that are the primary reasons for Borneo's rapid deforestation. Fires that have ravaged pristine rainforest on the island are often set illegally by companies that are then able to purchase the degraded land at a significantly reduced cost. In recent decades, the rise in global demand for biofuels has intensified deforestation, as more plots of rainforest are converted to oil palm plantations.[34] Unfortunately, palm oil is not a clean, viable alternative to petroleum: the burning of the forest for conversion releases vast amounts of carbon into the atmosphere and destroys critical habitat for wildlife, such as elephants and orangutans, bringing them into ever greater conflict with the local human population. Pan Yutong's stories draw attention to these conflicts: in "Riverbank Legends" ("He'an chuanshuo," 2002), Hakka migrant construction workers convert an ecologically valuable 4,000-acre peat swamp along the Sungai Kinabatangan into oil palm and teak plantations. The story raises awareness about how these plantations ravage the sources of food for Borneo's elephants and disrupt their natural migration patterns, forcing them to trample across the newly planted fields in order to reach food and water.

To protect its crops, the construction company sends out some of its workers to poach the elephants.[35]

In depicting these conflicts, Pan Yutong does not allow the rainforest to simply play a passive role: while it continues to "sacrifice," it also responds, becoming an agent, rather than a mere object, of its own elemental transformation. As a shadowy, swift, shape-shifting macro-organism, the rainforest emerges in Pan's ecopoetics as an elusive protagonist that carries out its own movements. Yet its "body" defies Pan's own depictions of it, which can only trace its circumference and cannot fully probe its depths or core. Consider, for example, the following depiction of the rainforest in "Riverbank Legends":

> The rainforest rushed down from the mountains to an abrupt stop at the riverbank. It cast a completely different arc that stretched to the horizon drawn across the peat swamp, where it protected the marsh from disastrous overflowing in the rainy season. . . .
>
> The rainforest on both sides of the river swayed violently in the monsoonal winds. As dusk came, it menacingly swallowed up the evening sun. Leaves blew about, finally leaving behind only broken, withered branches. These branches eventually all fell into the river and tumbled over and over as they followed the torrential river downstream. In the dark of night, the withered branches changed unpredictably, transforming into entwined water sprites that climbed up onto the riverbank.[36]

Interspersed rather sparingly in Pan Yutong's narratives, such depictions pan out to an overhead long-shot of the rainforest's shape, which is shown to be in motion, then focalize on certain natural elements, such as the two branches. As a giant and potentially anthropomorphic organism, the rainforest sways and hovers, sometimes menacingly, sometimes seductively (like a Dayak water sprite), over everything within and around it. The protagonists and minor characters of the inner two concentric circles of the narratology are helpless in the presence of its raw transformative power.

Pan Yutong's rainforest narratology, with its constellation of various agents and interests from migrant workers and environmental researchers to indigenous women and logging companies beholden to multinational corporations, eclectically combines settler and indigenous, modern and mythological relations to the rainforest ecology in an elaborate but tightly bound modernist short-story structure. Although neither Borneo nor Taiwan is his birthplace or current home, these two sites play a vitally generative role in the formation of

Pan Yutong's Sinophone Malaysian ecopoetics. In Pan's ecopoetics, the South Seas becomes symbolic not of human migrations between an original and new homeland, but of an interdependent global network of critical rainforest habitat and tropical ecologies connected by a "red line" across an equatorial oceanscape.

RAINFOREST OF RESEMBLANCES: BORNEO AS MOTHERLAND

Chang Kuei-hsing (Zhang Guixing, 1956-) is Sinophone literature's foremost architect of the Borneo rainforest. Of Hakka descent, Chang, unlike Pan Yutong, is originally from Borneo, as he was born and raised in Lutong, Sarawak (located between the city of Miri and the Brunei border). In his fiction, Chang specifically cultivates an image of Borneo as motherland and towns like Lutong and Daro—coastally situated between the rainforest and the South China Sea—as "home villages" (*guxiang*). Like Pan, Chang Kuei-hsing left Malaysia for higher education, enrolling at Taiwan Normal University in 1976; unlike Pan, Chang chose to settle in Taiwan permanently and adopt ROC citizenship. It was not until the late 1980s that Chang began writing seriously about Borneo. That was when he realized the uniqueness of his childhood experiences, such as his camping trips with young Dayak friends and classmates in the Borneo rainforest.[37]

In contrast to the concise, indirect, macrocosmic portrait of the rainforest in Pan Yutong's concentric narratology, Chang Kuei-hsing's ecopoetic modernism is more prolific and detailed: his fiction produces a lush catalogue of copious words and nature images in a seemingly boundless chain of metaphors and similes that metonymically links language/culture and landscape/ecology in their potentially inexhaustible variation. Jing Tsu describes Chang's writing as embodying "a physical medium of biodiversity," as the author details even the most microcosmic degrees and subtle hues of Borneo's ethnic (skin shade), linguistic (pidgins, creoles, dialects), and ecological (plants, fungi, insects) diversity, hybridity, and chameleon-like metamorphoses.[38] Structurally, Chang Kuei-hsing's heftier novels (as opposed to Pan Yutong's more concise short fiction) are labyrinthine, giving the reader "rainforest sensations" of directional uncertainty and leading one down many "tributary streams" of tangential anecdotes, stories, and myths.

Chang Kuei-hsing's novels about the Borneo rainforest—which include *Siren Song* (*Sailian zhi ge*, 1992), *The Wayward Clan* (*Wanpi jiazu*, 1996), *The Elephant Herd* (*Qun xiang*, 1998), *Monkey Cup* (*Hou bei*, 2000), and *My South Seas Sleeping Beauty* (*Wo sinian de changmian zhong de Nanguo gongzhu*, 2001)—showcase a richer and deeper cultural and historical genealogy of Borneo than Pan Yutong's short fiction, which is more concerned with evincing present-day environmental crises. Chang's series of novels are connected by theme and historical backdrop rather than continuity of character and storyline. They are all adolescent male coming-of-age narratives set in and around the Borneo rainforest during the time of Sarawak's transition from British colony to Malaysian state,[39] with extensive forays into the protagonist's family history as well as an ancient, colonial, and contemporary history of Borneo.

In tying place, nature, and ecology to family, culture, and history, Chang's fiction produces a dualistic interplay between China as the patrilineal ancestral land (*zuguo*)—denoting a manmade chronological history of clan, genealogy, and descent along a southward path of migration—and the Borneo rainforest as the "earth mother" (*dadi zhi mu*)—denoting a site of "primitive warmth" whose natural history is concealed in circuitous myth and arboreal density.[40] In his preface to *Monkey Cup*, Chang writes about desperately trying to find his way back into the Borneo rainforest of his memory. He addresses the rainforest as his mother, offering gratitude to her from afar as the "lungs of the earth" that imbue him with the breath of life.[41] Here, the Borneo rainforest becomes the "most maternal of lands" (invoking Yu Kwang-chung's modernist verse on China) that cradles the author's dreams and nurtures his imagination.

The mother is a revered figure in Chang Kuei-hsing's fiction: she is a siren who sings with the "humid, fertile breath" of Borneo's rainforest, summoning Chang back home into the womb.[42] In *Siren Song*, the protagonist, who growing up in colonial Sarawak goes by his English name, Ryan Chang, describes his mother as an incredibly fertile provider of life. Having already birthed seven children, she was pregnant with Ryan for ten months before he finally emerged.[43] The desire for a soothing, dark, maternal, and womblike environment consumes Ryan's childhood, as the swampy lake behind their family home becomes his nocturnal playground:

> In the lake behind the newly built pigpen, we planted floating duckweed that we used to feed the pigs. The lake was small, but all-inclusive: pond skaters, mole crickets, mayflies, earthworms, and chiggers thrived in there. The lake's small size made its bounty

> exquisite, and the manure and urine from the pigpen that flowed into it made it fertile. The smell of piss and manure from the lake penetrated all corners of our house, and it diluted my nerves and veins. . . . The coconut, jackfruit, rambutan, and mangosteen trees surrounding the lake dangled their roots into its fertile waters. Their branches were moist and tender, their knotty, bulbous trunks sappy, and they bore fleshy, juicy fruit. The smell of pig manure sweetened my sleep and revitalized my awakening. Its fragrance penetrated my every orifice and made me fidgety. I sat up from the bed upon which my older brothers lay spread-out, left the oppressive heat and sweaty stench of the mosquito netting, put on my loose-fitting, pee-stained shorts, and, while swatting mosquitoes with my bare arms, trampled snails and centipedes. . . . I munched on the duckweed and pig manure while my teeth chattered and my entire body shivered. Though I stood in the middle of the lake, I was only submerged up to the chest.[44]

The warm, amniotic embrace of the tropical swamp "fertilizes" the feverish boy and enchants his dreams. As Chang Kuei-hsing's "virgin work" (*chunü zuo*) on Borneo, *Siren Song* paints the rainforest in Odyssean "waterscapes" of enchanted swamps, rivers, and seas inhabited by alluring female figures.

Chang Kuei-hsing configures the archipelagic trope of the South Seas as an intersection between Western imperial, Chinese settler, and indigenous Dayak relations to the Borneo ecology: the Nanyang is a route of passage, navigation, negotiation, and conflict between the three systems. The worldview of Chang's protagonists is greatly influenced by the importation and imposition of both Western and Chinese culture, literature, art, and education in Borneo, yet these only contribute to shaping and illuminating the adolescent's view of the local, rather than stirring his desire to escape elsewhere. In *Siren Song*, the adolescent Ryan is aroused by European classicist paintings: he even steals an image of British Victorian painter John Waterhouse's "Hylas and the Water Nymphs" from a book at the public library in Lutong.[45] While seemingly a mode of erotic escapism, viewing these images of water sprites in his tropical surroundings only intensifies the protagonist's feeling that they are part of the local fabric of Borneo.

Whereas in *Siren Song* it is Western maritime imperial modes of aestheticizing, eroticizing, and feminizing the landscape that are absorbed into the protagonist's cultivation of South Seas sensibilities, in Chang Kuei-hsing's *The Elephant Herd* it is totems of continental Chinese culture and geography—such as the Yangzi River, Confucianism, the dragon, and the classical landscape painting—that fulfill this function. Chang's narrative experimentation—through poetic wordplay, mythmaking, and the interventions of anthropology and the natural sciences—reconfigures Chineseness as "a fluid designator" that destabilizes its geographical origin, producing what E. K. Tan calls a "haunting tension between the two competing homelands—the motherland, Malaysia, and the imaginary homeland, China."[46] The novel's ecopoetics also *resolves* this tension, as it dissolves the potency of China and Chineseness as the imaginary homeland of the protagonist's (and by extension the author's) desire and longing.

There are two main strands of evidence for this dissolution and resolution in *The Elephant Herd*. First, there is the doubling of the Chinese Malaysian protagonist, Shi Shicai, and his young Dayak friend (from the Iban tribe) Zhu Dezhong, who not only shadows and protects Shicai upon his journey into the rainforest but also extends to the boy a rite of passage into manhood as an indigenous warrior. Second, there is the historical superimposition of the Nanyang onto China and Chineseness in the lessons and artifacts bequeathed by Shicai's former Mandarin-language teacher. Here, Shicai's Sinophone education enhances and illuminates his relationship to his tropical surroundings (as opposed to China and his Chinese heritage). Textually mediated through the author's ecopoetic imagination, the history, myths, and anecdotes the boy learns cultivate a stronger cultural affinity to Borneo and the South Seas.

In the novel, Shicai, who is from the coastal town of Daro, and Dezhong, who is from the town of Kapit upriver on the mighty Batang Rajang, work together hauling timber along the river. While Shicai is welcomed warmly into the Iban community in Kapit, where he allows a sense of Dayak indigeneity to inform his rite of passage into manhood, Zhu Dezhong speaks fluent Mandarin, a phenomenon that baffles Shicai.[47] The curiously patriarchal "Chinese" traits of Dezhong's name—evoking Confucian "virtue" (*de*) and the Middle Kingdom as "center" (*zhong*)—are here superimposed with the masculine qualities of a loyal and righteous indigenous warrior and brother. Invited to celebrate Dezhong's homecoming festivities, Shicai becomes intoxicated on *tuak* (Dayak rice wine) and hypnotized by the music and dancing around him. In a drunken stupor, he transforms into an Iban warrior by seizing a *parang* (an aboriginal dagger) and shouts that he is going to behead "that pig" before he finally passes out.[48]

"That pig" refers to Shicai's uncle Yu Jiatong, leader of the notoriously rebellious "Yangzi River Brigade," a cell group of the Sarawak

Communist Organization (the SCO, also known as the Sarawak People's Guerrilla Forces) fighting British, Malay, and Australian counterinsurgency forces from 1961–65 during Malaysia's "Confrontation" with Indonesia over the two nations' competing claims to Sarawak and Sabah. Shicai's drunken pronouncement is a ceremonious commencement to his mission to track down the secret base camp of the Yangzi River Brigade so he can kill his uncle, whose neglect and abandonment of the goal to promote positive relations with the indigenous Dayaks led to the deaths of Shicai's four older brothers, all of whom were under Jiatong's command. Duplicitously, Jiatong advocates cooperation with the Dayaks, only to later tell Shicai that intermarriage with the "barbarians" is merely a political "strategy." In the past, Jiatong had first introduced Shicai's oldest brother, the timid Shinong, to Shinong's Iban wife, who welcomed Shinong into the longhouse community and prompted his transformation into a brave, tattooed Iban warrior before Jiatong's betrayal of him led to his death. Jiatong also tells Shicai—who has grown close to Dezhong's enchanting sister Fadia—that he should not let "the filthy skin color of the natives seep into his purebred yellow skin."[49]

Upon his mission to track down his uncle, Shicai is shadowed and mysteriously protected by Dezhong, who seeks the government reward money for Jiatong's head as payback for communist exploitation of the Ibans. When Shicai finally locates the camp off a tributary stream of the Batang Rajang deep in the rainforest, he must wait in a hut for several days for his uncle to return from his elephant-hunting trip. On the wall of the hut, Shicai discovers a Song dynasty painting entitled "Stormy Landscape" ("Fengyu shanshui"), once the prized possession of his Mandarin teacher, Mr. Shao. Mr. Shao bequeathed the painting to Jiatong, his star student, before he was deported to China for spreading communist propaganda in his classes. As night falls in the raised wooden hut, Shicai's vision becomes obscured by the lamp:

> Under the light of the kerosene lantern, "Stormy Landscape" revealed a different charm, morphing into a hot, humid tropical landscape, like the view the boy saw on the two riverbanks of the Batang Rajang. A gibbon and a monitor lizard scaled the cliff walls of the mountain. Durian and rambutan decorated the banks of the river islets. Longhouses and raised huts replaced the delicate and exquisite Chinese architecture. Literati and their young attendants wandering in the mountains transformed into half-naked adolescent Iban girls playing in the water. An entire landscape painting from the Southern Song transformed into a batik painting splattered with a colorful South Seas style.[50]

In the tropical hut deep in the rainforest, the Southern Song Chinese landscape is gradually superimposed with the Nanyang batik painting of the Borneo rainforest. Ancient totems of Chineseness are refigured as tropical ones native to Borneo.

This process of cultural and historical superimposition occurs throughout *The Elephant Herd*. In his flashbacks of studying Mandarin, Shicai only recalls lessons that gave him local referent points for understanding China's cultural and natural history. In Mr. Shao's lecture on the history of the crocodile, the ecology of prehistoric China becomes that of the tropical South Seas, and the dragon, a classic totem of Chinese culture, becomes the crocodile, the most feared overlord of Borneo's waterways:

> Before the Xia and Shang dynasties, the climate of the Chinese Central Plains was akin to the subtropics, especially the mid and lower regions of the Yellow River delta. This area, filled with marshes, humid and rainy, and where dense jungles gathered, was an ideal habitat for both herbivorous and carnivorous animals, providing the crocodile with the most ideal conditions for its existence. . . . During the Xia and Shang periods, the climate in the Central Plains changed drastically. It got colder. There were droughts. The lakes and marshes dried up. The crocodiles diminished, and in the end disappeared from North China. . . . All that was left behind was a multitude of crocodile legends. As the crocodile was gradually replaced by myths, it became the primal image of the dragon.[51]

By superimposing diasporic totems of China and Chineseness with those of Borneo and Dayak indigeneity (Shicai with Dezhong, the Yangzi River with the Batang Rajang, the Song landscape with the Nanyang batik painting, and the dragon with the crocodile), Chang Kuei-hsing dissolves patrilineal relations with the ancestral land into a cross-cultural communion with the tropical motherland. The novel's ancient mythology bends and obscures the "arrowlike" trajectory of diasporic, migratory, and settler history that leads from ancestral homeland (center) to the new frontier (periphery),[52] allowing a Chinese Malaysian boy to come of age as a native son of Borneo.

Even the original Sinophone title of the novel, *Qun xiang* (The Elephant Herd), reflects a kind of reciprocity between (the settler's) language and (the native) ecology. The title refers to the elusive, mysterious, diminishing Borneo elephant herd that continually migrates throughout the rainforest and piques the protagonist's imagination. In the novel, the herd's scars and suffering allegorize the island's historical victims of colonial and state violence, namely indigenous Dayak and Chinese settler communities. According to Andrea Bachner, the novel's title further "proposes a logic of resemblance," since the word *xiang* (elephant) can also mean "to resemble" and is used in the words for "imagination" (*xiangxiang*) and "pictograph" (*xiangxing wenzi*): as the story of *xiang*'s etymology goes, the character evolved from an ancient *pictograph* depicting what one *imagined* an *elephant* to look like.[53] Such resemblances between language and ecology make Chang's Sinophone ecopoetics a visual example of the "wilderness script" (*huang wen ye zi*) he describes in *The Elephant Herd*: an idiomatic expression of Chang's own invention, this phrase describes the writing among cockroach corpses and skeletal leaf veins that Shicai discovers in the pages of his uncle's elephant-hunting diary.[54] Through Chang's invention of such expressions, the rainforest (*yulin*), as a natural embodiment of ecological biodiversity, comes to resemble a "word forest" (*yulin*), or a literary labyrinth of linguistic multiplicity and novelistic heteroglossia.[55]

Chang further develops these ecopoetic relations and resemblances in his subsequent novel, *Monkey Cup*, which reflects on Sinophone writing by "mapping it onto the tattoo art of the indigenous Dayak tribe,"[56] once again superimposing one of the "essences" of continental Chinese culture with an indigenous totem of Borneo. Beyond such aesthetic practices, *Monkey Cup* and its follow-up, *My South Seas Sleeping Beauty*, are the most ecocritical and historically incisive of Chang Kuei-hsing's rainforest novels. The interrogation of family histories in the two novels unveils an orgy of colonial (both European maritime and Chinese settler) and postcolonial violence, which includes ecological devastation and sexual exploitation in Borneo. In *Monkey Cup*, the colonial plantation system allows the Chinese settler to stand in as the face of British colonization: it gives the protagonist's great-grandfather the title deed to an expansive plot of land, indentured coolie labor to work the plantations, and weaponry and mercenary forces to defend against raids by dispossessed and displaced Dayaks. When the protagonist must defer to the navigational skills of his Dayak guide during his quest into the rainforest to find his part-Dayak half-sister, the space of the rainforest in the novel inverts the power hierarchies of the plantation society, thus presenting readers an alternative countercolonial mode of being, surviving, and thriving in the local environment.[57]

In Chang's *My South Seas Sleeping Beauty*, these conflicting modes of being—and confrontations between colonizer, settler, and native—are embodied by the figures of the protagonist's mother and father (and by extension the father's best friend) in their respective relationships to the family garden. The garden is a symbol of an indistinct, liminal space of confrontation between colonial plantation, settler homestead, and indigenous rainforest. The narrator, Su Qi, grew up on his family's estate on the outskirts of Lutong, Sarawak, at the edge of the Borneo rainforest along the Batang Baram, across the river from Brunei. Su Qi's mother is Taiwanese, as she was brought back to Borneo by his father, Su Huan, who returned to the island after attending university in Taiwan. As a former horticulture major, Su Qi's mother cultivates an immaculate garden on the estate property, attempting to make it her pure "Garden of Eden." Her passion for gardening intensifies with the death of the narrator's baby sister: feeling she has lost control of her life and her fate, she plants "all sorts of strange and exotic flowers, plants, and trees," as she becomes consumed by "the near-mad pioneering spirit of centuries of Chinese settlers."[58] Here, Chang Kuei-hsing conceives of Su Qi's mother and the garden as allegorical representations of the Chinese settler and her frontier homestead. Su Qi's mother attempts to replace the "native weeds" with "tropical plants," calling to mind efforts by colonial regimes to introduce tropical cash crops from Latin America and Africa in Southeast Asia, such as coffee, chili pepper, rubber, and eucalyptus.

However, as the growth and strength of the "jungle weeds far outpaced those of the tropical plants my mother transplanted," Su Qi's mother is forced to adapt by adopting an annual slash-and-burn technique used by the indigenous population. As the garden grows under the mother's watch, it transforms into a place of near-constant change and regeneration. It becomes difficult to navigate—its pathways obscure and mazelike—a fragrantly intoxicating death trap for outsiders who lack a keen, multisensory knowledge of the environment. Reading a magazine article about his mother's garden, Su Qi discovers that she originally arranged the plants in each of the garden's seven zones "in the shape of a giant Chinese character," though she does not tell the journalist what the characters were:

> I always felt that certain paths looked like the brushstrokes of Chinese characters: it was as if Mother had been using her shovel and hoe as a brush for over a decade, with flowers and leaves as ink and the virgin soil as her calligraphy scroll.[59]

As a written expression and outward manifestation of the mother's secret dreams, inner desires, and silent sufferings, the garden project is symbolic of the settler's struggle to impress upon the new environment a language, culture, and epistemology imported from the old land. As Su Qi looks down on the garden from an airplane, he notices that it has become virtually indistinguishable from the surrounding rainforest.[60] Following the same ecopoetics of cultural superimposition in *The Elephant Herd* and *Monkey Cup*, the obscure "Chinese characters" of the garden decay, transform, and biogenetically regenerate into a different language and script altogether. The "maternal language" (or "mother tongue") is no longer that of the ancestral homeland, but that of the primitive rainforest that the maternal "Garden of Eden" has gradually come to resemble.

For Su Qi's father and his friend Lin Yuan, the garden is both the "death trap" and "enchanted palace" that Su Qi's mother designed for them. They desecrate its "womblike sacred darkness," transforming the garden into "another labyrinthine vagina for them to defile."[61] The garden and the surrounding rainforest are their colonial playgrounds, where they exploit exotic animals and young indigenous girls on their "sex safaris" to Dayak longhouses. Like the great-grandfather in *Monkey Cup*, Su Huan usurps a role akin to both colonizer and sultan (the two characters of his name can be metaphorically understood as "returned sultan") as the colonial period ends and Sarawak joins Malaysia. As an architect who designs grand estates for wealthy clientele, such as the Brunei royal family and Shell Oil magnates, Su Huan also frequently entertains his guests—Westerners, Chinese, and Malays alike—with lavish parties on his own estate, in which he hires indigenous girls to play the role of maidservants, releases exotic animals on the garden property, and allows his guests to gruesomely hunt them. When Lin Yuan succeeds Su Huan as the "master of ceremonies," he begins "taming" his adolescent Dayak maidservants with an electric prod almost identical to the one he uses on his livestock.[62] Su Huan and Lin Yuan treat the indigenous Dayaks and the rainforest fauna as one and the same: they desire them as commodities for their pleasure and titillation, and scorn them as barbaric jungle beasts that need taming. Just as Su Huan murders his wife's "bastard son"—fathered by a Dayak warrior—by leaving him for a crocodile in the jungle, Su Huan and Lin Yuan toss a baby macaque—purchased as a pet from a Dayak longhouse—to distract a mother crocodile while stealing her egg.

Observing these escapades from a young age, Su Qi notes how even the "descendants of coolie beasts"—Chinese migrants who were once treated like slaves by Western colonial masters—have begun to act like "white authors who followed the cannon blasts of the imperial ships to dock in the South Seas, where they drank wine in lavish estates and hotels and were waited upon by countless servants."[63] This historical imagination in the novel, situated at the confluence of migration/diaspora, maritime imperialism, and settler colonialism, informs its postcolonial ecocriticism. The environment of brutality and oppression stifles and suffocates Su Qi, estranging him from his father and stirring his desire to escape. Yet unlike Su Huan's journey to Taiwan, which the author describes in ironic quotation marks as a return to the "ancestral homeland,"[64] Su Qi's decision to study there seems happenstance, unplanned, a mere technicality: he is not in Taipei out of cultural affinity (he describes himself as a tropical fish out of water), but for the educational and employment opportunities the Sinophone metropolis offers.

In the novel, Chang Kuei-hsing links Borneo and Taiwan together in an island duality of resemblance and stark contrast, thus drawing Taiwan into a new mode of imagining the South Seas.[65] A more literal translation of the novel's long title is *The Sleeping Beauty of the Southern Kingdom, For Whom I Pine*. Here, the "Southern Kingdom" (Nanguo) can refer to both Borneo and Taiwan, as the term alludes to both imperial China's mode of referring to Southeast Asian kingdoms and the Japanese name for Taiwan during its fifty-year colonization of the island. Despite such resemblances, the two islands are depicted in stark contrasts: Borneo is rustic, Taiwan metropolitan. Whereas the passages on Borneo are full of lush images of nature, those on Taiwan emphasize manmade objects. Chang's depiction of Su Qi's dormitory is essentially a long list of such objects:

> Books, magazines, newspapers, cups, plates, toothbrushes, washbasins, plastic bins, fruit knives, teapots, guitars, basketballs, rackets and paddles, dumbbells, curtain rods, cassette tapes, fish tanks, bottles and cans scattered across the floor, adorning the dorm rooms as if they were a refugee camp, but serving no real purpose.[66]

Su Qi describes his Taipei dormitory paradoxically as a vigorous "amusement park" and an inert "nursing home."[67] The contrast between the two environments of Borneo and Taiwan guides the seemingly oppositional writing style of the novel in its two locales. The Taiwan portion follows a clear, chronological plot development that is largely dialogue-driven. The Borneo sections are full of myths, tangential anecdotes, and speculation over the truth or correct version of a story.

In *My South Seas Sleeping Beauty*, Taiwan represents a period of dormancy for Su Qi, yet it is also the place that activates and awakens his (as well as the author's) memories of Borneo, where he comes to discover the island is his true motherland, and where he learns to appreciate the bountiful, life-giving nature of its rainforest. Su Qi's return to the Borneo rainforest at the end of the novel is also a return to oral storytelling and imaginative mythmaking. In a final instance of cultural superimposition, Su Qi resembles the gentle, good-natured Brunei prince who comes to tell Su Qi that he loves the "same girl" (or the identical twin that stood in for Su Qi's childhood sweetheart when her sister was ill).[68] While the "Su" in Su Qi's surname is also the first character in the Sinophone transliteration of "sultan" (*sudan*), the "Qi," literally meaning "his," also alludes to his surrogate "other" (as in *qita*). Su Qi resembles a South Seas prince and the Borneo motherland his sleeping beauty.

In the ecopoetics of Chang Kuei-hsing and Pan Yutong, the Nanyang imagination posits the relationship between Borneo and Taiwan as a curved archipelagic trajectory between a rustic, tropical, fertile motherland and an adopted homeland (for Chang) that is also a metropolitan center of transnational Sinophone education and publication (for both Pan and Chang). This new migratory route across the South Seas comes to bear as much (and more immediate) significance, in the authors' evocation of the Nanyang than the ancestral migration from China to Southeast Asia. As a contribution to Taiwan's literary environment, their modernist attempt to dislodge the Chinese script from its continental cultural hegemony and reroute/re-root it through the tropical Borneo rainforest offers creative possibilities for using such linguistic experimentation to imagine, craft, and reaffirm Taiwan's own ancient archipelagic ties to the South Seas. The modernist cultivation of this historical imaginary might, on the one hand, appear in the form of linguistic creolization, mixing standard Chinese with other Sinitic languages as well as non-Sinitic languages (such as the Austronesian aboriginal languages of Taiwan) to highlight the ongoing creation of Taiwanese culture from interethnic contacts. On the other hand, this project might involve cultivating an ecopoetics that aesthetically and visually links language and culture to ecology and landscape to make a sense of place the basis for the form as well as the content of creative literary narrative. In Sinophone Malaysian literature, Malaysia and Taiwan are no longer the margins of China and continental Chineseness, but rather island and peninsular centers of creolized Sinophone cultures formed from interactions with non-Sinophone cultures and native ecologies in a South Seas network.

CHAPTER 5

De-Racializing Cultural Legibility in Postcolonial Singapore

Unlike Malaysia, which favors a single national language and officially defines "national literature" as Malay-language literature,[1] the Republic of Singapore recognizes four official languages (English, Mandarin, Malay, and Tamil), formally constituting its national literature as a multilingual enterprise. This stems from Singapore's heritage as a former British colony that encouraged immigrants from elsewhere in Asia to settle and base their trading, shipping, and other commercial activity there. Lacking a large indigenous population whose historical presence predates British colonialism (even among Malays who mostly migrated there), Singapore defines itself as a multicultural nation of immigrants. The Chinese Singaporean majority (roughly 75 percent) is the result of mass migration to the colonial Straits Settlements and Malaya, encouraged by the British "Forward Policy" of 1874, which gave Chinese settlers a majority in not only Singapore but other Malayan urban centers such as Penang, Taiping, and Ipoh. Colonial Singapore developed as the primary "transshipment" hub for Chinese migration and mercantile activity throughout Asia.[2]

From this history, postcolonial Singapore has fashioned a national identity based on a meritocratic ideal of "multiracialism" that opposes the preferential standards of nativism and affirms the settler foundations of the republic. Multiracialism encourages the equal preservation, celebration, and peaceful coexistence of multiple cultures differentially classified according to their official "race"—Chinese, Malay, Indian, and "Other" (the "CMIO" model).[3] Presuming that one's cultural heritage is primarily determined by one's descent from a single ancestral homeland, these designations are derivations of colonial categories that perpetuate racialist thinking. As Nirmala Puru-Shotam argues, multiracialism, though designed to create "a level playing field for all" Singaporean citizens, has never dismantled the "racial structures that under-girded the colonial system," thus negating "any measure of recognition that race is a social construct."[4]

For a nation that outside observers commonly refer to as a "nanny state" because of its relentless interventions in civil society (through the implementation of strict laws, public service campaigns, land reclamation projects, and so on), multiracialism is also a mode of social engineering. The state's approach to national culture is based on the same pragmatic, developmental scheme it has applied to issues of economic progress, housing, and environmental sanitation since its unplanned independence in 1965. In the wake of its expulsion from Malaysia that year, Singapore, under the leadership of Lee Kuan Yew (PM 1959–90) and the People's Action Party (PAP), embarked on a project to refashion the "backwater" colony as a global financial hub that would prosper through productive exchange with the outside world. Within thirty years of independence (as the popular narrative goes), the isolated island city-state, lacking an agricultural hinterland and possessing few natural resources, mobilized its greatest assets—human will, ingenuity, and manpower—to become an economic miracle, a bastion of First-World stability in an otherwise volatile region.[5] As the cultural policy behind this postcolonial "makeover," multiracialism was devised not only to expediently redress residual socioeconomic inequities and crises from the colonial era, but also to fashion the nation as culturally intelligible and inviting to the developed world.

Multiracialism sanitizes, but does not eliminate, cultural diversity to make it neat, legible, and orderly. It racializes culture and homogenizes the terms for inter- and intraethnic communication. It intentionally ignores and in some cases attempts to eradicate expressions of culture arising from intermingling *between* racial groupings or from pluralism *within* them. As Cherian George, a former *Straits Times* journalist, acknowledges, Singapore's administrators, "continuing a tradition started by British colonists, apply stark categories that caricature people's ethnic heritage, and equate ethnicity with both culture and language in ways that fail to reflect the cultural diversity and richness on the ground."[6] This is most evident in Singapore's language and education policies. Three of the nation's official languages—Mandarin, Malay, and Tamil—are designated "mother tongues," charged with transmitting cultural knowledge and values associated with their racial grouping—Chinese, Malay, and Indian. As the fourth official language, English is not a "mother tongue," but rather a "common working language" that presumably bridges the "unintelligibility" gap between the mother tongues (and thus between the racial groups themselves). English also provides a linguistic vehicle for globalization, deemed necessary for the nation's economic survival and technological prosperity.[7] Ideally all Singaporeans, regardless of racial or socioeconomic background, reap the benefits of an improved standard of living that fluency in English allegedly brings.[8]

On the one hand, Singaporeans' ability to tolerate racial differences and participate successfully in a global society is largely determined by their proficiency in English. On the other, their sense of cultural grounding, kinship, propriety, and self-worth as "Asians" (not "pseudo-Westerners") is determined by their proficiency in their racially designated mother tongue. Multiracialism not only mandates bilingual education (English plus the mother tongue),[9] but also suggests that the measure of one's "Singaporeanness" derives from one's ability to first discern the appropriate venue for using a given language and to then successfully communicate in that language without confusing or "cross-pollinating" the languages in a way that might alienate outsiders.

Within the framework of multiracialism, the transcendent value ascribed to English does not ghettoize the mother tongue's role in Singapore by demoting and confining it to a communal, subnational status. Rather, the demand for proficiency in the mother tongue—certainly Mandarin for the Chinese Singaporean majority, but also Malay for Malay Singaporeans and to a far lesser extent Tamil for Indian Singaporeans—plays a *transnational* function: in a post–Cold War environment, it is intended to revitalize bonds and establish lucrative reciprocity with the ancestral homelands.[10] For many students from mainland China, Hong Kong, Taiwan, Malaysia, Indonesia, Brunei, India, Sri Lanka, and Bangladesh, Singapore represents not only an important educational center and workplace, but also a gateway to the West that advertises a semblance of cultural familiarity as well. For Singaporean students, the emphasis on mother-tongue proficiency preserves the cultural capital of the various ancestral homelands in the national imagination: multiracialism ensures that Singapore is not a "motherland" for its citizens, a term reserved "exclusively for the ancestral countries of origin" designated by CMIO.[11] Mother-tongue proficiency further encourages citizens to cultivate the presumed kinship they share with those other Asian nations to capitalize on their rapidly developing economies and lower labor costs.

With its designation of appropriate languages for discrete venues of transnational exchange, multiracialism has imparted a tangible impact on the production, reception, canonization, and interpretation of Singaporean literature. National literature in Singapore is the sum total of its literatures in the official languages of English, standard Chinese (based on spoken Mandarin), Malay, and Tamil, each engaging a discrete literary tradition so as to be culturally legible to a certain transnational cross-section of readership. The "pioneers" of the Singaporean canon are authors inculcated in the literary traditions of either the former colonial power (Anglophone writers) or their respective ancestral homelands (Malay, Tamil, and Sinophone writers).[12] Tailoring its "Singaporeanness" to a particular "elsewhere," each literature—compartmentalized by language of production—"writes back" to separate sites of cultural and linguistic heritage: for example, Sinophone literature—in order to access a wider publication network and readership beyond Singapore—orients itself toward China, Hong Kong, and Taiwan.[13] A similar case can be made for the "outward orientation" of Singaporean literature in English (toward the West), Malay (toward Malaysia and Indonesia), and Tamil (toward southern India and Sri Lanka): narratives presumably produce little ground for comparison, as they share few "socio-historical commonalities."[14] Multilingual anthologies of Singaporean literature are rare, and translingual comparisons are even rarer.[15] Reading Singaporean literature across languages risks becoming an unwieldy task, as each language possesses its own storehouse of literary allusions and aesthetic conventions. The "parallel yet fragmented approach" to literary production "in the four official languages," as described by author Shirley Geok-lin Lim, treats Singaporean literature as "four distinct species" possessing "little in common."[16] Ideologically undergirded by multiracialism, this approach produces hyphenated, segregated literary categories in much the same way that the CMIO model assigns hyphenated, segregated Singaporean identities.[17]

The question of how Singaporean literature creatively responds to multiracialism presents an inviting point for translingual analysis, since all Singaporeans, regardless of background, confront this discourse. How do Singaporean authors from the different literary traditions internalize, navigate, and rebuff multiracialism's demands for global relevance, cultural legibility, proficiency in English and one's official mother tongue, and a Singaporean national identity that must be articulated through one's racial inheritance and genealogical link to the ancestral homeland? One way that Sinophone and Anglophone Singaporean authors have approached such questions is by reconfiguring the Nanyang as a postcolonial trope that undermines multiracial logic. The Sinophone writers Yeng Pway Ngon and Chia Joo Ming, as well as the Anglophone author Suchen Christine Lim, evoke the Nanyang by crossing linguistic, national, and racial boundaries in Southeast Asia to complicate the cultural self-representation of Singaporeans lumped into the "Chinese" racial category.

Yeng, Chia, and Lim reclaim the Nanyang from the confines of Chinese ethnic communalism and chauvinism. During the Cold War period, the term "Nanyang" became associated with the socialist political activism of Sinophone institutions in Singapore, such as Nanyang University, which waged resistance to state hegemony over issues of culture, language, education, the economy, and urban development. Accusing Sinophone institutions of ethnic chauvinism and caricaturing the Nanyang as the communalistic fantasy of a "New China" settlement in Southeast Asia, Lee Kuan Yew and the technocratic Anglophone wing of the PAP granted educational and economic supremacy to English and implemented campaigns of social and environmental makeover. Wresting the Nanyang from these overly simplistic caricatures, Yeng, Chia, and Lim retrace the "messier" historical trajectories of the South Seas in their fiction to evoke a translocal, transethnic, and translingual heritage rooted in maritime Southeast Asian (not continental Chinese) cultures and landscapes. Their Nanyang disrupts the neat orderliness of official multiracialism, on the one hand using the Sinophone to transmit postmodern ennui (rather than vital, deep-seated racial knowledge), while on the other "contaminating" the global Anglophone by summoning unofficial creoles and dialects—namely Singlish and Hokkien—as "languages of the soul."[18] They invoke the South Seas to de-racialize Singaporeanness, thus forming translingual bonds across literary boundaries.

SINOPHONE DEPOLITICIZATION AND CULTURAL LANDSCAPING

Though postcolonial Sinophone Singaporean literature shares a common heritage with its Malaysian counterpart in the vernacular "New Literature" published in colonial Malayan newspapers,[19] it pursued a different trajectory following Singapore's independence in 1965. At that time, Singapore's Nanyang University played a crucial role in developing local Sinophone writers, many of whom were Nanyang graduates. The school sponsored literary competitions and published popular literary journals such as *Mangrove* (*Hongshulin*).[20]

Nanyang University was established in 1956 as the first Sinophone university in Southeast Asia. The institution was a cornerstone for the Sinophone-educated community, without whose support the PAP would have been unable to consolidate power in postcolonial Singapore. By establishing the PAP as a coalition of Anglophone-educated technocrats and Sinophone-educated leftists in 1954, Lee Kuan Yew knew his political future depended upon winning over Singapore's Sinophone-educated majority. A Cambridge-educated lawyer who lamented the "apathy, self-centeredness, and lack of self-confidence" of his fellow students in colonial Singapore's Anglophone schools, Lee admired Nanyang University as a hotbed of political activism and envied the` Sinophone-educated as a "vibrant, vigorous, self-confident community," full of "discipline" and "political commitment."[21]

Despite the alliance, there was disagreement between the Anglophone and Sinophone factions of the PAP, particularly over the proposal for the Malaysian merger. Once the PAP achieved power in 1959 and Lee assumed the prime ministership (even though the British still handled foreign affairs), the two factions clashed over issues of culture, language, and education, which Lee felt the "Chinese-educated communists" had manipulated to their advantage: "It was not a proletarian issue; it was plain, simple chauvinism. But the communists knew it was a crowd-winner that pulled at Chinese heartstrings and they worked on it assiduously."[22] Lee painted the Sinophone faction as ethnocentric and unable to achieve the required unity to sustain a "multiracial Singapore," effectively downplaying its concern that British sponsorship of the Malaysian merger indicated a perpetuation of the colonial economic order. Splitting from the PAP to form the Barisan Socialis or "Socialist Front" after the initial call for the Malaysian merger in 1961, much of the Sinophone faction was more amenable to possible merger with Indonesia, where they received tacit support from President Sukarno and the Indonesian Communist Party (PKI), a multiethnic organization.[23]

Though the Malaysian merger lasted only two years, Lee Kuan Yew's victory over the Barisan Socialis—compounded by the failure of Indonesia's communist movement in 1965 and mass violence (with anti-Sinitic overtones) against suspected communists there—moved the PAP into position to dictate the ideological agenda. While graduates of Nanyang University continued to raise "the issue of Chinese language and culture" during each election cycle for more than a decade following Singapore's independence, Lee accused the Nanyang curriculum of failing to impart a "Singaporean" identity and of being obsolete, rendering its graduates unemployable and susceptible to communist persuasion.[24] Citing Nanyang's failure "to convert its teaching from Mandarin into English," Lee moved to merge the institution with the University of Singapore in 1980 to form the National University of Singapore, where "teachers and students would be forced to use English" and become "subsumed within the larger numbers of English-speaking staff."[25] Since "merge" was a euphemism for "close," many Nanyang alumni felt betrayed.[26]

This history—along with the charges of ethnic chauvinism, narrow-minded obsoleteness, lack of "Singaporeanness," and a communalist desire for a "People's Republic of China" in Southeast Asia—became dominant associations with the Nanyang and the institutions that bore the name in postcolonial Singapore.[27] Undercut by the bilingual education policy and the closure of Nanyang University, postcolonial Sinophone Singaporean literature lost important resources and vitality to challenge these dominant characterizations. Yet some Sinophone Singaporean writers have made their sense of defeat, decline, depoliticization, and marginality the subject of literary composition, weaving together personal and political history to reclaim the Nanyang from its relegation to an ethnic communalism of the "pre-Singaporean" past.

In his fiction, Sinophone author Yeng Pway Ngon (Ying Pei'an, 1947-) allegorizes postcolonial decline as the forcible removal of one's political voice and the constant confrontation with official dictates that mold individuals into "parrots" and "decorative flowers" for the nation. A poet, playwright, critic, and novelist, Yeng launched his eclectic writing career in the 1960s.[28] His works, including the novels *A Man Like Me* (*Yi ge xiang wo zheyang de nanren*, 1986), *A*

Lonely Face (*Guji de lian*, 1989), and *Unrest* (*Saodong*, 2002), as well as the volume of short stories, *The Non-Existent Lover* (*Bu cunzai de qingren*, 2007), evoke isolation, withdrawal, and persistent ennui.

Among Yeng's satirical and allegorical works of short fiction, "The Garden City" ("Huayuan chengshi," 1990) addresses the Singaporean's daily confrontation with the social engineering of national identity, which the author likens to environmental makeover. The story playfully illustrates Cherian George's description of Singapore as the "air-conditioned" nation: its official "branding as a Garden City" is "a perverse Singaporean irony" because it has little to do with preserving the island's "natural heritage" and is more about reclamation, sanitation, development, and decoration.[29] In the story, the unnamed male narrator meets a "foreign friend" for a beer at the Botanic Gardens. They discuss the "birdsongs and floral fragrances" of the "Garden City," an appellation that evokes "the most pride" among Singaporeans. The foreign friend then asks: "What do its people smell like?" Confused by the question, the narrator walks out to the sidewalk to inhale deeply, yet he still only smells the sweet fragrance of flowers. He also discovers something artificial about the floral scent because of its singularity and ubiquity, thinking perhaps it is not really a flower but a brand of laundry detergent that all Singaporeans have started using.[30] Then it dawns on him that this is the only scent he has ever known:

> When I'm out on the street, at home, in the office, opening the newspaper, flipping on the television, or even on the toilet (of course I remember to flush when done!), I smell that same fragrance![31]

The narrator becomes paranoid that he has lost his ability to smell anything but this pervasive floral detergent. Later, he confides in an artist friend his suspicion that, since Singaporeans apparently have no "body odor," they are not actually humans but flowers. The artist responds that "in the Garden City, everyone is both a human *and* a flower" and "therefore everyone must bear the responsibility of decorating the city."[32] Even though a freethinking artist ironically proffers this admonition, one's responsibility to "decorate" is not to create "art" but to conform to state directives such as the parenthetical interjection cited above—to flush the toilet or face a fine—as a psychologically ingrained reflex.

Prior to going to sleep, the narrator relates to his wife his Kafkaesque fear that when he wakes up, he will have transformed into a flower. Responding to his wife's question as to what is so frightening about flowers, the story concludes with the narrator's observation that flowers "cannot speak, at least not in the language of humans."[33] Challenging state directives that sculpt Singaporeans as "mute" flowers whose sole function is to decorate the Garden City, Yeng Pway Ngon draws a correlation between political suppression, social engineering, and the "Green Singapore" campaign. Although the PAP led the drive to clean up the heavily polluted rivers it inherited from the colonial era, the explicit goals of the campaign were to turn the island into a Southeast Asian "oasis" where "business-people and tourists" would base "their business and tours of the region."[34] The Green Singapore campaign not only targeted polluted spaces, but also treated the island's "most valuable natural resources," such as its tropical rainforest, as "wasteland" to be "reclaimed" from nature and converted into condominiums, golf courses, and "decidedly man-made parks" and beaches with "pruned hedges and orderly rows of trees."[35] Yeng's "The Garden City" demonstrates the mirroring processes of social and environmental landscaping by which the state preens, prunes, and sanitizes the island and the citizenry.

Though Yeng Pway Ngon's male protagonists outwardly rebel against Singaporean pragmatism and social engineering by pursuing artistic idealism, acting aloof and individualistic while shunning material success, their creative and intellectual pursuits ultimately reproduce many of the same dynamics as their social milieu. Reflecting the very processes of continual cultural makeover they outwardly detest, the protagonists' creative self-cultivation tends to be fleeting, superficial, and narcissistic, often resulting in boredom and self-loathing. This is particularly the case in Yeng's first novel, *A Man Like Me*, which won Singapore's National Book Development Council Award for Chinese Fiction in 1988.

Drawing its title from a short story also published in 1986—"A Woman Like Me" ("Xiang wo zheyang de yi ge nüzi") by Hong Kong author Xi Xi—*A Man Like Me* is a postmodern work that indefatigably borrows from—or ransacks—the protagonist's global literary and cultural influences in an intentionally haphazard and superficial way. The plot revolves around a love triangle between the male narrator, Zhou Jiansheng, and his two romantic partners, Zijun and Meifen. As an admirer of the modern Chinese author Lu Xun, Jiansheng is a poet who borrows the name of the protagonist from Lu Xun's short story "Regret for the Past" ("Shangshi," 1925), Juansheng, as his penname. Zijun, who shares the same name as Juansheng's love interest in Lu Xun's story, writes to Jiansheng after reading one of his poems in a local newspaper, noting their "Lu Xun connection." Yet the outward passion the couple shares for highbrow literature, cinema, and the arts provides an unstable foundation for their rocky romance, with their coffeehouse discussions devolving into mere name-dropping. The many references (among countless others) to Lu Xun's "Regret for the Past," Arthur Miller's *Death of a Salesman*, Erich Fromm's *The Art of Loving*, Simone de Beauvoir's *The Second Sex*, and even the primary allusion to Xi Xi's "A Woman Like Me," appear as depthless diversions. These empty allusions gesture at the postmodern irony of the novel's title, which refers to a man "like" the narrator, but not necessarily the narrator himself, as he is only able to articulate his subjectivity through an imagined affiliation with the emotions and experiences of fictitious characters from elsewhere: "I'm moved to tears by the plight of characters in novels and movies but am totally indifferent to the people I meet in real life."[36]

Like the dominant caricature of Singapore itself, Jiansheng is a "global hub" that diverts and refashions his identity through an outward cultural orientation—primarily Western and Chinese—that does not really take root. Jiansheng's continual self-makeover with a different fictional doppelgänger is meant to hide feelings of impotence, inferiority, and jealousy that derive from perceived failures: his economic failure as a bookstore owner (prompting him to repeatedly borrow money from his parents and friends), his emotional failure as a lover, and his creative failure as a Sinophone poet in a nation that places little value on literary pursuits. Instead of intellectual and creative maturation, Jiansheng uses "highbrow culture" as an "avenue for escape and for making unrealistic choices," acknowledging that his self-comparison to Lu Xun "is as ridiculous as saying the Singapore River is like the Yellow River." He laments that Zijun is "not the Zijun in Lu Xun's story" but a "product" of an education system and society that holds a "pragmatic view of love," demanding he conform to "the values of the social class she is striving to be a part of."[37]

A Man Like Me comments on the impotence of Singaporean literary, intellectual, and political involvement, as well as the postcolonial decline of Sinophone literature. Jiansheng's friend Zhiqiang, a journalist, comments on how press censorship stifles creative thinking, saying that "writers with any real talent" are ultimately "fixed" by the "parrots" who run the press: "Our newspapers aren't just government mouthpieces—they are more like the propaganda wing of the PAP."[38] Jiansheng likewise comments on the decrepit state of literature and culture in Singapore: "Here, as long as you can break sentences into lines, you can call yourself a poet."[39] At the end of the novel, Jiansheng's trip to Kuala Lumpur in a pathetic attempt to see Meifen, who has left him to marry a Malaysian man due to Jiansheng's infidelities with Zijun, provides a comparison between the postcolonial trajectories of Sinophone literature in Singapore and Malaysia. At a bookstall in the Jalan Petaling market, Jiansheng notes in mild surprise that "even though the Malay language dominates Malaysian society, there are still far more Sinophone publications than in Singapore."[40]

Escaping from his claustrophobic life in Singapore, Jiansheng's journey by train through the "endless jungle" of Peninsular Malaysia opens the novel's conclusion onto a new plane of possibility. It offers him a critical physical distance from Singapore to soberly reflect on his life there, making his previous troubles, dramatized through the lives of fictional characters, seem overly affected. Ironically, his observations of the people on the train and the environment around him compel him to question his constant, outward-oriented search. Abandoning his impulsive decision to find Meifen, he opts to return to Singapore, reinscribing its cityscape as "his jungle" where he will now release his insecurities about being hurt.[41]

Jiansheng's trip to Malaysia in the last chapter of *A Man Like Me* would seem a merely circumstantial plot device if it did not recur in Yeng Pway Ngon's novels. His next novel, *A Lonely Face*, follows a very similar trajectory. The unnamed protagonist is an alumnus of Nanyang University's Chinese Department who finds himself with few career prospects: "He never thought that this department, besides preparing one to teach Mandarin, was, as someone of importance had said, the most useless." The "someone of importance" alludes to Lee Kuan Yew and his pessimism about the employability of Nanyang's graduates that prompted him to close the school. As the protagonist laments, the study of "script, rhyme, exegesis, the Confucian *Analects*, Mencius, and Laozi" dictated by his Sinophone education left him with only "words of another world" that strain to find relevance and value in a pragmatic, Anglophone-dominant modern Singapore.[42]

In the final chapter of *A Lonely Face*, the protagonist returns to the Sinophone bookstore he used to frequent in his Nanyang days when he and his wife (who has now left him) were first dating. He recounts nostalgically all the imported revolutionary songs and works of May Fourth literature from China that the couple used to discuss, even though he admits they only looked at the titles of the books and did not actually read them. The narrator discovers that the "deserted atmosphere of the store could no longer conjure up the vitality of its heyday."[43] This is his final observation of contemporary Singapore before taking a bus to the Genting Highlands in Malaysia, where, in a depressed stupor, he gambles away all his money at the casino playing slot machines. Though treated empathetically, the protagonist is a satirical caricature of the type of former Sinophone-educated leftist who, once political activism was no longer viable, became materialistically devoted to self-enrichment.

As opposed to *A Man Like Me*, the trip to Malaysia fails to reinvigorate the hapless protagonist's creative idealism, yet it alludes to the commonalities and divergences of the cultural, political, and national heritage that Singapore shares with its neighbor. A fellow gambler tells the protagonist that he should, like "all Chinese Singaporeans," pay a visit to China to expand his business prospects and become properly "cultured." The protagonist responds that, based on his "meager salary," he "only has enough money to go to Genting or the Cameron Highlands" in Malaysia.[44] Internalizing the Singaporean discourse of multiracialism, in which Malaysia only possesses cultural value for Singapore's Malay minority, the narrator's dismissal of his surroundings is a selective negation of Malaysia's physical, historical, and cultural proximity, which once contributed to his leftist "Nanyang idealism." Attributing his protagonists' cultural disillusionment to this selective negation highlights Yeng Pway Ngon's poignant reinscription of the Nanyang imagination in his fiction, particularly in the novel *Unrest*, winner of the 2004 Singapore Literature Prize.

Similarly entailing midlife crises during the materialist 1980s, *Unrest* features flashbacks to the leftist politicization of colonial Singapore in the 1950s, tracing the personal histories of four former Sinophone-educated activists who participated in student boycotts against the British authority's forcible closure of labor unions and cultural organizations. One of the teenage protagonists, Weikang, is expelled from school and, on several occasions, detained and interrogated by the British police on suspicion of communist subversion. Feeling abandoned by classmates who avoid him because of his political taint and proclaiming that nowhere is more insufferable than the colony, Weikang decides to "repatriate" to China, his "socialist motherland," to join the revolution. Illustrating the more illicit passages across the South Seas during the Cold War, *Unrest* details how Weikang is able to illegally slip through Singaporean customs, board a ship to Hong Kong, and enter China through Swatow.[45]

Any hope for Weikang's discovery of cultural belonging in China's "new society" is shattered by the hardships he experiences there. In Swatow, he finds only a dilapidated, dimly lit town overrun by beggars: a comrade derogatorily dismisses them as "dregs of humanity." Treated as "a trivial black splotch from the South Seas" with doubtful loyalty to Chairman Mao, Weikang and the other "Repatriated Overseas Chinese" (Guiqiao) in Guangdong are severely persecuted during the Cultural Revolution. The Red Guards knock at Weikang's door in the middle of the night, ransack his house, and physically assault him. The episode uncannily replays a trauma from his Malayan childhood when the British rounded up his family during the anticommunist Emergency period and relocated them to the quarantined "New Village" of Chaah in rural Johor: whether "weeding out communists" or "counterrevolutionary elements," the two experiences were the same, making Weikang feel "as if he had committed a mortal sin."[46]

The flashback prompts a wave of more fond childhood memories of carefree mischief rooted in a pastoral Malayan landscape. Sketching a portrait of the New Village, a nostalgic Weikang draws the fruit trees outside the fenced perimeter: durian, rambutan, star fruit, guava, mangosteen, and soursop. Trying to recall their tropical flavor and the location of his house in the encampment, he is transported back to Chaah and its multiethnic, multilingual environment:

> The majority of the New Village residents were Chinese Malayans, and over half of those were Hakka, but there was a minority of Indians and Malays. The Indian and Malay children with whom he played could all speak a little Hakka. When Weikang was young, he could speak some Malay and even a little Tamil. He still remembered some Malay, but could only recall a few words of Tamil and was unsure whether he could pronounce them correctly. Besides playing in the field surrounding his family's shop, Weikang and his friends from the New Village also often went beyond the village fence to roam by the small river.[47]

Here, Yeng Pway Ngon shows how the children, regardless of racial background, partook of each other's "mother tongues," including nonstandard Sinitic languages such as Hakka. As Weikang recalls, the children would sneak off into "a thick plot of jungle haunted by Malayan Communist Party guerillas," where they encountered some

Sakai (Orang Asli) nomads "baring their upper bodies, wearing only loincloths, brandishing machetes and blowpipes." The children, led by the "guide to their sexual awakening"—a young Chinese Malayan "with such tan skin" that "he was easily mistaken for a Malay"—would explore the jungle until the sounds of MCP guerillas and counterinsurgency forces clashing with machine-gun fire chased them back to the New Village, trembling with fear and excitement.[48]

Excavating these buried memories, the Nanyang imagination of *Unrest* fords the Johor Strait to reopen the historically porous border between Singapore and Peninsular Malaysia. Contrasted with Weikang's alienated experience of China, the intimacy of his Malayan memory diagnoses the common stereotype of "culturally rootless" Singaporeans not as a symptom of separation from the "racial" heritage of the ancestral homeland, but as the politicized negation of a common past shared across a geopolitical boundary in postcolonial Southeast Asia. The novel's nostalgia for the rural, multicultural Malayan childhood and charged idealism of anticolonial activism denotes the author's refusal to repackage his identity along the neatly drawn outlines of multiracialism. Yeng's fiction demonstrates that when Sinophone education in postcolonial Singapore becomes depoliticized, severed from its shared local heritage in the Nanyang and relegated to the confines of Chinese ethnic communalism, it *loses* its cultural vitality. Yeng's postmodern fusion of pseudo-intellectualism and pop-culture sentimentalism, along with his frank depictions of homosexuality, masturbation, and adultery among both his male and female protagonists, are Sinophone exhibitions of Westernization, materialism, self-indulgent exploration, nihilism, and ennui in Singapore, rather than a pragmatic bulwark of conservative Chinese "mother-tongue knowledge" to defend against them.

Further challenging the relegation of the Nanyang to the confines of ethnic communalism in postcolonial Singapore, the fiction of Chia Joo Ming (Xie Yumin, 1959-) also represents a transethnic and translocal rewriting of the South Seas imagination. As deputy editor of the Sinophone newspaper *Lianhe zaobao*,[49] Chia is author of several collections of short fiction, including *A New Language* (*Shishuo xinyu*, 1994; winner of the 1996 Singapore Book Prize) and *Reconstructing an Image of the South Seas* (*Chonggou Nanyang tuxiang*, 2005; winner of the 2006 Singapore Literature Prize).[50] The latter work voyages into Singapore's neighboring landscapes in Southeast Asia to evoke a rich breadth and depth to a past—as part of a

Nanyang archipelago—that the nation has lost in its march toward globalization and cultural/environmental makeover.

As the concluding story to the *Reconstructing* volume, "Holiday in Ambon" ("Anwen jiaqi") is the tale of a hypermodern Singaporean's unintended discovery of his interethnic and translocal South Seas heritage in the wake of the 1997 Asian Financial Crisis. The narrator, referred to by his surname in Romanized script as "Choo" (Zhu), leads a fast-paced life as a stockbroker in Singapore. Choo reluctantly accompanies his father on a trip to the far-flung island of Ambon in the Maluku Islands (which the Dutch called the South Moluccas and "Spice Islands") of eastern Indonesia. While Choo regards the trip more as a vacation getaway from the pressures of work to an underdeveloped tropical island, his father's mission is to fulfill a lifelong request entrusted to him by his own father to locate relatives from whom their family has been separated for several generations. Of mixed Chinese and Ambonese (Malay and Papuan) descent, Choo is a sixth-generation Peranakan.[51]

"Holiday in Ambon" is inspired by a fictional travelogue from the Qing dynasty entitled *Encounters in the South Seas* (*Nanyang shuyu*, c. 1877), written by Wang Xiqi. The travelogue chronicles an imperial Qing fleet that sails to Ambon in the late eighteenth century and discovers among the native population a nobleman claiming Chinese descent. The nobleman, who continues to use his Chinese surname, Zhu, traces his ancestry to the Ming loyalist crew of a sailing junk that, when fleeing the Qing to Taiwan, was blown off course southward by a typhoon, making accidental landfall on Ambon. In the travelogue, the nobleman, who can speak Hokkien, serves as an interpreter between the Qing dignitaries and the Ambonese chief. In "Holiday in Ambon," Chia Joo Ming cleverly appropriates this marvelous tale—a popular novel showcasing imperial China's Nanyang imagination—as if it were an actual historical account in order to frame his protagonist's journey: the exotic "southern barbarian" with a paternal Chinese lineage becomes Choo's Ambonese ancestor.

In "Holiday in Ambon," the fantastical *Encounters in the South Seas* becomes a family document passed down through the generations. When the Qing fleet departed Ambon, the nobleman left his family behind and accompanied the dignitaries back to China, where he started another family and a new lineage. This new family in China passed down the legend of the Ambonese connection from one generation to the next:

> My grandfather left China for the Riau Islands, not to make a living, but to search for roots. My great-grandfather must have once told him that we had relatives on Ambon Island, and because of that my grandfather came south to Indonesia. For political reasons, he was forced to leave. Sensing that he would never return, he left behind my father [in Singapore] just in case, simply for the purpose of this trip to Ambon. It took three generations, or four if you include me, to fulfill a simple wish.[52]

Vis-à-vis a work of popular fiction from the Qing dynasty, Chia Joo Ming appropriates the imperial Chinese imagination of the South Seas and resignifies it to specifically address issues of culture, nationality, and globalization in postcolonial Singapore. Chia reconnects Singapore to its maritime location in the Riau Archipelago, a cluster of Indonesian islands nearly as close to the city-state as Peninsular Malaysia, and engages Singapore's discourse on the cultural heritage of an "immigrant" population. The ongoing, indeterminate, and cyclical—rather than terminal, simplistic, and linear—trajectory of the Choo family saga plays on the clichéd narrative of the Chinese immigrant to Singapore who has left his roots behind to find a better living in the South Seas. Even though "Holiday in Ambon" is a fictional flight of fancy, it nevertheless reverses the typical direction of the Singaporean's roots-seeking search for racial heritage and cultural orientation: rather than going "back to the ancestral homeland" of China, the narrative leaves China not for economic reasons but to search for roots on a peripheral island locale in the Nanyang.

Chia's novella determines roots—and maps the search for them—according to the cross-cultural routes of history, not the normative monoethnic standards of Singaporean multiracialism. Noting their mixed descent from "Indonesian natives" and "Ming dynasty aristocrats," Choo's father suggests to his son that, "if you were to search back far enough, we may not even be Han." Responding to his son's question about his own cultural identification, Choo's father responds:

> When you live in a place for a long time, you belong to that place. Whether you are willing to accept it or not, your behavior and mannerisms are that way. Of course, it is easiest to identify with the place you live during the formative period of your personality and beliefs.[53]

His father's statement of "I am where I am" prompts Choo to reflect on how his own "formative period" in Singapore has shaped the rather cynical perspective he brings to his father's roots-seeking mission in Ambon.

Both the historical turmoil in Southeast Asia (such as the mass anticommunist violence in 1965 in Indonesia following the September 30 Movement,[54] to which the author hints as the "political reason" Choo's grandfather's had to leave) that scattered the protagonist's family across three countries (China, Singapore, and Indonesia) and Singapore's national discourse about its defiant out-modernization of its Southeast Asian neighbors color the protagonist's reconstruction of his interethnic Nanyang heritage. On the trip to Ambon, Choo confronts his own cynical perspective on the Third World, fashioned by postcolonial Singaporean discourse, as it uneasily intersects with and departs from the Orientalist discourse of European colonialism as manifest in the attitudes of Western tourists to the region. At the Ambon airport, a Dutch woman named Jolanda, who works as a reporter for a travel magazine back in the Netherlands, asks Choo to take a picture of her. Striking up a conversation, the two realize they are staying at the same hotel and decide to meet for a drink after Choo's father has gone to bed. They go to a touristy bar whose specialty drinks conjure up colonial clichés of the East Indies: "Spice Lady," "East India Hero," and "Amboyna Love."[55] Such Orientalist clichés complement the exotic Nanyang imagination of the Qing dynasty imperial travelogue that frames the novella.

Jolanda and Choo form an odd pair: both of them primitivize the landscape and its inhabitants in their own particular ways. Jolanda tells Choo that Dutch tourists prefer Indonesia as a travel destination because it is a former Dutch colony that gives them colonial "spice" nostalgia. Romanticizing and idealizing the landscape and the natives, Jolanda admits she is drawn to the "temptations" of the "beach, blue sky, sunshine, and simple, honest people." Yet she harbors doubts about the images she has carried with her from the Netherlands, where she learned that the Dutch benevolently brought civilization to its colonies. She seeks to obtain a "true local's perspective" from Choo, even though he is a Singaporean citizen of part-Indonesian descent and is also new to the island.

For Choo, the landscape and architecture of Ambon remind him of the Singapore kampongs of his youth, which the state has now entirely converted to high-rise government housing—HDB (Housing Development Board) flats—and private condominiums. However, Ambon's sky is "even greener and bluer" than old Singapore, and a deeper pitch-black at night. For Choo, the landscape "stirs up some dusty memories" of his maternal grandmother's house. Despite the hint of nostalgia, Choo informs Jolanda of the mass violence and instability characterizing Indonesia's history, such as the colonial enslavement of native populations and massacres against settler populations in places like Java.[56] Unlike Jolanda, who sees the natives as uncorrupted, Choo goes to the other extreme, suspecting they all have been corrupted due to their extreme poverty and proximity to tourism dollars. Choo is very suspicious of an "overly" friendly and helpful taxi driver, who makes inquiries in the town on behalf of Choo's father and claims to know the location of their Ambonese relatives. He offers to drive Choo and his father to a small village in the jungle outside the town where their relatives allegedly live, prompting Choo's suspicions:

> Who knew whether the driver was duping us, and would just drive us to a spot in the jungle, rob us, or even take our lives? In a matter of life and death, I could not possibly be like Jolanda and naively assume the driver's pure innocence.[57]

When the taxi gets stuck in the mud, Choo yells at the driver, ordering him to remain still. Shortly thereafter, some villagers come to help remove the stuck vehicle. Choo then realizes that his distrust of the "impoverished" Ambonese, which caused his father embarrassment, is misplaced and misguided.[58] Just as far-fetched as Jolanda's patronizing Orientalism, Choo's attitudes are a by-product of the hypervigilance with which postcolonial Singapore views relations with its neighbors, a view reflected by the state's micromanagement of ethnic relations.

By recuperating memories of kampong childhoods that evoke the creolized Malaysian and Indonesian upbringings or ancestries of many Chinese Singaporeans, and by confronting the interethnic stereotypes regarding Singapore's Southeast Asian neighbors, the Nanyang imagination in the Sinophone fiction of Yeng Pway Ngon and Chia Joo Ming suggests that Chinese Singaporeans, contrary to the official dictates of multiracialism, do not have to scour the history of Chinese civilization in order to become culturally grounded and ethnically conscious citizens. Yeng and Chia reclaim the translocal and transethnic affiliations of the Nanyang from the postcolonial charges of ethnic chauvinism and the discourse of political decline.

SCULPTING A TRANSLINGUAL, TRANSETHNIC, TRANSLOCAL NANYANG

Like their Sinophone counterparts, Anglophone authors lumped into the "Chinese" racial category in postcolonial Singapore explore their translocal and cross-cultural heritage in neighboring Southeast Asian landscapes and personal histories. They also add a translingual dimension to their evocation of the Nanyang trope that simultaneously challenges the racialization of the mother tongue and the attempted eradication of dialects and creoles that the state's "Speak Mandarin Campaign" and "Speak Good English Movement" reflect.

The Singaporean government launched the Speak Mandarin Campaign in 1979. While the government's closure of Nanyang University around the same time symbolized the decline of Sinophone education and political activism, the Speak Mandarin Campaign recognized the need to address a perceived "over-Westernization" of Singaporean youth. Continued economic growth throughout the first two decades of independence coincided with increased demands for "greater participation in the formulation of the public policies" affecting all Singaporeans: calls for Singaporeans to continue supporting the PAP's more repressive legislation—exchanging individual liberties for the sake of "survival" and "pragmatism"—lost much of the appeal they generated in the volatile 1960s.[59] The PAP sought a relegitimizing mandate to preserve not only its political hegemony but also its style of rule. The buzzword became "Asian values," and the mother tongues were designated the site of their transmission. If Anglophone education already fulfilled the technocratic goals of the nation's globalizing economy, Mandarin education played the complementary function of transmitting "moral and social values . . . based on Chinese traditions, values, and culture" for the Chinese majority, as the PAP argued that English alone failed to reinforce "Confucian values of the family."[60] According to campaign logic, only Mandarin allowed Chinese Singaporeans to disseminate Confucianism "without the use of English" (which "intruded" upon communication across various Sinitic languages) and "without the dilution and distraction" that Sinophone multiplicity represented.[61]

Guided by the rationale that students of the "Chinese race" could not handle three languages at once (English and Mandarin in school, other Sinitic languages or Baba Malay at home), the campaign used slogans such as "Speak Mandarin, Less Dialect," "Mandarin is

Chinese," and "If You Are Chinese, Make a Statement in Mandarin" throughout the 1980s.[62] To drive home the goals of the campaign, Lee Kuan Yew stopped making speeches in Hokkien and ordered "all dialect programs on television and radio" (except the news) to cease.[63] The campaign construes Mandarin as the repository of a timeless racial heritage that offers Chinese Singaporeans a seamless link to "cultural roots" in the ancestral homeland.

Despite its appeal to racial heritage, which is the antithesis of the government's valuation of English, the campaign's push for Mandarin shares some latent commonalities with the promotion of English as a "common working language"—to globalize and remain relevant to the world. It is no coincidence that the Speak Mandarin Campaign occurred alongside Singapore's establishment of diplomatic and economic ties to the PRC in the post-Mao Reform era.[64] With ethno-linguistic ties giving Singapore's racial majority a comparative advantage in partaking of mainland China's capitalist reforms, Singaporean professionals "who knew both English and Mandarin commanded a premium."[65] Despite recognizing the international economic advantages of promoting Mandarin, the Singaporean government was wary of appearing to advocate Sinicizing its ethnic minorities and thus reiterated the campaign's specific racial orientation, as English was to remain the "common" interethnic language.[66]

In its relationship to globalization and fears of cultural illegibility, the Speak Mandarin Campaign is similar to the "Speak Good English Movement" launched by Goh Chok Tong (Lee Kuan Yew's successor) in 2000 to eradicate widespread use of the Singlish creole, considered unintelligible to outsiders. Like the rationale suggesting that Chinese Singaporeans could not properly learn Mandarin while speaking other Sinitic languages at home, the Speak Good English Movement assumed that many Singaporeans confused Singlish with "proper" English and could not communicate effectively with the large pool of foreign talent that sustained Singapore's status as a global hub.

Directly challenging the logic of the Speak Mandarin Campaign and the Speak Good English Movement, Anglophone authors evoke the "Singaporeanness" of Singlish as the "language of our souls." Using Singlish, these authors not only "contaminate" English,[67] but their transliteration of terms from Hokkien, Cantonese, and other Sinitic languages into the Romanized phonetic alphabet used to transcribe Singlish bypasses the Mandarin "mother-tongue" pronunciation altogether. A determination to retrace the messy, complicated relationship between language and cultural heritage, as well as a refusal to cede the terms of national culture to state-sponsored campaigns, is particularly prevalent in the fiction of Suchen Christine Lim (1948-). Returning to her roots in the Malaysian countryside and refusing to prioritize Chineseness over cultural affinities with her South and Southeast Asian neighbors and confidantes, Lim's work engages in a translingual resignification of the Nanyang.

Lim's novels, including *Rice Bowl* (1984), *Gift from the Gods* (1991), *Fistful of Colours* (1992), *A Bit of Earth* (2004), and *The River's Song* (2013), straddle the personal and the political, the colonial and the postcolonial, the (inter)ethnic and the (trans)national, and the past and the present in Singapore and Malaysia.[68] Born in Malaysia, Lim spent the early part of her childhood in Penang and Kedah. At fourteen, she moved to Singapore and later attended the National University of Singapore. This rural-to-urban, Malaysia-to-Singapore migration resembles that of Suwen, Lim's protagonist in *Fistful of Colours*, a novel that won the inaugural Singapore Literature Prize in 1992.

As an Anglophone-educated painter trained in Malaysia, Scotland, and Singapore, Suwen belongs to an informal clique of progressive Singaporean intellectuals and artists,

> a group of like-minded English-educated malcontents who got together every weekend to grouse about the sanitized politics of Singapore, and dissect the plays they had attended and the paintings they had seen as they drank beer till the wee hours of the morning in one another's pads.[69]

Although they are kindred spirits, they come from diverse ethnic backgrounds, representing not only the respective components of Singaporean multiracialism, but also inter- and intraethnic histories that disturb the legibility of Singapore's official racial categories. The novel's characters are very aware of their "hybrid cultural inheritances" that do not conform to the "racialized identities" delineated by state discourse in the 1980s.[70] Though they share a common distaste for Singapore's "sanitized politics" and cultural conservatism, their debates reflect different attitudes toward history, language, and the arts. *Fistful of Colours* is a novelization of Suwen's current art project: "marrying two mediums—the word and the picture—to make art" that retells Singaporean history as "the sum total of ethnic and personal histories woven into a common strand" neither wholly triumphant nor blatantly cynical. Her friends advise against doing a "pretty" propaganda mural of multiracial harmony one finds in an MRT station but to paint the past "for what it was. Unadorned by political myths, they had urged."[71]

Using the stories of her and her friends' forebears as Suwen's artistic muse, the novel frames the group's present-day relationships (and their attitudes toward contemporary Singaporean society) within a web of personal histories gleaned from conversations, old photographs, newspaper clippings, and observations of soon-to-be demolished or renovated architectural sites in Singapore. These histories inform each modern-day character's unique social outlook on the island, counterbalancing discontent with appreciation. Though critical of patronizing British attitudes about Malay "laziness," Zulaiman, the Malay journalist in the group, is more forgiving of the colonial past: his grandfather, who despite royal lineage worked as a waiter at the Cricket Club, earned the trust of a colonial official from Scotland who financed his son's (Zul's father) Anglophone education at the elite Raffles Institution. Zul's father, who felt abandoned by the British during the Japanese occupation, rescued a Chinese victim of an air raid and the two developed a lasting friendship that would survive the ethnic polarization of the volatile 1960s.

These histories inform Zul's comparatively strong sense of Singaporean patriotism, his appreciation of his Anglophone education, his sense of Malayness (tempered by an aversion to ethnic extremism), and his willingness to marry Janice Wong, a Chinese Singaporean professor. Zul's relationship with Jan forces him to confront prejudices underneath the multiracial veneer of the "global hub":

> For as long as we mix and mingle in the comfortable confines of the marketplace, all is well; move beyond that into the personal and the intimate areas, then the hub quivers and shakes like a machine into which one has accidentally poured water instead of oil.[72]

Zul exposes the superficiality of multiracial tolerance, which assigns appropriate venues for interethnic contact and tacitly labels others off-limits.

His fiancée Jan (Suwen's colleague) is even more critical. Her father's "pig-headed" ethnocentrism (he disowns her for her engagement to a Malay) and his violent treatment of her mother prompt Jan to question the motives of settlers who, like former colonizers, enforce their culture upon the new homeland, rather than adapt to the environment:

> I'm beginning to question why when people migrate here, to Southeast Asia, they want to change it to suit themselves. The Chinese want to recreate a China here, the Indians want an India and the English want another Devon or Hampstead Heath. . . . I've never felt that I was from China. My father does. But I grew up here.[73]

Identifying as "Southeast Asian," Jan chose to major in Southeast Asian history at her university. In order to marry Zul, she opts to convert to Islam.

Of Suwen's friends, her primary art mentor Nica Sivalingam possesses the most "colorful" and contentious personality. Suwen attributes Nica's strength of character to her "mixed Baba Chinese and Indian heritage," which from a young age forced her to straddle "two or three cultures within the home" while developing a thick skin to deflect racism from different directions.[74] The novel explores the history of several of Nica's forebears, including Tan Boon Wee, her maternal granduncle who worked as a chief clerk in the transportation department of the colonial bureaucracy, and Dr. Susantha Menon, her paternal grandaunt who was a physician at a clinic in Singapore's Little India district. Inspired by the freedom fighter Chandra Bose of the Indian National Army, Dr. Menon "actually helped to train a regiment of Indian women to fight the British in World War II."[75] When Nica's father, a surgeon, chose to marry a local Nyonya, it caused a scandal in the small Indian community in Alor Star, the Malaysian city where Nica spent the early part of her childhood. As a child, Nica was berated for picking up Cantonese from her amah, as she was ordered to speak only English and the "pure" Tamil of her Sri Lankan forebears. Turning to art, Nica "sculpted" herself away from "the narrow-mindedness and pettiness of Alor Star" to seek cosmopolitan tolerance in Singapore.[76]

The debates and comparisons between Nica and Suwen throughout *Fistful of Colours* form the backdrop to the novel's commentary on Singaporean politics, culture, and art. Whereas Suwen is emotionally maladroit, sensitive, sexually reserved, and unable to release or forgive the past (she was molested by her stepfather), Nica is open, outgoing, forthcoming, unsympathetic, and future-oriented, easily releasing past hurts and dissolving relationships that have ceased to interest her:

> Next to her, Suwen felt weak and pale, like the duller shades of earth colours. The greens and browns of the lichens one finds along the drains, she thought ruefully, whereas Nica's personality had the vibrant reds and yellows of tropical blooms.[77]

Nica's criticism of Suwen's art project, which Suwen initially proposes as a collage of words and images detailing the ascendance and decline of her stepfather's family and their estate, ultimately inspires the broader ambition that the novel represents. Nica disparages Suwen's "clan" mentality and her cause-and-effect, chronological approach to history that mirrors official narratives. Reminding Suwen that they live in an age of "cultural lobotomy," Nica insists:

> The Singapore artist must see beyond his clan and his race. Society can be ethnically myopic. But the artist shouldn't. If society looks right, the artist should look left. And then right. And back and front too.[78]

The juxtaposition and montage of personal histories and present-day stories in the novel reflects the Singaporean artist's determination to observe sidelong, against the tunnel vision of the chronological macronarrative.

Despite this reminder, Nica—as a sculptor and self-proclaimed free "spirit floating above the Indians and the Chinese"—embraces the engineered nature of the Singaporean national character and the "human will" for cultural makeover inspiring the country to "build dams, reclaim the land and bulldoze hills and mountains." Calling the "true Singaporean" a sculptor who "shapes and moulds his environment like nobody else," Nica is dismissive of Suwen's nostalgia for "the romance of the trees and hills of Perak," which was inspired by Suwen's boredom at the "utility and efficiency" of Singapore's "straight and definite" towers.[79]

One of the primary points of disagreement between the two artists regards Lee Kuan Yew's closure of Nanyang University and the persecution of suspected communists. Whereas Nica believes the institution had to be closed, Suwen is more empathetic toward those who harbor bitterness over its closure. Her relatives had donated to its establishment as a "place for the Chinese of Nanyang," and a few joined socialist movements that were brutally suppressed, leading to their incarceration, disappearance, and presumed deaths. Nica suggests that Suwen can only take such a naïve perspective because Suwen was away in the Scottish countryside during the most volatile period of communalist violence.[80]

Nica is also shocked by Suwen's sensitivity and lingering resentments over issues of language and culture, including the politicization of the mother tongue, the Speak Mandarin Campaign, and patronizing assumptions about her use of English, Cantonese, and Hokkien.

Suwen's outlook on language is not only framed through her conversations with Nica, but also with Mark Campbell, who as a Scot is the only non-Singaporean in her inner circle. Mark's presence as an outside observer in the narrative creates an implied reader for whom the narrative selectively "translates" some "insider knowledge" about Singapore—particularly its language politics—while at the same time intentionally leaving him partially in the dark. This aesthetic of partial intelligibility is exhibited in the novel's use of Singlish: when Suwen and her friends facetiously speak "the street-smart slang of the Ah-Beng-and-Ah-Huay variety," Mark is left out, just as the reader receives no explanation of what an "Ah-Beng" or "Ah-Huay" is.[81]

The novel traces Suwen's language debates with Mark back to their first meeting when she was a student in Scotland in the late 1960s. During an "International Night" festival at the university, the school's foreign students performed the "national cultures" of their respective countries. The difficulty of the Singaporean students in determining a common language and culture to perform, and the subsequent disparaging remarks by Mark, lead to a heated exchange:

> Most people sang or recited something in their national language. But the three of us from Singapore didn't know what to do. . . . [T]he two girls from Malaysia had already recited a Malay pantun. And two guys from China recited some poems in Mandarin. The girl from Hong Kong even sang an aria from a Cantonese opera. So one of the Singapore girls wanted to sing "Burong Kakak Tua." She was from a Baba family. But that's not a Singaporean song, the Malaysian lady told us. Anyway, the two of us didn't know the words. So, in the end, we sang "Sing Your Way Home." The applause, well, was lukewarm. Some of the Caucasians wondered why we sang in English. I was so embarrassed. Then later that night, Mark said something stupid . . . , something like I had no tongue of my own, and that I had to use a borrowed tongue. . . . You are a Scot, I said. And your English is not a borrowed tongue?[82]

The passage highlights the problematic necessity of reducing one's cultural and linguistic heterogeneity to a single, legible, unique sound-bite to perform on a global stage. By virtue of their Anglophone education, the students' common language is English. Yet the bewildered Western audience assumes narrow-mindedly that the Singaporean students have no language of "their own." Additionally, the Chinese students patronizingly refer to the Singaporeans as "daughters of China, married into other families."[83] Noting their refusal to acknowledge English, Malay, or Cantonese as also belonging to her (or to Singapore), Suwen is embittered by the notion that the languages she speaks are somehow "borrowed tongues."

In the contemporary setting of the novel, Suwen aims her lasting bitterness at the postcolonial Singaporean state, whose language campaigns internalize many of these imperialist assumptions. Pointing to the early Chinese settlers of the Nanyang as "illiterate non-Mandarin speakers" who "came from the riffraff strata" and the "rough-and-tumble world of the poor and lawless," she berates the Speak Mandarin Campaign as empty talk about "our Chinese virtues and values."[84] Piecing together Suwen's personal histories—those of her own childhood as well as of her stepfather's family—*Fistful of Colours* creates a "sidelong," translingual correlation between the historical relationships of English to Singlish and Mandarin to other Sinitic languages in Singapore. The story of Suwen's step-grandfather Ong Ah Buck is that of a rags-to-riches rickshaw coolie who becomes the wealthy owner of his own transport company. After Ong Ah Buck donates money to the colonial government to support the Allies in the anti-Japanese war effort, a local Sinophone newspaper prints an article praising his contributions. Ong Ah Buck's son reads the article aloud to other family members and servants of the Ong estate in Mandarin, which in the novel "translates" directly into more formal English:

> His transport company, the largest Chinese-owned company on the island, has been a consistent supporter of the government's war fund. Mr Ong has been contributing five dollars for each of the twenty buses owned by his company. This letter which came with his latest cheque expresses regret over his delay in sending his monthly contribution.[85]

Using euphemistic phrases such as "expresses regret over his delay," the article assumes a high degree of formality. However, the audience does not understand what Ong's son has read to them, so he "paraphrases" the article in spoken Hokkien, which the author "translates" directly into Singlish: "A good man, ah! Always gives the angmoh money. The angmoh fight the Jepun people, our father pays them. He gives the angmoh money to buy war planes and guns, ah!"[86] This causes the family to roil with laughter.

In addition to using common Singlish terms such as *angmoh* ("red-hairs," from the Hokkien term for Caucasians) and *Jepun* (from the Malay term for Japan/Japanese), the Singlish paraphrasing of Hokkien is cruder both in its exaggerated embellishment ("money to buy war planes and guns") and in its elimination of mundane details like specific numbers and figures. The novel's transliteration of common Singlish vocabulary from Hokkien, Malay, Cantonese, and Tamil to convey the intimacy of "Singaporeanness,"[87] rather than the outward-oriented formality of Mandarin and English, flies in the face of the Speak Mandarin and Speak Good English campaigns. The defiant recognition of a linguistic heterogeneity whose inter- and intraethnic heritage is irreducible to the state's racialization of the mother tongue paints a messier, more colorful social portrait in which the island's true mother tongues are its unofficial creoles and dialects.

Refusing to accept the terms of cultural legibility designated by the state, Suwen identifies as an Anglophone-educated, Hokkien-Cantonese Malaysian Singaporean. Fed up by responses to her art exhibit questioning her "Asian values" and "identity as a Singaporean Chinese,"[88] she seeks solace and solitude in her "roots" at the end of the novel, returning by train to the Malaysian village of Kuala Jelai where she grew up. At Singapore's old, art-deco Tanjong Pagar Railway Station (which, at the time the novel was written, was operated by the Malaysian national railway and designated as Malaysian territory),[89] Suwen looks up above the station platform to observe

> the familiar wall mural of tin miners, dulang washers, rubber tappers and padi planters; a myriad of minute mosaic tiles had gone into the making of the mural, a tribute to the work of the humble folks. She drew comfort from that work although it had little artistic merit. But the mural served its purpose, reminding people like her that Peninsular Malaysia was still the home of simple rural folks, the home of farmers and rubber tappers, the homeland of her maternal grandparents, and part of her own roots. Neither Communist China nor the literary China found in Chinese literature was her spiritual home, she concluded. Standing amidst the noisy crowd waiting for the afternoon train to Kuala Jelai, she had the curious sensation that she was going home at last.[90]

Lacking the type of "artistic merit" lauded by her cosmopolitan clique, the mural at the old train station (not the sleek new MRT stations) lends a final visualization to the cross-cultural breadth and depth Suwen discovered in her and her friends' personal histories. Made from colored rubber tiles through a process patented by the Singapore Rubber Works, the murals (there are actually six of them, each in a triptych style) offer a cultural panorama of colonial Malayan labor circa 1930, connecting images of Singapore's history as a port city in the South Seas—one mural shows Chinese junks and Malay boats in the harbor next to a modern passenger steamship as Indian coolies haul fruit onto shore[91]—to the agricultural and industrial peninsular hinterland (images of Chinese tin miners, Indian rubber tappers and fruit gatherers, and Malay padi farmers).[92] Despite the seeming abandonment of Singapore associated with Suwen's presence at the station, the murals provide another sidelong glance at Singaporean history, invoking its cultural, climatological, maritime, and terrestrial confluences with Malaysia.

Sculpting the Nanyang, not as an ethnically myopic "new China" settlement in the South Seas, but as the transethnic and translocal historical affinities Singapore shares with its Southeast Asian neighbors, Suchen Christine Lim's *Fistful of Colours* forms a translingual bond with works of Sinophone literature that similarly de-racialize the cultural landscape of postcolonial Singapore. The novel highlights the ways in which the Nanyang has been translated and transliterated into English—the former colonial language—as part of a creolizing decolonization process to claim the language as one's own. This translingual process (from Sinophone to non-Sinophone) of rewriting dominant national narratives in Southeast Asia can also be seen in the work of authors who write in languages indigenous to the region as well.

CHAPTER 6

Popular Sino-Thai Integration Narratives

In Southeast Asian historiography, the Kingdom of Thailand is commonly portrayed as a "success story" for its integration of Chinese immigrants and settlers into the national culture. Historians attribute this success to Thailand's evasion of Western imperial annexation, as Chinese settlers were absorbed into a native Thai social hierarchy rather than a colonial system that distinguished them as middlemen or temporary foreign laborers, as in British Malaya and the Dutch East Indies. The semicolonial or neocolonial statuses that Thailand historically assumed (particularly in its relationship to the British Empire at the turn of the twentieth century and under US patronage during the Cold War) do not negate the most celebrated tenet of "Thai exceptionalism": its status as Southeast Asia's only "uncolonized" nation.[1] This status forms a key backdrop to the South Seas as a trope of Chinese integration in Sino-Thai literature, which here indicates both Sinophone and Thai-language narratives about the Sino-Thai community.

Thailand's evasion of colonial rule supposedly explains why the country has "the least violently ethnicized politics in the region."[2] Whereas in Singapore and Malaysia, postcolonial policies of multiculturalism (whether ideally egalitarian or admittedly hierarchical) perpetuate British racialism, Thailand has never thoroughly internalized or consistently reinforced such logic, even if it has not been immune to it. As the land of the "Thai"—audibly indistinct from the name of the kingdom's ethnic majority, the "Tai"—the imagined nation-state has obvious ethnic connotations.[3] Yet the perception that the Tai majority is more "Thai" than the nation's internal "others" has competed with more pluralistic visions of modern nationhood since its inception.

In evading colonialism, Siam (as Thailand was known prior to its official renaming in 1939) adapted its own colonial style of nation-state territoriality and administrative bureaucracy.[4] Successive governments strove to assimilate a diverse populace to the normative cultural and linguistic standards of the Tai-Thai (or Tai-Siamese) majority. The Sino-Thai population, scattered throughout the country though predominantly concentrated in the urban capital of Bangkok, was the largest among these non-Tai (or in many cases part-Tai) communities.[5] The Sino-Thai community represents a successful, nonviolent, and nonsegregationist example of immigrant integration in Southeast Asian history.[6] Yet "integration," as the formation of a unified whole, has two competing connotations: it functions both as a transitive verb—an action carried out to assimilate the Other, requiring conformity to the preset standards of the majority—and intransitive verb—an accommodating expansion of the boundaries that define the whole. Sino-Thai popular novels, written both in standard Chinese and Thai, evoke the South Seas to reflect upon the historical impact of the oppositional tensions embodied by national integration, adapting to while also redefining what it means to be "Thai."

During the Cold War era, or Thailand's "American Era" from the 1950s to the mid-1970s,[7] an assimilatory agenda prevailed. Beginning in the 1980s, a historical rewriting of the assimilation narrative reasserted notions of cultural plurality suppressed by the martial-royalist nationalism of the Cold War. An integral component of this pluralist revisionism, reexaminations of Sino-Thai histories insisted upon the dogged persistence of a fluid Sino-Thai biculturalism, even throughout the Cold War when the direct South Seas link between Swatow and Bangkok no longer sustained and replenished the local Sino-Thai community's strong Teochew affiliations.

A leftist, working-class, Bangkok-centered, often collaboratively authored, and highly Teochew-inflected Sinophone literature survived the assimilationism of the Cold War, in spite of its severed ties with mainland China, its relative marginality in the Sinophone literary world, and the forcible closure of local Sinophone newspapers that sponsored literary production. This literature attests to a Sino-Thai biculturalism that bridges a presumed cultural gap between the era of immigration and settlement (ending in 1945) and Thailand's "Chinese cultural revival" beginning in the 1980s. This literature receives scant scholarly attention in transnational Sinophone literary studies and generally is not included in Thailand's national literary archive. Read alongside Thai-language popular novels, Sinophone Thai fiction—as the popular, serialized, collaboratively authored "sequential novel" (*jielong xiaoshuo*)—provides a complementary narrative of Sino-Thai integration. Thai-language popular novels span the entire arc of modern Sino-Thai history with archetypal, soap-operatic domestic sagas of Sino-Thai immigration, assimilation, upward mobility, and national influence. By contrast, the Sinophone sequential novel addresses the disenfranchisement of the migrant working class that accompanied national development during the Cold War. It is a slice-of-life snapshot of a community in a transformational time and place, rather than a family epic of cultural evolution and long-term change.

The South Seas trope (whether the Sinophone Nanyang or literally translated into Thai as *thale tai*) informs the theme of Chinese integration in both Sinophone and Thai-language popular novels. In its Thai usage, the term evokes a specific trajectory of mass migration between China and Southeast Asia in the late nineteenth and early twentieth centuries: the Swatow-Bangkok corridor that facilitated the migration and settlement of predominantly Teochew-speaking immigrants in Siam. The allusion to this corridor affirms Teochew cultural and linguistic continuity afforded by migration to Siam over other places (including elsewhere in China). The closure of this overseas route after 1945 shifts connotations of the South Seas to the commercial and educational links that working-class and bourgeois Sino-Thai communities established with Sinophone centers in Southeast Asia (namely Penang and Singapore) and Hong Kong. Here, the Nanyang (or *thale tai*) signifies a regional affiliation that allows for bicultural continuities because it skirts compulsory national assimilation. These regional affiliations in the South Seas also bypass mainland China (and even reference to China) as outlets for cultivating biculturalism.

In their translingual signification of the South Seas trope, Sino-Thai popular novels also challenge prevailing definitions of biculturalism as the simultaneous embodiment of two mutually distinct and "uncontaminated" cultures and languages. Creolizing processes in Sino-Thai narratives undermine the polarities of assimilationist and bicultural understandings of Sino-Thai integration, revealing the impossibility of separating the "Sino" component from the "Thai" affiliation it modifies. The discursive pitfall of the bicultural model is that it perpetuates the very "Chinese" versus "Thai" dichotomies of an assimilationist discourse that demands erasure of the former in favor of the latter. Sino-Thai biculturalism is not an alternative to creolization (a model more often applied to the syncretic "third spaces" of colonial contexts), because here biculturalism is the formation of two creolized (rather than impenetrable) spheres. Sinophone and Thai-language popular novels are cross-pollinated with intriguing linguistic hybridizations between the Thai and Chinese scripts (particularly in their Teochew readings). Such processes suggest that the South Seas trope in Sino-Thai narratives is not simply an affirmation of a biculturalism meant to revise the "success story" of Chinese assimilation. As the site of multiple creolizations, Sino-Thai popular novels recognize a plurality, flexibility, and syncretic potential of Thai national culture that neither assimilates to a majority standard nor staunchly adheres to fixed definitions of two mutually impervious cultures.

NATIONAL ASSIMILATION AND SINO-THAI BICULTURALISM

Thailand's "absorption" of Chinese immigrants and their descendants, the "Sino-Thai" or Lukčhin,[8] has made Thailand a historical success story of Chinese integration. Yet the integration narrative has two competing versions: one emphasizes assimilation and conformity (from Chinese to Thai), the other accommodation and flexibility (the expansion of "Thainess" to incorporate biculturalism). The assimilationist narrative of Chinese integration suggests that Chinese settlers migrated to the kingdom and assimilated to some predetermined notion of what constituted "Thai" or "Siamese." In other words, they adopted the Thai language, Thai names, the Theravada Buddhist religion, reverence for the Thai monarchy, and Thai social customs and graces, all the while "mixing Thai with Chinese blood until they were virtually indistinguishable."[9] The assimilationist narrative celebrates these historical processes as the triumphs of Thai martial-royalist dictatorships in quelling the threat of "contamination" posed by externalized "others" in order to "achieve progress/development" for the nation. It views the nation as "a mystical unity" (*samakkhitham*) and "a distinctly graded hierarchy in which some are more Thai, more 'national' than others."[10] Adhering to the Thai "official nationalism" of "Nation-Religion-King" (*chat-satsana-kasat*),[11] the assimilation narrative draws its colonial legacy from the royalist absolutism of King Vajiravudh (Rama VI, r. 1910–25) and finds postcolonial expression in regimes of military generals-cum-prime ministers such as Plaek Phibunsongkhram (Phibun, PM 1938–44 and 1948–57), Sarit Thanarat (PM 1958–63), and Thanom Kittikhachon (PM 1963–73).

By contrast, the accommodation narrative does not attribute any "mystical unity" to the nation, but rather "embraces its diversity," highlighting the nation's "variety of peoples bundled together" to deconstruct "myths of unity and continuity."[12] This "civic nationalism" draws from the legacies of decolonization and constitutional democratization in the prewar 1930s and early postwar 1940s. Opening Thainess to the plurality of ethnicities, languages, and regional or metropolitan cultures encompassed within the nation, this narrative nevertheless attempts to "domesticate its ideas by finding parallels" in Theravada Buddhist teachings,[13] particularly notions of compassion and karma. Sino-Thai popular novels explore the historical tensions between the assimilation and accommodation narratives, providing allegorical episodes (ranging roughly from the 1910s to the present) that attest to the influences of both discourses. Both the "absorbable" category of the "Sino-Thai" (Lukčhin) and the "othered" category of the "Chinaman" (*čhek*) figure into this historical tension between assimilation and accommodation in Thailand's transition from kingdom to modern nation-state.

Until the turn of the twentieth century when diasporic Chinese nationalism took hold in Southeast Asia, the otherness of Chinese settlers in Siam did not pose a threat to the Tai-Siamese royalty because the settlers were not citizens of a modern Chinese nation-state. Chinese settlers, primarily from the Teochew (Chaozhou, pronounced "Taečhiu" in Thai) region of China (northern Guangdong province), came to Siam as early as the eighteenth century, where they filled a commercial niche running the rice trade. Although some settlers intermarried with local Siamese, "their relations with the Thai were confined to a single dimension, namely trade."[14] Some wealthier entrepreneurs among the Sino-Thai merchant community established symbiotic relations with (and often married into) the Tai-Siamese nobility, gaining bureaucratic appointment in the royal hierarchy.[15] This benefited Tai-Siamese elites, who, according to the Sino-Thai historian Nidhi Eoseewong, could profit through patronage of wealthy merchants without having "to work hard, face hardship, or take business risks." The Sino-Thai merchant class profoundly influenced the inception of an urban, bourgeois Siamese (and later Thai) culture.[16] Throughout the nineteenth century, Thai remained the sole linguistic avenue to privilege and power in Siamese society, as Chinese settlers "had to learn Thai to speak to members of the elite," while in neighboring Western colonial territories "they learned French, Dutch, or English" to enter elite ranks.[17] Other cultural factors promoted the ease of transition for Sino-Thais: Teochew settlers in Siam readily adopted Theravada Buddhism, which they saw as differing only slightly from the Mahayana traditions of rural southern China. "Conversion" did not require abandoning older customs, but simply involved adding or blending them with new ones.[18]

The term "Sino-Thai" (Lukčhin) historically denotes a culturally integrated category in the Thai national narrative that predates the ethno-nationalist construction of a racialized "Chinaman" (*čhek*) in the early twentieth century. Just as Siam's late nineteenth-century transformation appropriated models of Western colonial administration in British India, Malaya, and the Dutch East Indies,[19] the application of "indelible 'racial' traits" to Chinese settlers also bears the influence of racialist discourse among Siam's Western-educated leaders.[20] This begins with King Vajiravudh, the first Siamese king to be educated in the West, where he studied at Oxford and Sandhurst. As the "chief ideologue of Thai royalist absolutism,"[21] King Vajiravudh promoted a monarchical nationalism defined *against* the Bangkok Sino-Thai merchant class, viewing Chinese immigrants as imminently subversive of the monarchy. In 1913, the king composed an essay entitled "The Jews of the Orient and Wake Up, Thailand" ("Phuak Yiu haeng burapha thit lae mưang Thai čhong tưn thoet"). Interestingly, the title refers to the "land of the Thai" two decades before Siam officially became Thailand, hinting at the increasing pervasiveness of ethno-nationalism among the Bangkok royalty. The king's anti-Sinitic essay reveals his initiation into the popular anti-Semitic discourse in Europe that accompanied his Western education, as he criticizes Chinese immigrants, particularly merchants, for regarding their residence as temporary, refusing to assimilate, retaining loyalties to China, neglecting responsible citizenship, and exploiting Siam's resources to serve their own greed.[22]

The king's paranoia stemmed from two drastic changes regarding Chinese immigration at the time. First, Chinese were arriving in unprecedented numbers. Intensified Chinese (especially Teochew) immigration dated back to 1861 when a passenger steamship port opened in Swatow providing direct travel to Bangkok. From 1876–98, nearly 185,000 Chinese passengers came from Swatow directly to Siam, with only about 27,000 returning. Between 1906 and 1918, the number of total Chinese arrivals increased substantially to more than 630,000, while the number of returnees also increased to nearly 250,000, showing the growth of circular migration after earlier pioneer settlement drew Siam into the South Seas network. In total, nearly 3.7 million Chinese settled in Siam throughout a century of emigration following the Opium Wars. The vast majority of them—60–80 percent (2.2–2.9 million)—were Teochew. By 1910, three years before King Vajiravudh composed his anti-Sinitic essay, Chinese immigrants and their families made up almost half of Bangkok's population: though they settled throughout the kingdom, Bangkok was their primary port of entry with the highest concentration of immigrants.[23]

The second change was the emergence of diasporic nationalism, which influenced the 1911 Republican Revolution in China. In addition to the greater number of settlers, the stronger and more frequent overseas connections worried the Siamese royalty. As in the other port cities of the Nanyang, settler communities in Bangkok began establishing Sinophone newspapers and, in the wake of the Chinese revolution, Mandarin-medium "Chinese schools." Though diasporic nationalism took competing forms, the bottom line for the Siamese king was that it was "Chinese," concerned foremost with China. Unlike the more "assimilated" Sino-Thais, the new immigrants could establish themselves in Bangkok's Chinatown in the Yaowarat Road and Sampheng Lane districts in such great numbers that they would not have to communicate with Tai-Siamese, remaining, in the opinion of the king, unassimilated "Chinamen" (*čhek*).

Yet there was a key difference between Siamese policies toward Chinese immigrants and those of the Western colonial powers in neighboring countries. Instead of insisting that the Chinese would only be temporary inhabitants, the Siamese aristocracy (much of which had Sino-Thai roots) recognized the possibility of assimilating a large Chinese minority. Rather than segregate settlers from natives, the Siamese monarchy imposed stricter measures to ensure the "Thainess" of the citizenry. The Nationality Act of 1913 and 1914 magnanimously defined as Thai "every person born on Thai territory," though it also enforced the adoption of Thai surnames.[24]

As surnames were a relatively recent phenomenon in Siamese society, there were few guidelines as to what constituted a "Thai" surname. At the very least, the name had to be written in the Thai script and involve some trace of Thai vocabulary. Many immigrants simply registered their Teochew surname, or *sae* (*shi*), in conjunction with the Thai word *trakun*, meaning "clan." Others combined their *sae* with auspicious meanings, such as *čharoen* ("prosperous"), or with their vocation, such as *phanit* ("commerce").[25] The Nationality Act was one of the first policy measures that attempted to define an official Thai nationalism against the increasingly visible *čhek* or Chinese Other.

Subsequent military dictatorships of the twentieth century, beginning with General Plaek Phibunsongkhram, put forth hardline assimilatory measures. "Phibun," as the general was known, was one of two key leaders of the People's Party that led the 1932 coup to overthrow the absolute monarchy and establish a constitutional monarchy in Siam. The other, Pridi Banomyong (PM 1946), who was of Sino-Thai descent, emerged as Phibun's primary political challenger and as the leading visionary of a more accommodating civic nationalism. As the civilian leader of the 1932 coup, Pridi was a democratic reformer who believed that the rule of law to establish citizens' rights would produce an "equitable and efficient society" that could serve as the discursive foundation of modern nationhood: "more practical than mystical," Pridi, who "saw no close connection between nation and race," described Thailand as "a mix of ethnic groups."[26] In his short stint as prime minister in 1946, Pridi oversaw passage of a new constitution to establish a parliament completely elected by popular vote.[27]

By contrast, Phibun was a field marshal who drew on the fascist doctrines of the German and Japanese regimes, causing him to briefly fall out of favor during the early postwar period. As prime minister, Phibun was responsible for Siam's official name change to Thailand in 1939, popularizing the slogan: "Thailand belongs to Thais," by which he meant the Tai.[28] The "Thai" to whom this land belonged, were, according to Phibun, "a race with martial characteristics, threatened by bad neighbours."[29] Additionally, Thais should speak Thai, which Phibun's administration officially standardized as Bangkok Thai (or Central Thai). Although creolized from the beginning (because Bangkok was largely a Sino-Thai settlement), Bangkok Thai became, in this conformist discourse, "pure Thai" (*Thai thae*). In the late 1930s, as Thai-language education became compulsory, Phibun closed, outlawed, and imposed severe restrictions on Sinophone schools and presses in Thailand, starting a precedent that would recur throughout the 1950s and 1960s under anticommunist pretenses.[30] The government even banned Teochew opera performances, popularly known as *ngiu*, in Bangkok.[31] Under Phibun, Chinese integration became an assimilatory mandate dictating that one adopt a Thai name (both first and last), receive a Thai education, and speak Central Thai.

Throughout the Cold War period, US neocolonial patronage brought together previously divided royal, military, and business factions in "a powerful alliance" under Phibun's successors, Sarit and Thanom, promoting a tripartite ideology of "Nation-Religion-King."[32] In the post-Phibun stages of the Cold War, the rhetoric of Thai nationalism was typically "conservative, conformist, and royalist."[33] Foreign investment, particularly from the United States but also Japan, Europe, and Hong Kong, transformed the military bureaucracy's previously antagonistic relationship with wealthy Sino-Thai businessmen. In this context, the menace of the *čhek* Other shifted from mercantilism onto communism: conservative Thai leaders painted Thai leftists as "a kind of alien minority" who were "really" Chinese or Vietnamese, and the anticommunist struggle became "a loftily national crusade."[34] In collaboration with the Thai military and bourgeoisie, the United States made Thailand a base for stopping the domino effect of communism in Asia.[35] Thailand's "American Era" had three major effects on the Sino-Thai community: loss of contact with the ancestral homeland, pressures of assimilation that intensified intergenerational conflicts, and the achievement of upward mobility.

The massive demonstrations of the 1970s marked the revival of dissenting views of nationhood that challenged the militaristic triumvirate of Nation-Religion-King and American neocolonialism. These years loom large in modern Thai literary history. The reprinting and widespread circulation of previously censored activist Chit Phumisak's *Art for Life, Art for the People* (*Sinlapa phưa chiwit sinlapa phưa prachachon*, 1956) spawned the highly influential "Literature for Life" (Wannakam phưa Chiwit) movement, which sought to depict "the real life of ordinary people" through social realism. These works contrast the economic and political marginality of the poor and working class with the crass materialism of business elites and military-government leaders benefiting under American neocolonialism.[36] Many Literature for Life narratives describe the poverty in the rural "outer provinces" (*tang čhangwat*), which influences a protagonist to migrate to Bangkok. Lured by media images of urban glamor and wealth, the protagonists are ultimately condemned to living in slums while working menial jobs. Overcome with nostalgia for family and rural simplicity, the protagonist is unable to return to a now transformed home village. The stories provide a bleak portrait and incisive critique of modern Thai nationhood under American economic investment and military involvement. These features of the Literature for Life genre are shared by much of the Sinophone Thai fiction from the Cold War era.

Despite violent "military-orchestrated" crackdowns that "portrayed any advocates of political or social change" as "communist," "un-Thai," and traitorous "enemies of nation, religion, and king" during the 1970s,[37] greater tolerance of social plurality became part of mainstream dialogue from this point onward, paving the way for the Sino-Thai "renaissance" of the 1980s. Thailand's establishment of diplomatic relations with mainland China in 1975 and the dissolution of the Communist Party of Thailand triggered by the Sino-Vietnamese split in 1978 also set the stage for the Sino-Thai historical revisionism of the 1980s. Examples include historian Nidhi Eoseewong's positive resignification of the pejorative *čhek* in his 1986 study of the part-Sino Thai King Taksin (r. 1767–82): rather than symbolizing King Vajiravudh's caricature of the greedy, parasitic "Chinaman," Nidhi argued that *čhek* stood for the diversity that is "the strength of Thai culture."[38] The author Suchit Wongthet's historical study *A Mixed Lao-Chinaman* (*Čhek pon Lao*, 1987) also revalorizes *čhek*: Suchit traces the historical mixedness of the Tai ethnic category in its integration of not only Lao and Chinese cultural elements but also Mon, Khmer, Burman, Malay, and Cham ones.[39]

Emphasizing an accommodation narrative of Chinese integration, some scholars refute the assumption that the Sino-Thai represent a model minority of assimilation, instead affirming a Sino-Thai "biculturalism" celebrating a specifically Thai vision of "Chineseness." In a 1993 survey of a cross-section of Bangkok Sino-Thais, sociologists Chan Kwok Bun and Tong Chee Kiong discovered that most members of the community, including third- and fourth-generation Sino-Thais, were multilingual, speaking one or more Sinitic languages (predominantly Teochew) in addition to Central Thai. Based on their data, Chan and Tong conclude that, rather than "total assimilation," Sino-Thais master a kind of situational biculturalism in four different social spheres: domestic-familial, formal-official, business-entrepreneurial, and educational-recreational.[40] Chan and Tong assert that, although situational, the "Sino" modifier in "Sino-Thai" acknowledges a "secondary identity" that is "not just momentarily conjured up and then displayed for occasion," but is one that "has been acquired, internalized and integrated as an integral part" of one's authentic cultural expression.[41] From this description, "Sino-Thai" appears as a relatively fluid "situational minority" identity within an accommodating multiethnic framework containing permeable interethnic boundaries.

Citing Chan and Tong's research, the historian Philip Kuhn argues that Sino-Thai biculturalism provides an alternative model of integration to creolization that attests to Thailand's historical evasion of colonialism. Thailand differed from neighboring colonial societies in Southeast Asia, where distinct creole groups historically occupied a third space in between but apart from both native and immigrant groups segregated by European colonialism: "Instead of creolization, there was widespread biculturalism and bilingualism among Chinese and Sino-Thai—a kind of Chineseness that resisted complete assimilation even while adding a layer of Thai behavior and speech to its cultural palette: Chinese speech in the home and with Chinese business associates, Thai speech with Thais."[42] The situational bicultural model of Sino-Thai integration is applicable to the different social spheres of Sino-Thai popular novels. Sinophone and Thai-language narratives occupy separate discursive arenas in and outside Thailand: the circulation of the former is largely limited to a small local community (based primarily in Bangkok) with some transnational literary ties to Hong Kong publishers and academic circles in Xiamen, while the latter is firmly and visibly entrenched in Thailand's national literary arena.

However, the linguistic and cultural expression of Sino-Thai popular novels suggests that biculturalism is not an alternative model *to* colonial creolization, but rather is an alternative mode *of* creolization. Placing biculturalism and creolization in a dichotomous framework presumes a narrow understanding of creolization as a process of cultural synthesis that produces a singular "third space" apart from two distinctly defined cultures and languages. A situational Sino-Thai biculturalism maintains clear distinctions between the first (Thai) and secondary (Chinese) identities that internalize, perpetuate, and celebrate (rather than challenge) the stark ethnic stereotypes of *čhek* in the assimilation narrative (such as mercantilism, thrift, and diligence). When posited not in opposition to biculturalism as a distinct third space but rather as the dynamic, formational process of culture and language through localization, adaptation, and exchange, creolization becomes a critical cornerstone of Sino-Thai biculturalism, acknowledging two interpenetrable spheres that creolize in analogous ways. This understanding suggests that Sino-Thai integration is *neither* a process of complete assimilation nor bicultural accommodation, but rather the production of *more than one* creole space. Evoking the trope of the South Seas, Sinophone and Thai-language popular novels illustrate two of these spaces.

A COLLABORATIVE SNAPSHOT OF SINOPHONE THAINESS

The Sinophone Thai author Fang Siruo (Phonlachet Kitaworanat, 1931–99), who wrote under the penname Nai Fang, identifies several challenges faced by Sinophone Thai literature at the outset of the Cold War: "Entering the 1950s, censorship became very strict: Sinophone education could only be offered through the fourth grade of primary school, and—from that time until the 1970s—all sorts of imported books, newspapers, and magazines were banned. In this type of cultural environment, how much literary accomplishment could writers attain?"[43] With intermittent measures taken by military dictatorships to close and censor Sinophone schools and presses, Sinophone literature had a tenuous existence in Cold War-era Thailand. Despite this, literary production continued sporadically throughout the Cold War with the reins over themes and trends passing from first-generation immigrant writers to younger authors born and raised in Thailand: these authors replaced the nostalgic "overseas literature" (*qiaomin wenxue*) with a "localized" (*dangdihua*) literature "reflecting the here and now" (*fanying cishi cidi*).[44]

Like the Thai Literature for Life movement in the 1970s, Sinophone Thai literature from this era engages in a similar critique of Thai society under American neocolonial capitalism, depicting the exploitation of the economically disenfranchised. Of course, the critique of capitalism was not new to Sinophone Thai literature, which inherited a leftist, social realist, vernacular tradition from the New Literature and left-wing literature movements in China. Such works originally appeared in literary supplements of Sinophone Thai newspapers in the 1920s and 1930s, prior to official censorship and severe restriction under Phibun. After the Thai government put a stop to all new Chinese immigration in 1945, local Sinophone literature followed the direction it went in neighboring Malaysia after independence: it was shackled by stricter policies toward Sinophone education and publication, yet freed from its "overseas" orientation toward mainland Chinese themes and trends. As in postcolonial Malaysia, this moment of crisis ironically doubled as a moment of creative liberation: Sinophone Thai literature transformed, becoming more focused on local settings, more multilingual, and more in sync with developing trends in Thai-language literature.[45]

In transnational Sinophone literary studies, Thai examples hold a marginal place at best,[46] with popular novels "reflecting the here and now" from the 1950s to the late 1970s garnering the most critical attention.[47] Set against the backdrop of Cold War anticommunism, American neoliberal economic development, and media censorship, these novels provide snapshots of (primarily urban) Sino-Thai society, depicting collaborative modes of being and becoming Thai that do not fully accord to the assimilatory standards set by state policy. Unlike their Thai-language counterparts, the Sinophone popular novels are not concerned with the theme of upward mobility, as "American Era" development does not bring the working-class protagonists the type of material success enjoyed by the Sino-Thai bourgeoisie.

Among the most cited examples is a 1960s popular novel, *Stormy Yaowarat Road* (*Fengyu Yaohuali*, 1963–64), which is the collective work of nine authors, all using pennames: Nai Fang (penname of Fang Siruo, 1931–1999), Chen Qiong (Wu Jiyue, 1905–92), Yi Fei (Chen Yingshang, c. 1915–84), Li Xu (Li Qingliang, 1922–93), Yi She (Ni Longsheng, 1927–2012), Bai Ling (Li Youzhong, 1931-), Hong Ying (Zheng Yuzhou, 1932-), Li Hong (aka Nian Lamei, penname of Xu Jinghua, 1934–95), and Shen Yiwen (Shen Senhao, 1936-). The authors include older, first-generation immigrants such as Chen Qiong, younger Thai-born authors such as Bai Ling who received some childhood education in China before returning to Thailand, and other local-born authors who received all their Sinophone training in Thailand and were avid readers of Thai-language literature, such as Shen Yiwen, who went on to translate several short stories from the Literature for Life movement into standard Chinese.[48] The authors were retirees, journalists, entrepreneurs, and corporate employees brought together by Fang Siruo,[49] who at the time was editor of Bangkok's *Sinophone News Weekly* (*Huafeng zhoubao*). *Stormy Yaowarat Road* was originally serialized in forty-one chapters in *Sinophone News Weekly* from 1963 to 1964, during which time the writers met weekly to discuss and plan the details of the novel. Not long after the novel's serialization, *Sinophone News Weekly* was closed down by the Thai government for its socialist leaning: *Stormy Yaowarat Road* was not published in book form until 1983 in Hong Kong.[50]

The authors of *Stormy Yaowarat Road* all shared a concern over the decline of Sinophone education and cultural production under the repressive conditions of military dictatorship in Thailand. The novel itself reflects this concern: for example, characters lament the decline of Teochew opera, which "used to be the soul of Yaowarat Road," as well as the corporatization of Sinophone newspapers, whose reporters have forsaken editing, accuracy, and objective journalism for advertising, sales, and other "nonsensical" responsibilities.[51]

Despite the seriousness of the authors' collective mission, *Stormy Yaowarat Road* is rather playful, imitating the style of the popular Hong Kong sequential novel and frequently employing dramatic irony for comedic effect. In the sequential novel format, each chapter typically ends with a cliffhanger: the author of that chapter then "invites" the author of the subsequent chapter to step in and resolve the issue. There are goofy villains, such as the greedy and corrupt Yaowarat "slumlord" (*cuozhu nai*) and widow from Swatow, Zheng Ah Zhen, and antiheroes, such as Liu Yafu, who always thinks of sly and dubious ways to procure the rent money owed to Ah Zhen. By a playful twist toward the end of the novel, Yafu turns out to be Ah Zhen's long-lost nephew. There are many slapstick scenes, such as Ah Zhen hiding her lover, a thuggish gang boss, underneath her bed, or Yafu dressing up as Zhu Bajie or "Piggy" from *Journey to the West* (*Xi you ji*) to advertise a Teochew opera performance of the sixteenth-century Chinese classic on Yaowarat Road.[52]

For all its good humor, *Stormy Yaowarat Road* is in many ways a typical Thai Literature for Life narrative: the term "stormy" in the title captures the tumultuous social changes brought about by the rapid economic development of Thailand in the 1950s and 1960s.[53] The protagonist, Li Jun,[54] is from the southern Thai city of Hat Yai on the Malayan peninsula. As a Sino-Thai from the South, Li's parents circumvented the suppression of Sinophone education, taking advantage of transnational connections in the Nanyang by sending their son to a Mandarin-medium secondary school in Penang. The son of a rubber tapper, Li leaves home when a steep decline in rubber prices, as well as the devaluing of the Thai baht, forces him out. Accompanied by his uneducated but streetwise friend Yafu, Li goes to seek his fortune in the capital. Arriving in Bangkok's Chinatown district along Yaowarat Road, Li Jun quickly becomes disillusioned with the "sin city." In addition to being pick-pocketed, scammed by a fake employer, and unable to find even menial work despite his education, Li discovers that Yaying, a childhood friend from Hat Yai whom he runs into, is now working as a prostitute. Wishing he could rescue her from her situation, but knowing he is barely able to rescue himself, the rather naïve Li Jun declares the metropolis a "monster" that "feeds on people."[55] He laments:

> Had I known it would be this difficult to make a living in Bangkok, that the people here would be so cruel, and that there would be so many traps to fall into . . . , I would have stayed at home to help my father and brothers with the rubber tapping![56]

Li's disillusionment with the modern capital resonates with the sentiments of most Thai Literature for Life narratives. The protagonist may regret his decision to migrate to Bangkok, but the conditions of economic instability that drove him from his nostalgically invoked home village in southern Thailand nevertheless remain. The main difference is that the disenfranchised rural communities depicted in Thai-language Literature for Life do not have the transnational Nanyang connections (such as Penang and Singapore) to which the Sinophone settler community in southern Thailand has recourse if necessary. This is where the Nanyang trope highlights the circumvention of compulsory assimilation.

In Bangkok, Li Jun's uncle helps him and Yafu find cheap residence in a Yaowarat communal hostel. After his unsuccessful attempts to find work, Li Jun decides to convert their small flat into a classroom, where he teaches many of the resident children Mandarin. His most diligent student, Xingmei, turns out to be the slumlord's daughter: she takes a liking to her new teacher. Soon thereafter, "Grandpa Bun" (Bao Laoye), a steamed-bun vendor who lives on the second floor, tells Li Jun that a merchant at a nearby Yaowarat clock shop is looking for an accountant and that he recommended Li for the position. Though Li's Bangkok prospects improve after he starts his new job, the slumlord discovers her daughter's admiration for Li and decides that she must quickly marry Xingmei off to the son of a wealthy bank owner, lest she become the future wife of the son of an impoverished rubber tapper. Knowing that her daughter will oppose the arrangement, the slumlord Ah Zhen hatches a devious scheme to make it appear as if she is taking Xingmei on a long vacation to Penang, Kuala Lumpur, Singapore, and Hong Kong. Yet the daughter of Li Jun's employer overhears Ah Zhen making arrangements with her go-between and reveals the plan to Li Jun and Yafu. They devise a counterplot to expose the corrupt slumlord, making it appear as though Xingmei has run away. Chastised by all her tenants, Ah Zhen experiences the terror of potentially losing her only daughter and comes to see the error of her ways. Li Jun writes a narrative about his experiences and submits his manuscript to a Sinophone newspaper in Bangkok. Impressed with Li's writing, the newspaper editor invites him to be a featured contributor. At the end of the novel, the editor reminds Li Jun that, since the Sinophone newspaper scene is "in shambles," he cannot expect fame or fortune from his endeavors, but instead the work represents a selfless contribution to cultural sustenance.[57]

With all its predictable twists and turns of plot, *Stormy Yaowarat Road* is a typical melodramatic young adventure narrative. Underneath its sensational exterior, it shares common concerns with other Sinophone popular novels and Thai Literature for Life narratives from the 1960s and 1970s, which expose many of the adverse effects of capitalist development under Thai military dictatorship and American neocolonialism: rampant corruption, drug addiction, gang violence, materialism, the displacement of working communities, and urban slum life.[58] The novels also attempt to reaffirm "life" through either an authorial appeal to or model demonstration of compassion, community, and cultural continuity. This often comes at the conclusion of the narrative, when the various criminals, slumlords, and corrupt businessmen are either dealt some degree of karmic justice or they repent and reform. The humanistic and compassionate Buddhism that permeated the social activism associated with the Literature for Life movement is a central theme of the Sinophone popular novel, in which characters earn a "second shot at humanity" (*chongxin zuoren*).[59]

Sinophone Thai novels also challenge the assimilationist view of Chinese integration by depicting various spheres and strategies of Sino-Thai biculturalism. Works such as *Stormy Yaowarat Road* shed light on less-visible sectors of Sino-Thai society that are clearly not upwardly mobile. These are lower- and working-class communities of hawkers and vendors, migrant workers, small restaurant and shop proprietors, and street performers and artists who inhabit the narrow, hidden alleyways that serve Yaowarat Road and other Bangkok thoroughfares.[60] As a testament to the social challenges facing, as well as contributions made by, poor working-class members of an already long-established Sino-Thai community, Sinophone narratives complement the themes of first-generation immigration and long-term upward mobility that are more central to the Thai-language popular novel. Although the Sinophone novels briefly comment on the decline of Sinophone literacy and fluency among the Sino-Thai community, the narratives do not posit this perspective as part of a zero-sum, cultural preservation-versus-assimilation scheme. Rather, the decline is a by-product of globalization and Westernization. The novels attribute the decline of Sinophone literacy more to the pervasive emphasis on English as a second language during the "American Era" than on compulsory Thai-language education: in fact, the protagonists of *Stormy Yaowarat Road* highly encourage excelling in Thai.

The extant scholarship on Sinophone Thai literature attributes the uniqueness of such works as *Stormy Yaowarat Road* to three aspects of their evocation of Teochew: their use of the Chaoyang-Swatow (Chaoshan) dialect of Teochew (particularly in the spoken dialogues of the texts), their depiction of specific Teochew cultural practices like the region's unique opera (*ngiu*) and tea ceremony (*gongfu cha*), and their emphasis on Teochew cultural and linguistic cultivation and preservation—an emphasis woven into the theme of the narratives. Among the many Sinophone literatures produced outside China, strong Teochew linguistic and cultural influences are particularly prevalent in Sinophone Thai literature.[61]

The Swatow-Bangkok cultural corridor is an important ingredient to the Nanyang imagination of Sinophone Thai literature: the majority of Sinophone authors in Thailand are of Teochew descent, including all nine authors of *Stormy Yaowarat Road*. Many members of the first generation of Sinophone authors (those who began writing in the pre-1949 period before diplomatic relations with mainland China ceased) traveled to Swatow for secondary or university education. During this earlier era, the Swatow-Bangkok corridor had reverberations at both ends, as an old folk proverb that spread across the Teochew-speaking regions of Guangdong province states: "When there is nothing left to eat, pack up your bags and head to Siam."[62] Teochew idioms and popular slang also find their way into the standard Chinese of Sinophone literature from Thailand. In *Stormy Yaowarat Road*, young male characters are called *ah shia* (*a she*), which means something akin to "bloke" in colloquial English. Adults curse children as *za shi gia* (*zao si zai*), or "boys who die young." Another Teochew idiom, *towkay kia lou* (*toujia zoulu*), literally meaning "the boss is leaving," describes the bankruptcy of a department store.[63]

Despite its emphasis on Teochew language and culture, Sinophone Thai literature is not a distinctly "Chinese" cultural or linguistic counterpart to a separate "Thai" sphere. Thai Teochew in fact differs from Teochew as spoken in China. Cut off from the ancestral land for more than thirty years during the Cold War, Thai Teochew remained more archaic, using older vocabulary that became "Mandarinized" in mainland China over the same period. Thai Teochew is also unique for its linguistic "Thainess," expressed by its prominent incorporation of Thai vocabulary: this is a key aspect of Thai Teochew in Sinophone Thai literature. Like Malay words in Sinophone Malaysian literature, Thai terms typically appear as phonetic transliterations into Chinese characters. It is the Teochew (not Mandarin) readings of these characters that most resemble the Thai pronunciation.[64] These Thai terms often appear in spoken dialogue and are sometimes followed by a parenthetical explanation, such as in the phrase *khun khru rap čhotmai* (*kun ke le zhumai*), or "the teacher has received a letter."[65] There are many instances in which no translation or explanation of Thai terms is provided. In *Stormy Yaowarat Road*, these include proper names of Thai places (Betong, Hat Yai, Ubon, and Talat Phlu) and people (Phanni). Beyond this, they also include specific Thai titles and terms such as *phi* (*pi*, an elder sibling), *ai* (an exclamatory prefix for a man, akin to saying "that damn . . ."), *khun* (*kun*, a polite form of address, such as "sir" or "miss," but literally meaning "you"), *nai* (Mr.),[66] *luang* (*luan*, "royal" or "noble," also an official ranking), *rai* (*lai*, a unit of land measurement, approximately 1,600 square meters), *talat* (*da le*, market), and *wat* (*yue*, a Buddhist temple). In the Chinese script, many of these nouns follow Thai (as opposed to standard Chinese) grammatical patterns, appearing before rather than after descriptive modifiers. Occasionally, there are redundant hybridizations like *batu yu*, a combination of *plathu* (Thai: mackerel) and *yu* (Mandarin: fish),[67] with *pla* and *yu* both meaning "fish."

As the Sinophone sphere of Sino-Thai biculturalism, Sinophone Thai literature is itself a site of creolization that cannot be culturally dissociated from its Thainess. Despite the narrative differences between Sinophone and Thai-language popular novels in their engagement with the history of Chinese integration, their processes of creolization are reciprocal: the Sinophone creolizes with the Thai and the Thai creolizes with the Sinophone in both languages of literary composition.

DOMESTIC SAGAS OF CULTURAL ADAPTATION AND UPWARD MOBILITY

The proliferation of Thai-language popular novels on Sino-Thai history beginning in the late 1980s refutes the hardline assimilation narrative of Chinese integration in Thailand by showing how Sino-Thai communities have adapted to their circumstances and maintained outlets for cultural continuity. These are invariably melodramatic narratives of penniless immigrant Teochew coolies (*čhapkang*) or petty merchants (*phokha*) who depart from Swatow to travel across the "South Seas" (*thale tai*) in the "piglet cabin" (*chan lukmu*) of a ship and who arrive in the "southern kingdom" (*phaendin thang tai*) of Siam/Thailand (Siam Lo/Mư̄ang Thai) between 1910 and 1945 with "a sleeping mat and a pillow" (*sư̄aphư̄n monbai*) as their only possessions.[68] By good fortune, these initially destitute men rise to become modern "merchant lords" (*čhao sua*).[69] Their upward mobility becomes the "Thai dream" of the translingual South Seas imagination in nearly every popular Thai-language novel about Chinese immigrants.

Despite being largely cut off from China after 1949, and despite grappling with periodic assimilation policies under successive military dictatorships, the immigrant protagonists' adaptation to life in Bangkok does not produce culture shock, nor does it require total assimilation. Rather, Siam/Thailand appears as a land of endless opportunity, despite the straitened circumstances under which the protagonists arrive and despite the domestic hardships they face. Rather than dashing the immigrant's dream of the "golden peninsula," these post–Cold War Sino-Thai narratives bring the dreams of even the poorest of coolies to sunny realization, thereby revising the generally bleak tone of Literature for Life or earlier Sinophone narratives describing urban relocation in Thailand.

As melodramatic family sagas aimed at a nationwide audience, popular Sino-Thai novels rewrite Thailand's national assimilation narrative through the lens of multigenerational Sino-Thai families, headed by an immigrant patriarch and spanning the twentieth century. Readers are invited to (re)learn and (re)claim biculturalism by imagining Sino-Thai identity "through the medium of the Thai language."[70] This allows Thailand to reimagine itself as a nation that has historically welcomed and accommodated Chinese immigrants, tolerated biculturalism by demanding neither segregation nor total assimilation, and provided a wealth of opportunities for upward mobility.

The 180-degree turn in Thai literature's Chinese integration narrative, from (lamenting) assimilation to (celebrating) accommodation, is best exemplified by the immigrant family sagas of the second-generation Sino-Thai author Botan (penname of Supa Sirising, 1945-). Botan has written more than fifty popular novels spanning five decades, including many that have won national literary awards, such as *That Woman's Name Is Boonrawd* (*Phuying khon nan chư̆ Bunrot*, 1981), a story about a "G.I. bride" in northeastern Thailand during the American War in Vietnam who struggles in the face of social stigma to assert financial independence. Besides writing novels, Botan has worked as a journalist and editor of women's magazines. Along with her husband, she founded Chomromdek, a publishing company that mainly publishes young adult and children's fiction, in the early 1980s.[71] Botan wrote her first novel, *Letters from Thailand* (*Čhotmai čhak Mư̆ang Thai*, 1969), while a student at Bangkok's Chulalongkorn University. Winner of the 1969 SEATO (Southeast Asian Treaty Organization) Prize for Literature,[72] this landmark work about a Chinese immigrant patriarch and his Sino-Thai family in Bangkok was the first of its kind in modern Thai literature. As a collection of a hundred letters written by the Teochew protagonist to his mother back in his home village, the novel exposes interethnic stereotypes in Thailand while critiquing urban bourgeois culture and the rampant spread of materialism under the military dictatorships of Sarit and Thanom. Though upwardly mobile as the owner of a Chinese confection chain, the protagonist interprets any objectionable social behavior he witnesses—such as excessive drinking, gambling, and fighting—as uniquely "Thai." Throughout the novel, he laments his alienation from his Sino-Thai wife and children, whom he has "utterly failed" to shield from what he sees as "complete assimilation" and the total surrender of their "Chinese identities" to Thai culture.[73]

Whereas *Letters* garnered attention for its critical portrayal of Thai society through the perspective of a hardheaded immigrant, another Sino-Thai novel by Botan, *Before the Fog Lifts* (*Kon sai mok lư̆an*, 1987), written two decades later during the period of historical revisionism, represents a major reversal in tone toward Chinese integration. Rather than signifying a forced "surrender" to assimilation, the South Seas imagination of *Before the Fog Lifts* portrays the Swatow-Bangkok corridor as an historical conduit of Teochew cultural continuity in the new homeland, where Teochew serves as the Sinophone lingua franca of all Sino-Thai communities, regardless of regional background.[74] Bangkok in the 1920s and 1930s appears as a place where Teochews feel even more "at home" than in other regions of Guangdong province. In this "land of plenty," where there is room for biculturalism, the protagonists are less resistant to appropriating Thainess.

At the beginning of *Before the Fog Lifts*, Botan introduces two distant cousins, Cheng and Nguan Seng, who emigrate from China together:

> In the year 2465 of the Buddhist Era [1922], two young men set out on foot from a small district in Chaoyang, Teochew for the port of Swatow, looking for a way out of China to go make a living in Siam.
>
> At the time, the Teochew region was experiencing a severe drought. . . . Seeking refuge in the provincial capital or other provinces was considered too risky as famine ravaged a number of other provinces and cities as well. Then there was the problem of accents and different dialects, which were basically separate languages. . . . Regional discrimination and intolerance was yet another consideration. . . .
>
> News came occasionally from relatives and friends who had made the voyage to the South Seas and returned to visit or sent their children back to study the language of their ancestors. The news was typically good, and it seemed that there was no better place than Siam.
>
> The Siamese did not demonstrate blatant hatred for the Chinese as in other countries. . . . The king managed affairs-of-state properly, asking only that his subjects demonstrate sufficient loyalty and that they act in accordance with the law. . . . Since they were considered foreigners, they did not have rights to buy land under their own names, but they could easily rent it from government officials whose children were not interested in farming even though they had inherited land.
>
> The Siamese were not at all troubled by the religious beliefs of the Chinese or that they upheld their custom of ancestor worship. They could erect small or large gravestones depending on their finances, and there were many shrines, vegetarian restaurants, and Chinese temples scattered there as well. For the most part, the language spoken in the Chinese communities of Siam was Teochew.[75]

Botan portrays Siam as a safe haven where specifically Teochew linguistic and cultural continuity is possible. Of course, unlike the protagonist of *Letters* who does not emigrate until 1945 and is immediately cut off from the family he left behind during the Cold War, Cheng and Nguan Seng emigrate during an earlier period when the Sino-Thai community is still in formation and the assimilatory policies of Phibun and his successors are not yet in place.

Nevertheless, throughout the more than sixty years covered in the narrative, *Before the Fog Lifts* downplays the cultural antagonisms magnified in *Letters*, emphasizing instead intercultural similarities (such as Buddhism) and mutual tolerance for bicultural expression. This ease of transition and accommodation, which serves as a thematic backdrop to the majority of popular Sino-Thai novels, is challenged by the policies of the right-wing dictatorships. Yet the upward mobility afforded by the "American Era" allows the protagonists some leeway to circumvent these policies, as the immigrant patriarchs slowly but daringly expand their investments and endeavors into bigger enterprises and emergent industries. Their wealth allows them to pay off officials as well as send their sons to Hong Kong and Singapore to evade compulsory military service and receive a Sinophone education.

The melodramatic conflict that develops in *Before the Fog Lifts* is not the result of interethnic tension and forced assimilation, but springs from a family feud between Nguan Seng and Cheng over how best to make a living in Siam. Their common ancestor was an innovative doctor who authored a Chinese medical text, but forbade his descendants from using the book to make money. After arriving in Bangkok, Nguan Seng invites Cheng to conjointly run a pharmaceutical factory producing remedies listed in the text, but Cheng refuses. The entrepreneurial-minded Nguan Seng accuses Cheng of being irrationally afraid of incurring the wrath of their ancestor. Nguan Seng reads passages to Cheng to prove to him that the wording in the text is not as strict as Cheng believes, and that its author anticipated that future modification of his instructions would be necessary:

> It is written down in ancient wording right here: "As the world continues to change, new diseases are born for which this text can be used. Reforms are acceptable but complete alterations are not. A doctor cannot oppress the people. Help humanity with diligence." All of this proves that the medical text can be reformed along with changing times and needs.[76]

Nguan Seng initially uses the text to hawk Chinese herbal remedies, but gradually he expands his business and eventually launches his own giant pharmaceutical company.

Since Cheng feels more suited to horticultural pursuits than mercantile ones, he decides not to get involved in comanaging Nguan Seng's business. He marries Kieo, the daughter of his Sino-Thai uncle and Tai-Thai aunt, in order to use her name and citizenship to purchase land. Whereas Nguan Seng commands a large fortune, Cheng and his family earn a respectable living managing a small herb, or *samunphrai*,[77] plantation that supplies Nguan Seng's company. Though he spends much of his life resenting his more prosperous cousin, Cheng witnesses Nguan Seng's spoiled children squander their money and opportunities, such as private schooling and study abroad. Cheng sends his children to Thai school, where they become diligent, upstanding citizens. In the early 1980s, long after Nguan Seng's death, Cheng's grandchildren collaborate with Nguan Seng's grandchildren by using their inheritance to open a hospital in Bangkok that provides charity care to poor patients. It is only at this point that an elderly Cheng, standing before Nguan Seng's grave, forgives his cousin and releases his lingering resentments (the metaphorical fog-lifting alluded to in the novel's title).[78] Allegorized by the modification of their ancestor's medical text, Cheng and Nguan Seng represent two modes of modest cultural adaptation and upward mobility in the historical process of Chinese integration in Thailand.

The upward mobility of the Chinese immigrant protagonists in the Thai-language popular novel always requires some degree of collaboration with the established Sino-Thai or Tai-Thai community. This often means marrying a local-born woman with Thai citizenship (either Tai-Thai or Sino-Thai), even if one already has a wife (and children) back in China. In many Sino-Thai popular novels, the immigrant protagonist's strategic polygamy is an important catalyst for the family melodrama that accompanies the protagonist's transition to the upper stratum of the Thai bourgeoisie. This is best demonstrated in *Through the Pattern of the Dragon* (*Lot lai mangkon*, 1989), a popular novel by Praphatson Sewikun (1948-) that represents the pinnacle of the Sino-Thai renaissance in the post–Cold War environment of historical revisionism.

Through the Pattern of the Dragon captures the extension of the translingual South Seas trope—and the archetypal Chinese immigrant figure in Thailand—beyond Sino-Thai authorship in the national imaginary. Of part-Tai and Portuguese descent, Praphatson is a former diplomat who has authored several best-selling novels. He is best known for *Time in a Bottle* (*Wela nai khuat kaeo*, 1985), a novel about living in a middle-class Bangkok household with divorced parents. Praphatson grew up in the Yaowarat district and was fascinated by the Sino-Thai merchant community that surrounded him. With an "overwhelming prevalence of dialogue," his novels are easily adapted for film or television.[79] *Through the Pattern of the Dragon* was made into a wildly popular television serial drama in 1992.

The novel, narrated by the granddaughter of the family patriarch, tells the story of Liang Sư̆phanit. After coming to Siam, Grandpa Ah Liang works as a coolie hauling rice at the Ratchawong Pier on the Chao Phraya River in Bangkok. He opens a coffee shop just before the 1941 Japanese invasion. Following the war, Ah Liang begins to produce textiles, market trendy clothing, and eventually opens investment, security, and banking firms in Bangkok. In the process of his upward mobility, Ah Liang makes the necessary adjustments to adapt and integrate in Thailand. He takes a Thai surname, combining his Teochew surname, Sư̆, with the Thai word for "commerce" to become Sư̆phanit.[80] He marries the Sino-Thai Ah Niam so he can purchase the land necessary to build his textile factory, even though he has a wife from an arranged marriage and two sons back in China.

The novel portrays Ah Niam as an idealized Thai mother: she is generous, respectful, self-sacrificing, and particularly wise in compassionate Theravada Buddhist practice. Once Ah Liang establishes himself, he provides (illicit) passage for his first wife and sons to flee the Communist revolution in China and join him in Bangkok. The arrival of the "China-wife," who is not depicted favorably, disrupts the family order. Devious, unscrupulous, greedy, uncultured, and constantly scheming to assert her position as the matriarch (*mia luang*) of the Sư̆phanit clan, she is a stereotyped caricature of the *čhek* or *Čhin mai* ("fresh-off-the-boat Chinese") in Thailand. As in other Sino-Thai narratives, the male patriarch's polygamy is not targeted as the source of domestic trouble: he is exonerated by the necessity of upward mobility. As for his two China-born sons, Ah Liang sends them to Hong Kong for higher education almost immediately after they arrive.[81] Ah Liang's children help him establish a transnational investment empire in Bangkok, Hong Kong, and Singapore.

However, Ah Liang has to repeatedly bail out his children after they make unwise and selfish decisions with the family's finances and businesses. The novel projects the immigrant figure as the unshakeable bedrock of frugality and simplicity in an environment of excess: Ah Liang's Teochew surname, Sư̆, means "stone" (*shi*). Yet rather than a critique of Thai society, the novel uses the immigrant figure to demonstrate respect and appreciation for the land of settlement. Liang Sưphanit repeatedly puts his feelings toward Thailand in Buddhist terms as the place to which he owes a karmic "debt of gratitude" (*mi bunkhun*). At the end of the novel, when his doctor suggests that he go abroad for what might be life-saving surgery, Ah Liang refuses, saying that it is his dying wish for his spirit to be reincarnated in Thailand.[82] The narrator overhears her grandfather's explanation to his children:

> Grandpa said he owed a debt of gratitude to Thailand, because it gave him food and tools, as well as the strength required to raise his children. Although Grandpa probably always believed he was Chinese, and did not overly try to behave like a Thai as some of his friends did, he believed he was a Chinese who "was grateful and recognized virtue" and therefore would always remember the merits of the land that had transformed him into somebody.[83]

As a hagiographical portrait of the self-made (yet eternally grateful) and upwardly mobile Sino-Thai patriarch and "merchant lord," Ah Liang in many ways demonstrates the proper bearing of a benevolent Thai king who gradually recedes from view as he ages but still occasionally steps in to resolve the disputes of his kingdom (his family and business).

In this sense, *Through the Pattern of the Dragon* participates in a cultural reevaluation of the historical role of the Sino-Thai "merchant lord" (*čhao sua*) vis-à-vis the traditional Tai-Thai gentry (*phudi*). Toward the end of the novel, as the narrative moves into the late 1970s and early 1980s, members of the Sưphanit family discuss the impending marriage of Ah Liang's grandson, Rawi, to a young woman from an aristocratic Tai-Thai family long in steep financial decline. The narrator's aunt remarks:

> I once heard a saying that "ten merchants cannot take care of you as well as one nobleman." But now they should say that "a thousand noblemen cannot take care of you nearly as well as one merchant." It seems these days that all the old aristocrats and royal officials are rushing to link themselves to big businessmen.[84]

Though properly demonstrating a "debt of gratitude" to Thailand's benevolent accommodation of Chinese immigrants, *Through the Pattern of the Dragon* also joins with the historical revisionists of the 1980s to challenge the martial-royalist monopoly on the narrative of national progress, celebrating the crucial contributions of the merchant and largely Sino-Thai urban bourgeoisie.

This revisionism emphasizes multigenerational Sino-Thai biculturalism as persisting through and outlasting demands for assimilation. As family melodrama, the Sino-Thai novel alternates between two spheres. The "inner sphere" involves the domestic intrigues of large, upwardly mobile Sino-Thai families. Here, demonstrations of "Chineseness," through the use of Teochew idioms and adherence to patriarchal values, such as preference for sons and arranged marriage, still mark a point of cultural difference and intergenerational tension. The "outer sphere" involves the public adoption and display of recognizably and acceptably "Thai" patterns of social behavior among Sino-Thai communities. The crossovers or passages between these two spheres are relatively seamless, absorbing Sino-Thai biculturalism into an accommodation narrative asserting the plurality of and fluid movements between cultures and languages.

Yet as in Sinophone Thai narratives, biculturalism in Thai-language popular novels does not depart from but in fact illustrates creolization. Authors frequently phoneticize Teochew words using the Thai script, especially when capturing spoken dialogue. Sometimes translations accompany the Teochew words, consciously highlighting lessons in exotic Chineseness for readers. In *Through the Pattern of the Dragon*, Ah Liang lectures his children on the meaning of *ngi* (*yi*, virtue) in front of a calligraphy scroll (with the character *yi* drawn on it) hanging on the wall under a framed painting of an ant (a homophone with "virtue" in Teochew). Ah Liang reveres the ant as a symbol of virtue in his lecture to his children: "The ant is a strong and hardworking insect. It knows endurance and industriousness. No matter how hard the rain falls or how hot the sun shines or how far it must travel, the ant never gets discouraged or tired in its search to find food."[85] Here, the ant (*mot*) becomes a totem of Sino-Thai virtue and diligence. Ironically, the narrative never mentions the dragon (*mangkon*), which is a more paradigmatic totem of Chineseness and part of the novel's title. Perhaps a more apt title for the novel is *Through the Pattern of the Ant*.

Ah Liang's lecture on *ngi* exemplifies how Thai-language popular novels often use Teochew terms, rather than more common Central Thai ones, to emphasize a creole worldview. For example, they refer to China as "Mount Tang" (Tưng Sua) instead of the standard Mưang Čhin. Newly arrived Chinese immigrants are the "new Tang" (*sin Tưng*) rather than "Chinamen" (*čhek*) or "fresh-off-the-boat Chinese" (*Čhin mai*). Sino-Thai children are called "children of the Tang" (*Tưng nang kia*) and Tai-Thai children are called "southern barbarian children" (*huang nang kia*). The presence of Teochew in the popular Thai novel is not simply a performance of a Chinese biculturalism that serves as a moment of exotic deviation from a Central Thai standard. Many Teochew words, as well as Sino-Thai patterns of speaking and writing Thai, are so creolized with Thai that they require no translation in the texts. These include familial terms such as father (*pa* or *tia*), mother (*ma*), grandfather (*a kong*), grandmother (*a ma*), older brother (*hia*), older sister (*čhe*), younger brother (*ti*), and younger sister (*muay*). Teochew personal pronouns in the Thai script best reflect these creolizing processes. Much of the Sino-Thai community uses Teochew words for "I/me" (*ua*), "you" (*lư*), and "he/she" (*i*) when speaking Thai to bypass the hierarchical or relational complexities that dictate personal pronoun usage in Central Thai. When these personal pronouns are pluralized, they do not take on the Teochew plural suffix *-nang*, but rather the Thai plural prefix *phuak-*, such as in *phuak ua* ("we/us"), *phuak lư* ("you" [plural]), and *phuak i* ("they/them"), thus representing pidginized and creolized vocabulary.

The South Seas imagination of Sino-Thai popular novels addresses the competing assimilation and accommodation "success stories" of Chinese integration in Thailand. Reflecting upon a persistent biculturalism aided by archipelagic Sinophone connections in the South Seas that help circumvent the assimilationist policies of successive Thai military dictatorships, contemporary Sino-Thai literature attests to a history of accommodation and plurality both within the ranks of the urban working class (reflected by the Sinophone sequential novel) and the upwardly mobile bourgeoisie (the Thai-language popular novel). However, the processes of translingual creolization that cross-pollinate standard Chinese with spoken Thai and written Thai with spoken Teochew reveal this biculturalism not as a representation of two immutable cultures, but rather as continually creolizing ones. The historical success story of Chinese integration cannot be reduced to a choice between biculturalism (preserving a distinct language and culture while wholly adding another) and assimilation (conforming to a normative Tai-Thai standard through erasure of difference). Rather, the popular Sino-Thai integration narrative recognizes multiple sites of ongoing creolization in Thai literature and culture.

Conclusion

On a Monday evening in early January 2009, approximately 1.7 million Singaporeans—just short of half the nation's population—tuned in for the grand finale of a hit television serial drama entitled *The Little Nyonya* (*Xiao niangre*). Over a span of thirty-four episodes on MediaCorp Channel 8 beginning in November 2008, *The Little Nyonya* averaged nearly a million viewers per broadcast, making it the most popular Singaporean television program aired in two decades. Subtitled in English, the show's appeal crossed ethnic, linguistic, and generational divides among Singaporean audiences: Suria, Singapore's primary Malay-language network, subsequently picked up the Mandarin-language drama and dubbed it in Malay. Both the Mandarin and Malay versions of *The Little Nyonya* were later broadcast nationally in neighboring Malaysia, where they similarly garnered high ratings in 2009.[1]

To understand *The Little Nyonya* phenomenon, one cannot simply look to its prototypically melodramatic plot line of romantic intrigue, its overwrought acting, or even its array of attractive celebrities. The show's appeal can be understood as one evolution in a Baba-Nyonya "renaissance" in Singapore, an ongoing but sporadic cultural revival that ironically emerged alongside (and in contrast to) official efforts to "re-Sinicize" Chinese Singaporeans in the 1980s through state campaigns demanding they speak Mandarin to each other and practice Confucian values. Following similar revivals across the Malaysian border in Melaka's Old Town and Penang's Georgetown (two cities which share a colonial heritage with Singapore as former Straits

Settlements), the Baba renaissance included efforts to restore and preserve the colonial Peranakan architecture in Singapore's predominantly Baba-Nyonya neighborhoods of Emerald Hill and Katong.[2] On the Singaporean theater scene, the renaissance included the staging of plays like Stella Kon's *Emily of Emerald Hill* (1985), in which the Nyonya protagonist not only speaks Baba Malay, Singlish, and English, but also offers an onstage cooking demonstration of *babi buah keluak*, a Peranakan dish made from pork and a kind of black, nutty, milky fruit from a tree grown in mangrove swamps.[3]

The Little Nyonya evidently tapped into this latent postcolonial fascination with the Peranakan figure among its Singaporean audience: imagining, recreating, and staging Baba-Nyonya material culture, the show generated devoted viewers across varying demographics. Detailed shots of Peranakan architecture, interior design, costume, and cuisine were just as vital to the production process as those of action and dialogue, whether highlighting the bright floral patterns of the Nyonya's *sarong kebaya* (Malay: skirt and blouse) or the ornate spread of a long dining table replete with colorful porcelain, embroidered cloths, and various pastries such as red and white *kuih* (Hokkien: cake). The show's theme song syncretized modern pop sensibilities and classical Southeast Asian styles, using the xylophonic notes of the gamelan—traditional Javanese orchestral music—to lead into and accent the keyboards and acoustic guitars of a Mandarin pop ballad.

The *Little Nyonya*'s reconstruction of Baba-Nyonya material culture demanded a significant financial investment from the show's producers and required its screenwriters and actors to conduct historical and ethnographic research, as few of them were of Peranakan background. Those who were, such as lead actress Jeanette Aw, admitted possessing little knowledge of Baba-Nyonya history and material culture.[4] Shot on-site in Singapore, Melaka, and Penang, the show's setting traversed the geopolitically partitioned boundaries of Singapore and Malaysia. *The Little Nyonya* narrates the two nations' common Peranakan heritage through twentieth-century historical events that precipitated a Baba-Nyonya cultural decline and general withdrawal from sociopolitical visibility in both countries: the Great Depression and economic strife of the 1930s under British colonialism, the Japanese invasion and occupation (1941–45), and Malayan (1957), Malaysian (1963), and finally Singaporean (1965) independence. From the outset, the show's setting imperatively shifts from a hypermodern, contemporary Singapore to the older, more preserved Peranakan spaces of Penang and Melaka, where a progressive young Chinese Singaporean visits her grandmother and (re)discovers her creolized Nyonya roots.

Although *The Little Nyonya* envisions creolization as a common, desirable national heritage and point of identification for its Malaysian and Singaporean audiences, its predominantly Mandarin dialogue (with English subtitling) draws attention to the pervasive influence of Singapore's policy of multiracialism in limiting the show's capacity to fulfill that vision. Conforming to a Singaporean law requiring Mandarin for all Sinophone television programming (Baba-Nyonyas are also racialized as "Chinese" in both Singaporean and Malaysian discourse) and reflecting Singapore's promotion of English as interethnic medium of translation and communication, actors perform and audiences consume Baba-Nyonya history and culture through the very structures of colonization and racialization that the Peranakan figure symbolically transcends. Although characters in *The Little Nyonya* were occasionally required to perform a traditional Malay *pantun* (lyric or folk song)—a forced rupture that registers noticeable discomfort on the actors' faces—the demand for Mandarin fluency certainly affected the show's casting (Qi Yuwu, a resident actor from China, played the lead Baba role of Chen Xi) as well as its presentation of Baba-Nyonya culture (Jeanette Aw, the show's most prominent Nyonya actress, initially played a mute character, a choice some critics attributed to her allegedly "bad Mandarin").[5] Historically, Mandarin was not a common language spoken by the Baba-Nyonya community, whose lingua franca throughout the colonial era was their Baba Malay creole. After Baba Malay, English followed by Sinitic languages such as Hokkien and Teochew were much more common among the Baba-Nyonyas than Mandarin, and this certainly would have been the case during the historical era portrayed in the television show.[6] In terms of the show's dialogue, it is not the creolized Peranakan culture and language of the past that bridges the racial divides of the (trans)national viewership in the present, but rather the English subtitles' translation of a racially Sinicized and linguistically Mandarinized postcolonial reimagining of Baba-Nyonya culture that does so.

The language issue in *The Little Nyonya* is of interest here not in regard to the program's historical inauthenticity, but rather as a reflection of how the show's postcolonial recuperation of creolization, like all narrations of the past, can never be a "pure" replication totally transcendent of the political present. By mediating Baba-Nyonya culture through the governing linguistic framework of Singaporean multiracialism, but also challenging that framework by envisioning a creolized heritage (as opposed to a collection of monoracial groupings) as a shared emblem of Singaporean and Malaysian national cultures, the show constitutes its own mode of creolization as an ongoing process of cultural formation and political (re)negotiation. *The Little Nyonya* crosses the Malaysian border to express a regional affiliation and common cross-cultural origin in the interethnic exchanges between settler and indigenous languages and cultures. Yet the show also reconciles such expression with the dominant visions of national culture that have respectively defined and governed those borders since independence. In this sense, *The Little Nyonya* highlights precisely the possibilities, desires, tensions, and contradictions inherent in what I have described throughout this book as the Nanyang imagination, or the trope of the "South Seas." The show brings to audiovisual life the transcolonial, transnational, and translingual significations of the Nanyang that seek to de-racialize national culture (specifically in Singapore).

The case of *The Little Nyonya* is an example of how the Nanyang trope can provide a potential space of critical inquiry in other modes of cultural production beyond written literature. Whereas written literature provides its own form of audiovisual experience, the visual arts, music, theater, television, and cinema represent distinct narrative and aesthetic possibilities (as well as limitations) for visualizing, vocalizing, and sensing the Nanyang in ways that complement or perhaps diverge from those of "writing the South Seas" as described here. From the Shanghai and Hong Kong-based Shaw Brothers' twentieth-century development of a media empire in the "various dependent territories in the South Seas,"[7] to Tsai Ming-liang's cinematic return to Malaysia from Taiwan in films such as *I Don't Want to Sleep Alone* (*Hei yan quan*, 2006); or from the recent cinema of Singaporean directors Royston Tan, Eric Khoo, and Jack Neo who mix Singlish, Hokkien, Malay, Cantonese, Mandarin, and Tamil in their spoken dialogue to twenty-first-century Thai television dramas that mix Teochew and Thai such as *The Last Petal of the Peony* (*Botan klip sutthai*) and *The Song Brothers Clan* (*Ti trakun Song*), the transcolonial, transnational, and translingual dimensions outlined in this book underscore these Nanyang representations as well.

Perhaps more critical to further exploration of the Nanyang imagination than its appearances in other media is its role as a postcolonial trope in the literatures of other Southeast Asian countries that remain beyond the scope of this book, especially Indonesia and the Philippines as two of the largest archipelagic states in the world. With respect to postcolonial analyses of the archipelagic consciousness, these two nations occupy important historical positions in the territorial and epistemological decolonization of the "Global South."[8] In 1955, following their ambassadors' attendance at the African-Asian Conference in Bandung, Indonesia, Presidents Sukarno and Magsaysay declared their countries "archipelagic nations" to oppose the homogenizing demands of the capitalist and communist nations in the Cold War formations of global blocs.[9]

The colonial histories of Chinese migration, settlement, and integration in Indonesia and the Philippines reproduce many of the settler-indigenous dynamics in the other Southeast Asian societies discussed here: the creation of commercial niches in colonial port cities such as Batavia and Manila, sporadic episodes of anti-Sinitic violence carried out by Western colonial regimes both suspicious of and reliant on Chinese laborers and middlemen (the Spanish on Luzon in the seventeenth century and the Dutch on Java in the eighteenth century), and the long-term localization and relative indigenization of mixed-ethnic creole communities (Peranakans and Mestizos) culturally distinct from the later wave of new Chinese immigrants who began arriving in the late nineteenth century. Likewise, the postcolonial histories of the two nations thematically converge with many of the national contexts discussed here, featuring nativist education and economic policies, US-supported right-wing dictatorships (Suharto's New Order and the presidency of Ferdinand Marcos) characterized by extended periods of martial law and anticommunist counterinsurgencies, military coups, and moments of massive civic demonstrations and calls for democratization.

Of course, policies and attitudes toward Chinese integration have differed significantly in the two countries: whereas anti-Sinitic violence has often been a feature of broader national violence (whether directed at communists in 1965 or the bourgeoisie in 1998) in postcolonial Indonesia, the postcolonial Philippines has pursued a trajectory more similar to that of Thailand, making possible "genuine assimilation" and "full citizenship."[10] In the post–Cold War (and post-Marcos) era, the Philippines has, much like Thailand, also witnessed a resurgent interest in epic narratives of Chinese integration, creolization, and upward mobility in popular national language (in this case Tagalog) media.[11] As archipelagic republics, Indonesia and the Philippines merit separate treatment to examine whether, or how, the Nanyang imagination contests or reflects visions of national culture and literature in the two countries.[12]

Unlike Indonesia and the Philippines, the national contexts discussed herein (China, Malaysia, Singapore, and Thailand) are not (officially or physically) archipelagic republics, yet this is precisely why the archipelagic organizational principle of the Nanyang imagination plays such a critical role in upsetting their dominant paradigms of national literature and culture, revealing how they are limited by views of ethnicity and language as bound to a single, primordial territory. Underscoring the archipelagic principle of the Nanyang in the various literary texts illuminates four critically repressed conditions of their national contexts. Emphasizing the centrality of the sea not as a static entity, obstacle, or barrier but as a fluid and dynamic space facilitating interchange, the archipelagic principle first demonstrates how the Nanyang, as a cross-cultural imagination, locates cultural roots in moments of contact resulting from overseas movements and arrivals. Though these overseas movements may not always literally occur by ship and link the same two points in one direction, writing the South Seas affirms the importance of historical sea-crossings and the multidirectional network they facilitated. Second, the Nanyang's archipelagic principle puts the postcolonial cultural and political dynamics of its ongoing resignification in conversation with other tropical archipelagoes of postcolonial literary evocation, namely the Caribbean and the Pacific Islands, where the centrality of the sea (and the contacts it has historically facilitated) has inspired the cross-cultural cultivation of regional, multilingual, creolized expressions of national literature as an ongoing process of becoming rather than being. Third, the archipelagic principle distinguishes the Nanyang (a maritime Sinophone concept foregrounding creolization) from Southeast Asia (a Western imperial projection emphasizing the historical partition and regional nonintegration of discrete terrestrial nations/national cultures). Finally, the archipelagic concept contrasts the Nanyang (a maritime New World network) with the continental organizing principle of Chineseness (the diasporic preservation or evolution of a culture prioritizing singular, monodirectional descent from an ancestral land). The archipelagic imagination resurfaces in key literary gestures in the various national contexts discussed here: these include the juxtaposition of the "sea realm" with the continental realm in modern Chinese literature (Chapter 1), the journeys between the islands of Borneo and Taiwan which circumvent the Chinese continent and the Peninsular Malaysian center (Chapter 4), and the reassessment of postcolonial Singapore's obfuscated and repressed cultural and historical ties with the islands of Indonesia (Chapter 5).

Extensions of geography (into other countries and literary contexts like Indonesia and the Philippines) and genre (into other audiovisual media) represent just two of the analytical possibilities for further exploring the Nanyang imagination through a transcolonial, transnational, and translingual framework. Despite the diverse ends to which the Nanyang has been appropriated and deployed by authors in different national and historical contexts, its comparative significance as a postcolonial literary trope can be summed up in terms of three important contributions. First, the Nanyang imagination draws attention to how the history of Chinese travel, migration, settlement, and creolization in Southeast Asia has impacted the formation of nation-states and national cultures in the region. Whether addressing the Republic of China (including its Taiwan incarnation post-1949), the Federated States of Malaysia, the Republic of Singapore, or the Kingdom of Thailand, the allusion to the Nanyang in creative works by authors from these countries reveals how their national imaginaries are not merely the result of modern confrontations and negotiations between Western imperialism and indigenous traditions. The Nanyang imagination exposes the diasporic, racialist, nativist, or assimilationist ideological underpinnings of these nations inspired in large part by histories of Chinese migrant/settler interactions, conflicts, and alliances with indigenous (and sometimes South Asian settler) communities in Southeast Asia. Furthermore, many authors from these countries invoke the Nanyang precisely to contest the ideological orthodoxy of these national imaginaries and reenvision them by articulating cultures of creolization based on localization and acclimation as well as translocal, transethnic, and translingual affiliations.

Second, framing the Nanyang as a creole New World of settlement and, in some cases, upward mobility for Chinese emigrants speaking different languages and arriving at different historical moments over many generations (much like European settlers in the Americas) should disabuse us of a singular notion and category of "Chinese diaspora," the "Overseas Chinese," and even the "Nanyang Chinese."

Rarely (if ever) are the terms "British diaspora," "French diaspora," "Spanish diaspora," and "Portuguese diaspora" applied to communities in the New World of the Americas, as histories of settler colonialism (especially where settlers organized revolutions against the ancestral homeland), intermixture with other settler or indigenous groups, and long-term creolization of languages and dialects have produced Canadians, Mexicans, Colombians, and Brazilians, with contextualized subgroupings such as "Anglo-American" and "French Canadian" among others. Though theories of diaspora emphasize its cultural diversity and heterogeneity (as well as its emergence from experiences of violence, trauma, dislocation, and colonial subjugation),[13] we should not assume that the cultural politics and discursive arenas of Chinese Malaysians, Chinese Singaporeans, and Sino-Thais are similarly or necessarily Chinese, forever pinned to expressions of Chineseness. Though certain transnational linkages may be oriented around the concept of a shared ancestral homeland and cultural heritage, it is the local contextualized use of Sinitic languages that are the legacy of emigration (such as Teochew) and racialist inculcation (such as Mandarin) that makes such communication possible, while differing inflections and admixtures of those languages with non-Sinitic ones produce Malaysianness, Singaporeanness, and Thainess in their respective expressions. As a postcolonial trope envisioning this New World, the Nanyang constitutes an archipelagic network of exchange among different national cultures inflected by processes of Sinophone creolization.

Third, and finally, the idea of the Nanyang reveals that, in addition to conceptual differences between continental and archipelagic imaginations, interregional relations and historical power imbalances between North and South (whether civilizational, imperial, or colonial) are integral to a comparative model of postcolonial studies that has, to date, largely focused on civilizational dichotomies of East and West and the imposition of Western languages and epistemologies on the "Rest."[14] When Sinitic languages or Chinese ethno-nationalist identities are imported by or imposed on settler communities in the Nanyang, or when settlers bring their own visions and modes of sustenance, livelihood, and wealth expansion from the ancestral homeland to bear on the natural environments of Southeast Asia, colonial processes are at work that add a Sinophone dimension to conditions of postcoloniality in the region. Rather than seeing these processes as an alternative to or separate from Western imperialism in Southeast

Asia, they should be understood as engaging and intersecting with (both influencing and influenced by) Western impositions, including industrial capitalism and regimes of racialization. By invoking the trope of the South Seas, Chinese and Southeast Asian postcolonial literature writes back, in time and space, to the confluences of ideological authority claimed by Western empire and ancestral homeland, in order to decolonize the regimes of discursive authority still dominating and delimiting the expressive possibilities of national culture in the present.

CHINESE AND THAI GLOSSARY

a kong อากง
a ma อาม่า
A Q zhengzhuan 阿Q正傳
a she 阿舍
ai ไอ้
ai 哎
Ananda Mahidol อานันท มหิดล
Annan 安南
"Anwen jiaqi" 安汶假期

Bai Ren 白刃
baihua wen 白話文
baihua yundong 白話運動
bainian guochi 百年國恥
Beiyang 北洋
Bao Laoye 包老爺
batu yu 巴土魚
bogong shu 伯公樹
Botan klip sutthai โบตั๋นกลีบสุดท้าย
"Buyi" 補遺

Can yexing 殘夜行
Cao Xueqin 曹雪芹
Caogen shushi 草根書室
chan lukmu ชั้นลูกหมู
čhao sua เจ้าสัว
Chaoshan 潮汕
Chaozhou 潮州
Chaozhou jiazu 潮州家族

čhapkang จับกัง
čharoen เจริญ
chat-sasana-kasat ชาติ ศาสนา กษัตริย์
čhe เจ๊
čhek เจ๊ก
Chen Lianqing 陳煉青
"Chen xing" 辰星
Chen Yingshang 陳英賞
Čhin จีน
Čhin mai จีนใหม่
Chin Sophonpanich ชิน โสภณพนิช
Chit Phumisak จิตร ภูมิศักดิ์
Chomromdek ชมรมเด็ก
chongxin zuoren 重新做人
chunü zuo 處女作
cuozhu nai 厝主奶

Da Po 大坡
da zuojia 大作家
dadi zhi mu 大地之母
da le 噠叻
"Dang wo si shi" 當我死時
dangdihua 當地化
de 德
dianying 電影
difang secai 地方色彩
dongfang 東方
Dongnan Ya 東南亞
Dongyang 東洋
dute xing 獨特性

ertong wenxue 兒童文學

fan 番 / 蕃
fanying cishi cidi 反映此時此地
"Feibang" 誹謗
"Fengyu shanshui" 風雨山水

gongfu cha 功夫茶
gongsi 公司

Guiqiao 歸僑
guofan 過番
guojia zhuyi 國家主義
guomin 國民
Guoyu 國語
guxiang 故鄉
"Guxiang" 故鄉

hai 海
"Hai shijian" 海世間
"Haijiao di guxing" 海角底孤星
Han 漢
"Han ba" 旱魃
Hanzu 漢族
"He'an chuanshuo" 河岸傳説
"He kou" 河口
Hei yan quan 黑眼圈
hia เฮีย
Honglou meng 紅樓夢
Hongshulin 紅樹林
Hua 華
Huafeng zhoubao 華風週報
huang nang kia ฮวงหนั่งเกี้ย
huang wen ye zi 荒文野字
Huang Zhengfu 黃征夫
Huang Zunxian 黃遵憲
Huaqiao 華僑
Huaren 華人
huawai 化外
Huawen 華文
"Huayuan chengshi" 花園城市
huiguan 會館

i อี

"Ji ge wenti" 幾個問題
Jiao feng 蕉風
jielong xiaoshuo 接龍小說
Jining ren 吉寧人
jiuguo 救國

jiuren 救人

"Kaiwang Zhongguo de manchuan" 開往中國的慢船
"Kan gao de jieguo" 看稿的結果
"Ke bei" 刻背
Kejia 客家
Kejia zhi ge 客家之歌
kenhuang 墾荒
Khamsing Srinawk คำสิงห์ ศรีนอก
khun คุณ
khun khru rap čhotmai คุณครูรับจดหมาย
koutou hua 口頭話
kouyu 口語
"Kuangren riji" 狂人日記
kun 坤
kun ke le zhumai 坤嗑叻祝邁

lai 萊
Lao Khamhom ลาว คำหอม
Le bao 叻報
Li Jun 李俊
Li Qingliang 李慶良
Li Youzhong 李友忠
Lianhe zaobao 聯合早報
Liu Na'ou 劉吶鷗
lư ลื้อ
lu shijian 陸世間
Lu Xun 魯迅
luan 鑾
luang หลวง
Lukčhin ลูกจีน
Luo Fangbo 羅芳伯
Luo Huasheng 落花生
Luo Maodeng 羅懋登
Luotuo xiangzi 駱駝祥子

"M de shizong" M的失蹤
ma ม้า
Ma Hua 馬華
"Ma Hua juyun de jinzhan" 馬華劇運的進展

Ma Huan 馬歡
Ma Sanbao 馬三寶
mada 馬打
mai zhuzai 賣豬仔
Maitian 麥田
Malai guniang 馬來姑娘
Malaiya de yiri 馬來亞的一日
man 蠻
mangkon มังกร
Maocheng ji 貓城記
mi bunkhun มีบุญคุณ
mia luang เมียหลวง
"Mingming niao" 命命鳥
Minjindang 民進黨
minzu zhuyi 民族主義
mot มด
mu 母
Mu Shiying 穆時英
Mưang Čhin เมืองจีน
Mưang Thai เมืองไทย
muay หมวย

Nahan 吶喊
nai 乃
nai นาย
nang หนั่ง
nanguo 南國
nanlai 南來
nanlai zuojia 南來作家
Nantian 南天
Nanxing 南星
Nanyang 南洋
Nanyang Bo 南洋伯
Nanyang Huaqiao 南洋華僑
Nanyang piaoliuji 南洋漂流記
Nanyang qikan 南洋期刊
Nanyang renmin gongheguo beiwang lu 南洋人民共和國備忘錄
Nanyang secai 南洋色彩
Nanyang shangbao 南洋商報
Nanyang shuyu 南洋述遇

Nanzhao 南詔
ngi หงี
ngiu งิ้ว
Ni Longsheng 倪隆盛
Nidhi Eoseewong นิธิ เอียวศรีวงศ์
nong de huabukai 濃得化不開
"Nong de huabukai (Xingjiapo)" 濃得化不開 (星加坡)
"Nong de huabukai zhi er (Xianggang)" 濃得化不開之二 (香港)
nüguo 女國

pa ป้า
Pan Guichang 潘貴昌
Peng Yuhe 彭玉和
phaendin thang tai แผ่นดินทางใต้
phanit พาณิชย์
phi พี่
Phibun พิบูลฯ
phokha พ่อค้า
Phonlachet Kitaworanat พลเชษฐ์ คีตวรนาฏ
phuak พวก
phuak i พวกอี
phuak lư พวกลื้อ
phuak ua พวกอั๊ว
"Phuak Yiu haeng burapha thit lae mưang Thai čhong tưn thoet" พวกยิวแห่งบูรพาทิศและเมืองไทยจงตื่นเถิด
phudi ผู้ดี
pi 丕
pla ปลา
Plaek Phibunsongkhram แปลก พิบูลสงคราม
plathu ปลาทู
po 坡
Pobishe waizhuan 破畢舍外傳
Poluozhou zhi zi 婆羅洲之子
Pridi Banomyong ปรีดี พนมยงค์
Putonghua 普通話

qi 其
Qi Yuwu 戚玉武
qiaomin wenxue 僑民文學
qiaomin yishi 僑民意識

qiaosheng 僑生
qimeng 啟蒙
Qiongyuan kafeixiang 瓊園咖啡香
qita 其他
Qiu Shuyuan 邱菽園

rai ไร่
"Redai yulin" 熱帶雨林
"Rouyan de Bali" 肉艷的巴黎

sae แซ่
samakkhitham สามัคคีธรรม
Sampheng สำเพ็ง
samunphrai สมุนไพร
Sanbao taijian xia Xiyang ji 三寶太監下西洋記
Sarit Thanarat สฤษดิ์ ธนะรัชต์
"Shanghai de hubuwu (Yi ge duanpian)" 上海的狐步舞 (一個斷片)
"Shangren fu" 商人婦
"Shangshi" 傷逝
Shen Senhao 沈森豪
Shenzhou 神州
shi 氏
shi 石
shi wu wai 示無外
Shi Zhecun 施蟄存
shijie 世界
shijie yu 世界語
Shishuo xinyu 世說新語
Shitou ji 石頭記
Shu Qingchun 舒慶春
Shuihu zhuan 水滸傳
"Si zai nanfang" 死在南方
Siam Lo เสี่ยมล้อ
"Sicheng (Beiping de yiwan)" 死城 (北平的一晚)
sihai zhi wai 四海之外
sin Tưng ซินตึ๊ง
Sinlapa phưa chiwit sinlapa phưa prachachon ศิลปะเพื่อชีวิต ศิลปะเพื่อประชาชน
Sư สือ
Su Huan 蘇還

sưaphưn monbai เสื่อพื้นหมอนใบ
sudan 蘇丹
Sun Zhongshan 孫中山
Supa Sirising สุภา สิริสิงห
Sưphanit สือพาณิชย์

Taečhiu แต้จิ๋ว
Tai ไท
Tai Hua 泰華
Taksin ตากสิน
talat ตลาด
tang čhangwat ต่างจังหวัด
Tang Daogeng 湯道耕
Tangshan 唐山
Thai thae ไทยแท้
thale tai ทะเลใต้
Thanom Kittikhachon ถนอม กิตติขจร
ti ตี๋
Ti trakun Song ตี๋ตระกูลซ่ง
tia เตี่ย
tianxia 天下
Tie Kang 鐵抗
Tongmenghui 同盟會
tongwen 同文
toujia zoulu 頭家走路
trakun ตระกูล
Tưng nang kia ตึ่งหนั่งเกี้ย
Tưng Sua ตึ่งซัว
tuohuang 拓荒
Tusheng Huaren 土生華人

ua อั๊ว

Vajiravudh วชิราวุธฯ
Vanich Chaiyawan วานิช ไชยวรรณ

waishengren 外省人
Wang Xiqi 王錫祺
Wannakam phưa Chiwit วรรณกรรมเพื่อชีวิต
Wanpi jiazu 頑皮家族

wat วัด
weixing xiaoshuo 微型小說
Wela nai khuat kaeo เวลาในขวดแก้ว
wenhua huigui 文化回歸
wenyan wen 文言文
"Wo de pengyou Yadula" 我的朋友鴨都拉
Wu'an ming 烏暗暝
Wu Jiyue 吳繼岳

Xi Ni Er 希尼爾
Xi Xi 西西
Xi you ji 西游記
xia Nanyang 下南洋
xiandai 現代
xiang 鄉
xiang 象
"Xiang wo zheyang de yi ge nüzi" 像我這樣的一個女子
xiangtu 鄉土
xiangxiang 想象
Xiao niangre 小娘惹
xiao Yindu 小印度
Xiaoshuo yuebao 小說月報
Xie Huiping 謝惠平
xifang 西方
Xiguan 惜官
Xin Ganjue Pai 新感覺派
Xin guomin ribao 新國民日報
Xin Hua 新華
xin sixiang 新思想
xing 星
Xingjiapo 星加坡
"Xingzhou ji xian, e Sudao kun guzhou zhong, fuci jianzhi" 星洲既陷, 厄蘇島困孤舟中, 賦此見志
Xingzhou ribao 星洲日報
Xingzuo 星座
Xinjiapo 新加坡
Xinjiapo wuding xia 新加坡屋頂下
xinke 新客
Xiyang 西洋
Xu Jinghua 許靜華

Xuesheng zhoubao 學生週報
Yan Bi 顏璧
Yaowarat เยาวราช
Yazhou 亞洲
"Ye dian" 野店
Ye Yalai 葉亞來
"Yelin" 椰林
yi 義 / 蟻
ying 影
ying'er guo 嬰兒國
Yingrguo 影兒國
Yingya shenglan 瀛涯勝覽
yiyu qingdiao 異域情調
Yongle 永樂
Youren 有人
yu 魚
Yuan Shikai 袁世凱
yuanshi qingyu 原始情欲
yue 越
yulin 雨林
yulin 語林

zao si zai 早死仔
Zhang Shunai 張叔耐
Zhao Rong 趙戎
Zheng Chenggong 鄭成功
Zheng He 鄭和
Zheng Yuzhou 鄭玉洲
Zhenghong qi xia 正紅旗下
zhiliu 支流
zhitu 迫迌
zhong 中
Zhong Hua 中華
Zhong Hua minzu 中華民族
Zhongguo 中國
Zhongguo renzhong 中國人種
Zhongguoren 中國人
Zhongwen 中文
Zhongyuan 中原
zhongzu de wenti 種族的問題

Zhu 朱
Zhu Bajie 豬八戒
"Zhufu" 祝福
zhugulü guniang 朱古律姑娘
"Zhuiwang laozhu" 綴網勞蛛
zuguo 祖國
zuoyi wenxue 左翼文學

NOTES

PREFACE

1. All figures on Chinese emigration are drawn from Amrith, *Migration and Diaspora*, 18–38.

2. See Ma Huan, *Ying-yai Sheng-lan*.

3. Ooi, introduction to *Southeast Asia*, 16–18.

4. Kuhn, *Chinese Among Others*, 21.

5. Amrith, *Migration and Diaspora*, 23.

6. Despite legends tracing their lineage to Zheng He's voyages, the Baba-Nyonyas did not emerge solely in Malaya. Peranakan communities also appeared in the Dutch East Indies in the sixteenth and seventeenth centuries (after initial Dutch contact and early Chinese settlement), such as Java and the Riau Archipelago, as well as southern Siam. The women these settlers married were not only Malay, but also other indigenous Southeast Asians. Many Peranakans later migrated to Penang, Malacca, and Singapore, colonial ports that the British grouped together as the "Straits Settlements" in 1826 (Rudolph, *Reconstructing Identities*, 55, 76–124).

7. Khoo Joo Ee, *Straits Chinese*, 24.

8. Wu Jin, *Redai fengguang*, 82.

9. Rudolph, *Reconstructing Identities*, 2.

10. Amrith, *Migration and Diaspora*, 4, 31–32.

11. In self-deprecation, Lee Kuan Yew, former prime minister of Singapore, describes Chinese Singaporeans as "descendants of illiterate landless peasants from Guangdong and Fujian" (*From Third World to First*, 645).

12. Guo, *Wu wang guochi*, 126.

13. Kuhn, *Chinese Among Others*, 12, 114, 146; Rudolph, *Reconstructing Identities*, 109; Rush, *Opium to Java*, 24.

14. Kuhn, *Chinese Among Others*, 58.

INTRODUCTION

1. See, for example, Yu Dafu's short story, "Sinking" ("Chenlun," 1921).

2. Yu Dafu, *Yu Dafu Nanyang suibi*, 64–65.

3. An example of such purging occurred in the early 1980s, when history textbooks no longer mentioned Yap Ah Loy (Ye Yalai), a poor Hakka trader who founded Kuala Lumpur in the mid-nineteenth century and rose to the position of "Kapitan Cina," representing the local Chinese settlement to the colonial authority (Ting, "Battle Over the Memory," 43).

4. Ng, *You dao zhi dao*, 325–54.

5. Ibid., 326, 334.

6. Suchen Lim, *Fistful of Colours*, 79, 186–87.

7. Ien Ang uses the phrase "haunted by Chineseness" to describe her conundrum as a Peranakan Indonesian living in the West who does not speak Chinese but must cope with her recurrent racialization as such (*On Not Speaking Chinese*, 21–36).

8. Praphatson, *Lot lai mangkon*, 42.

9. This process reflects the postcolonial imperative of "writing back to empire" described by Ashcroft, Griffiths, and Tiffin in *The Empire Writes Back*.

10. The volume *Global Chinese Literature* (2010), coedited by Jing Tsu and David Der-wei Wang, is an example.

11. This view of national literature is particularly evident in Pascale Casanova's *The World Republic of Letters* (*La république mondiale des lettres*, 1999).

12. Tsu, *Sound and Script*, 12.

13. E. K. Tan, *Rethinking Chineseness*, 3.

14. Groppe, *Sinophone Malaysian Literature*, 19–21.

15. Bachner, *Beyond Sinology*, 16.

16. In area studies, the idea of "Southeast Asia" coalesced around "an aggregate of nations—individually distinct and collectively a battleground in, first, the Pacific War, then the Cold War" (Emmerson, "'Southeast Asia,'" 10). The Southeast Asian Writers (or S.E.A. Write) Award, reinforces this definition, annually awarding its prizes to representative works from each member nation. Anglophone anthologies (mostly in translation) of Southeast Asian literature, such as *Virtual Lotus* (edited by Teri Shaffer Yamada), are generally organized by nation.

17. Fanon, "On National Culture," 170, 185.

18. Ibid., 177.

19. Ibid., 161, 164.

20. Hall, "When Was the 'Post-Colonial'?" 250.

21. Hall, "Cultural Identity," 227.

22. Ibid., 232.

23. Glissant, *Caribbean Discourse*, 5, 248.

24. Ibid., 8, 16, 88, 154, 203, 221, 234.

25. Ibid., 67, 95, 98, 139, 150, 249.

26. Ibid., 3.

27. Hau'ofa, "Our Sea of Islands," 10–16; De Loughrey, *Routes and Roots*, 154.

28. Lionnet, "Continents and Archipelagoes," 1508.

29. Sears, "Postcolonial Identities," 62; Chua, "Southeast Asia in Postcolonial Studies," 232. For comparative analyses of Anglophone literature from

the Philippines, Malaysia, Singapore, and Hong Kong, see Patke and Holden, *The Routledge Concise History of Southeast Asian Writing in English.*

30. Bowen, "Contributions Development," 387.

31. Casino and Shin, "South China Sea," 43.

32. Murray, Boellstorff, and Robinson, "East Indies/West Indies," 221, 225.

33. In *Ancient Indian Colonization in South-East Asia*, R. C. Majumdar describes Suvarnadvipa as a gilded seascape attracting Indian travelers in classical Sanskrit texts: "The heroes of most of these stories are merchants and . . . princes, or chiefs in straitened circumstances, who wanted to acquire wealth by trade or other means" (7).

34. Using the same two Chinese characters as Nanyang, the Nanyō "vaguely refers to the tropical sphere of seas and islands to the 'south' of the Japanese mainland" (Naoto, *Nanyo-Orientalism*, 2). The twentieth-century "southward advance" of the Japanese military and its incorporation of a maritime empire into the "Greater East Asian Co-Prosperity Sphere" coincided with the rise of popular exoticism of the Nanyō, "a region into which the burgeoning population of Japan could expand in an Asian version of colonial empires then maintained by all the major European powers" (Kleeman, *Under an Imperial Sun*, 11).

35. *Hanyu da cidian*, 894. In China, Dongnan Ya has replaced the more outdated Nanyang, while Sinophone communities in Southeast Asia continue to use the latter term.

36. Lixin Sun, "Chinese Maritime Concepts," 329.

37. Ibid., 328; Casino and Shin, "South China Sea," 59.

38. Fiskesjö, "On the 'Raw' and the 'Cooked,'" 141–42.

39. The Tang dynasty travelogue *Book of the Southern Barbarians* (*Man shu*, 868–73) documents military expeditions into the kingdoms of Nanzhao and Annam, cataloguing local topography, flora, fauna, peoples, governing structures, laws, and exotic tribal customs such as teeth lacquering, body piercing, and face tattooing (Fan, "Man shu," 17).

40. Wang Gungwu, "Early Ming Relations," 53–55; Wade, "Zheng He Voyages," 123–24.

41. In contrast to the "South Seas," the Xiyang ("Western Seas") traditionally denotes the Indian Ocean and Arabian Sea. For a comparison of the maritime imperial perspective in Luo Maodeng's novel to a Portuguese one of the same era, see Finlay, "Portuguese and Chinese Maritime Imperialism."

42. Ma, *Ying-yai Sheng-lan*, 93, 107–10.

43. Wang Gungwu, "Early Ming Relations," 56–57.

44. Ma, *Ying-yai Sheng-lan*, 90.

45. Chen Chen, *Shuihu houzhuan*, 1: 150–59, 2: 147–77. In the novel, the Siamese king claims to be a descendant of the general Ma Yuan, who led a conquest of Annam in 42 AD to bring it under Han suzerainty. In China, Ma Yuan was posthumously revered as "master of ships and oceans" and "conqueror of the barbarians of the Four Seas, sometimes figured as fish, sea serpents, and dragons" (Schafer, *Vermilion Bird*, 97–98).

46. Widmer, *Margins of Utopia*, 37, 69. Widmer argues that Li Jun is a fictionalized embodiment of Zheng Chenggong, the Ming loyalist who

captured Taiwan in 1662, and that Siam in the novel simply serves to "screen the reference to Taiwan" (*Margins of Utopia*, 24, 55–60).

47. Wang Gungwu, "Early Ming Relations," 61.

48. *Hanyu da cidian*, 894.

49. Said, *Orientalism*, 3.

50. Eric Hobsbawm identifies this period as 1875–1914 (*Age of Empire*, 56–83).

51. Stewart, "Creolization," 1, 6–8, 18.

52. Anderson, *Imagined Communities*, 47–59.

53. For example, see Skinner, "Creolized Chinese Societies."

54. Stewart, "Creolization," 8.

55. Lionnet, *Autobiographical Voices*, 8–14.

56. Chaudenson, *Creolization*, 5–13, 95; Glissant, *Caribbean Discourse*, 53, 182.

57. Eriksen, "Creolization ,"172–73.

58. Quoted in Nair, "Creolization," 238.

59. Moore-Gilbert, "Spivak and Bhabha," 463.

60. Ibid., 461; Goldberg, "Heterogeneity and Hybridity," 73.

61. Prabhu, *Hybridity*, 5–6.

62. Nair, "Creolization," 239, 242.

63. Glissant, *Poetics of Relation*, 11, 34, 144, 163; *Caribbean Discourse*, 140–42.

64. Most labels for these communities in the national languages of Southeast Asia bear some derivation of "Chinese" (English), *Chinees* (Dutch), or *Chinês* (Portuguese), such as the Malay *Cina* and the Thai *Čhin*. The exception is Vietnam, where the Sino-Vietnamese minority is officially classified as the "Hoa."

65. Ng, "Sinophone/Chinese," 74–75.

66. Shih, *Visuality and Identity*, 4; Shih, "Concept of the Sinophone," 710.

67. Ghosh and Kennedy, introduction to *Decentring Empire*, 2.

68. Trivedi, "Postcolonial or the Transcolonial?" 270.

69. On this subject, see E. K. Tan, *Rethinking Chineseness.*

70. Kellman, *Translingual Imagination*, 3, 9.

71. Ibid., 15.

CHAPTER 1

1. Literary historians acknowledge the roots of modern Chinese literature in late-nineteenth-century works documenting the introduction of Western science and technology, the ascendancy of Western imperialism, and the collapse of the Qing dynasty. Canonical histories of the New Literature movement include Zhou Zuoren's *Zhongguo xin wenxue de yuanliu*, Lu Yongheng's *Zhongguo xin wenxue gailun*, and Wang Zhefu's *Zhongguo xin wenxue yundong shi.*

2. For a detailed account, see Chow Tse-tsung, *May Fourth Movement.*

3. Schwarcz, *Chinese Enlightenment*, 1.

4. Tani Barlow defines "colonial modernity" as a "complex field of relationships or threads of material that connect multiply in space-time" across discrete units or borders (such as nation-states or civilizations) of historical inquiry ("On 'Colonial Modernity,'" 6).

5. Schwarcz, *Chinese Enlightenment*, 1, 6.

6. Wagner, "Canonization of May Fourth," 96.

7. Schwarcz, *Chinese Enlightenment*, 2–3.

8. Goldman, introduction to *Modern Chinese Literature*, 1; Wagner, "Canonization of May Fourth," 106.

9. Hsia, *History of Modern Chinese Fiction*, 533.

10. Schwarcz, *Chinese Enlightenment*, 2; Tang, *History of Modern Chinese Literature*, i.

11. Tang, *History of Modern Chinese Literature*, i.

12. Wagner, "Canonization of May Fourth," 105.

13. For more on the development of fictional realism, see David Wang, *Fictional Realism in Twentieth-Century China*.

14. In *Primitive Passions*, Rey Chow explores the "mutual reciprocities between literary and visual modes of representation" in the canonical work of Lu Xun, the "founding father" of modern Chinese literature (7).

15. Goldman, introduction to *Modern Chinese Literature*, 1.

16. Schwarcz, *Chinese Enlightenment*, 5.

17. Around 1870, the steamship revolution "ushered in a transformation in the scale of migration," particularly following the opening of the Suez Canal, which expedited ocean transit between Europe and South, Southeast, and East Asia (Amrith, *Migration and Diaspora*, 25–26).

18. Studies of Chinese nationalism have historically generated the same paradigm (Karl, *Staging the World*, 6).

19. Qin Xianci, "Xu Dishan nianbiao," 388.

20. Owen Wong asserts that the story's female protagonist, Minming, is of Chinese descent, while the male protagonist, Jialing, is Burman (ethnic Burmese) (*Zhongguo zuojia yu Nanyang*, 37). Yet in the text, Xu Dishan offers no hints as to Minming's ethnicity, nor does he mention any ethnic difference between the two main characters. Regardless of ethnic lineage, they are—by all measures of culture, place, and language—Burmese.

21. Xu Dishan, *Xu Dishan xiaoshuo xuan*, 44–45.

22. Kai-wing Chow, "Narrating Nation," 67.

23. Said, *Orientalism*, 3.

24. A short list of tribute items from Southeast Asia in Cao Xueqin's novel, which is also known as *The Story of the Stone* (*Shitou ji*), includes Borneo camphor, Siamese tea, a cypress-smoked Siamese sucking-pig, and Saigon cinnamon (*The Story of the Stone*, vol. 1, *The Golden Days*, 478, 499, 519; *The Story of the Stone*, vol. 2, *The Crab-Flower Club*, 398).

25. Langao zhuren, *Qilou chongmeng*, 260–62.

26. Widmer, "*Honglou meng* Sequels," 130.

27. Schafer, *Vermillion Bird*, 80–81.

28. Popular Vietnamese lore contradicts Chinese official history, claiming the sisters committed suicide by throwing themselves into a river rather than

succumbing to the authority of the Han. I am grateful to George Dutton for sharing this version of the story.

29. Langao zhuren, *Qilou chongmeng*, 259.

30. Woodside, *Vietnam and the Chinese Model*, 46.

31. Wong Yoon Wah, "Chongxin huanxiang," 19.

32. Leo Lee, *Romantic Generation*, 124–35.

33. Lin Wanjing, *Zhongguo zuojia zai Xinjiapo*, 35.

34. Owen Wong, *Zhongguo zuojia yu Nanyang*, 13, 68. The postcolonial Singaporean author Yeng Pway Ngon parodies this Nanyang trope of the ubiquitously rich floral fragrance in his short story "The Garden City" (1990), which I discuss in Chapter 5.

35. Unlike the Singapore-based story, the Hong Kong-based sequel to "Insolubly Rich" does not habitually apply the term to the scenery and the protagonist's desire. Whereas tropical Singapore embodies an erotic lust for the Other, Hong Kong evokes stock allusions to the fantastic from the classical Chinese literary repertoire, such as Penglai Island, the mystical habitat for Taoist immortals (*Xu Zhimo quanji*, 205).

36. The sensory experience of Beijing as a "dead city" contrasts Lianfeng's experience of Singapore. Rather than a rich explosion of the senses, the quartet's finale evokes a chilling of the senses with its gothic depiction of a cold, dark, snowy, and eerily quiet winter's night in a Beijing cemetery in 1928 (*Xu Zhimo quanji*, 212–16). Unlike the other travel pieces, this story is more an expression of political pessimism about China's conditions at the time.

37. Xu Zhimo, *Xu Zhimo wenji*, 58–60.

38. Xu Zhimo, *Xu Zhimo quanji*, 197.

39. Ibid., 199.

40. A great example of this is the short story "The Shanghai Foxtrot (a Fragment)" ("Shanghai de hubuwu [yi ge duanpian]," 1932) by Mu Shiying.

41. Xu Zhimo, *Xu Zhimo quanji*, 197.

42. Ibid., 200–202.

43. Clifford, *Routes*, 5, 31–40.

44. Amrith, *Migration and Diaspora*, 30, 38.

45. Ibid., 48.

46. The southbound trajectory of the 1930s left-wing author Ai Wu (pseudonym of Tang Daogeng, 1904–92) represents a bold exception to this standard. Leaving his home in Chengdu in 1925, Ai Wu trekked south overland (on foot!) across the frontiers of Yunnan and Burma, and did not "sail the South Seas" until British colonial authorities in Rangoon deported him back to China via Hong Kong in 1931. Ai Wu fictionalizes these experiences in his collection of short fiction, *Travels in the South* (*Nan xing ji*, 1935).

47. Lin Wanjing, *Zhongguo zuojia zai Xinjiapo*, 78.

48. Riep, "Xu Dishan," 251.

49. Qin Xianci, "Xu Dishan nianbiao," 391–93.

50. Xu Dishan, *Xu Dishan xiaoshuo xuan*, 57.

51. Ibid., 101–4.

52. Qin Xianci, "Xu Dishan nianbiao," 387.

53. Xu Dishan, *Xu Dishan xiaoshuo xuan*, 105–9.

54. Ibid., 86–87.
55. Ibid., 88–89.
56. Ibid., 59.
57. Ibid.
58. Ibid., 61–62.
59. Ibid., 63.
60. Ibid., 65–66.
61. Ibid., 65.
62. Ibid., 72.
63. Ibid., 73.
64. Ibid.
65. Teng, *Eurasian*, 112–34.
66. Lu Xun's narrator continues to replay the encounter, and his answer to the widow of "I am not sure," over and over in his head: "such a chance meeting could have no great significance, and yet I was taking it so to heart; no wonder certain educationalists called me a neurotic" (*Selected Stories of Lu Hsun*, 128).
67. Xu Dishan, *Xu Dishan xiaoshuo xuan*, 72.
68. Ibid., 73.

CHAPTER 2

1. Lu Xun's novella *The Real Story of Ah-Q* (*A Q zhengzhuan*, 1921) is the canonical example of such a satirical portrayal.
2. Kenley, *New Culture*, 29–40.
3. In this scene, Lu Xun, as a student at Sendai University in Japan, sees a newsreel in his microbiology class showing a slide of the Japanese military in Manchuria executing a Chinese accused of spying for the Russians during the Russo-Japanese War (1904–5). The author contrasts the apathetic, monochrome faces of the Chinese onlookers who gathered to watch the spectacle with the fervent Japanese students around him cheering triumphantly: "Though they [the Chinese onlookers] were all of them perfectly sturdy physical specimens, every face was utterly, stupidly blank" (*Real Story of Ah-Q*, 16–17). Standing among Japanese spectators in Japan and watching a slide positioned to replicate the subjective (and superior) gaze of the colonizer engendered Lu Xun's interpretation of the Chinese condition, one that inspired him to take up the pen.
4. Huang Jianli argues that the historical reputation of the South Seas Chinese as "mothers of the revolution" was more of an exhortation intended to rally support than an accurate interpretation of reality ("Umbilical Ties").
5. Mullaney, *Coming to Terms*, 25.
6. The concept of the "Chinese race," promoted by staunchly anti-Manchu late-Qing intellectual reformers, envisions China as "a natural unified country" with "racial homogeneity" and "uniform custom" (Kai-wing Chow, "Narrating Nation," 74).
7. Bergère, *Sun Yat-sen*, 352. In this early formulation of Han ethnonationalism, there is an assumed "historical equivalence between Manchu

and Western colonial power" that, according to Rebecca Karl, "led to a narrowed recentering of 'Chinese-ness' around ethnicity, which allowed for 'the people' to be specified *not* through either political consciousness or revolutionary activism but through an essentialized ethno-racial designation" (*Staging the World*, 117–18, emphasis in the original).

8. Quoted in Bergère, *Sun Yat-sen*, 358. As Bergère writes, "The interaction between ethnicity and national identity had not been made clear. On the basis of the numerical weakness of the minorities (which he reckoned at ten million), Sun proclaimed the purity of a race of four hundred million Chinese" (ibid.).

9. Kai-wing Chow, "Narrating Nation," 55.

10. *Minzu zhuyi* specifically expresses a form of "ethno-nationalism," whereas *guojia zhuyi* expresses the "statist concept" of nationalism as a "citizenry" (Karl, *Staging the World*, 117).

11. Kuhn, *Chinese Among Others*, 16, 49.

12. Bergère, *Sun Yat-sen*, 3.

13. Hsia, *History of Modern Chinese Fiction*, 167.

14. Quoted in Wong Yoon Wah, *Post-Colonial Chinese Literatures*, 134.

15. In his memoirs, Lao She admitted that he went to Singapore because he could only afford a third-class ferry ticket there ("Wo zenyang xie *Xiao Po de shengri*," 303). Xu Dishan (see Chapter 1) may have also inspired Lao She's interest in the Nanyang, as the two writers were lifelong friends and roommates in London when Xu attended Oxford (Witchard, *Lao She in London*, 31).

16. Lao She, *Er Ma*, 12.

17. Lao She, "Wo zenyang xie *Xiao Po de shengri*," 303–4.

18. Wong Yoon Wah, *Post-Colonial Chinese Literatures*, 104.

19. Lao She, "Wo zenyang xie *Xiao Po de shengri*," 304–5.

20. David Wang, *Fictional Realism*, 111.

21. It is also possible that Lao She's use of *po* in the three names alludes to "Pooh," as in Winnie-the-Pooh. Lao She was likely aware of A. A. Milne's *Winnie-the-Pooh* (1926), which was published in London during Lao She's residence there. In terms of their innocent wisdom and playful interrogation of logic, Little Po and Xianpo are reminiscent of Milne's characters.

22. Lao She, "Xiao Po de shengri," 3–4.

23. Turnbull, *History of Singapore*, 19–21.

24. Roff, *Origins of Malay Nationalism*, 111.

25. A public servant of the British Empire, the historian J. S. Furnivall identified this racial division of residence, education, and labor as integral to successful colonial rule in his comparisons of the British and Dutch administrations in Burma and the East Indies (*Colonial Policy and Practice*, 1–22).

26. Lao She, "Xiao Po de shengri," 4–5, 12–13.

27. Ibid., 3–4.

28. Ibid., 5.

29. Ibid.

30. Ibid., 61–67.

31. Ibid., 6–8.

32. Ibid., 9, 13.
33. Lao She, "Xiao Po de shengri," 13–14.
34. Ibid., 14.
35. Ibid., 7, 73–74.
36. Ibid., 54, 63–69.
37. Ibid., 37–43.
38. Ibid., 32.
39. Ibid., 13, 23.
40. This foreshadows the somewhat dystopian plot of Lao She's next novel, the science fiction *Cat Country* (*Maocheng ji*, 1932).
41. Lao She, "Xiao Po de shengri," 86, 89–98.
42. Lao She, "Wo zenyang xie *Xiao Po de shengri*," 305.
43. Jiang, "Lao She *Xiao Po de shengri*," 29.
44. Farquhar, *Children's Literature*, 27–36.
45. Reiterating Lao She's own comment that the novel contains "ideas which do not belong to the world of children," Wong Yoon Wah praises *Little Po's Birthday* for not only accurately satirizing colonial Singapore's racialized structure, but also for keenly anticipating the nation's postcolonial future as a multicultural "Garden City" where second-generation children reject the ethnic stereotypes of their immigrant parents and work toward the desegregation of schools along ethno-linguistic lines (*Post-Colonial Chinese Literatures*, 105–10).
46. Jiang, "Lao She *Xiao Po de shengri*," 29.
47. Lao She, "Wo zenyang xie *Xiao Po de shengri*," 306.
48. Owen Wong, *Zhongguo zuojia yu Nanyang*, 22. Other than "Little Po" and "Big Po," the novel does not identify local place or street names. While Lao She gives Little Po's Chinese Singaporean friends very generic names like Nanxing ("Southern Star," with *xing* also alluding to the first character in the old Sinophone name for Singapore, Xingjiapo), he simply refers to Little Po's Indian and Malay friends as the "little Indians" (*xiao Yindu*) and the "Malay girls" (*Malai guniang*) ("Xiao Po de shengri," 39).
49. Jiang, "Lao She *Xiao Po de shengri*," 32. "Kling," or "Keling," was a generic term for Indians in colonial Malaya which derived from the historical misconception that "all Indians—be they Bengali, Tamil, Hindustani, Sindhi, Sikh, or Gujerati—came from the coastal region of Kalinga" (now known as Orissa) in India. Though the term referred mostly to Tamil Indians in Malaya, it was inaccurate and derogatory (Khoo Kheng-Hor, *Nanyang*, 177).
50. Lao She, "Xiao Po de shengri," 17.
51. "Diary of a Madman" concludes with the narrator's plea: "Save the children." In "My Old Home," the narrator returns to his village to find a "lamentably thick wall" between him and a childhood friend who was the son of the narrator's household servants. Seeing their two young sons now playing together freely, the protagonist expresses hope for a future free from class divisions: "I hope they will not be like us, that they will not allow a barrier to grow between them. . . . They should have a new life, a life we never experienced" (*Selected Stories of Lu Hsun*, 18, 60, 63).

52. Lao She, "Wo zenyang xie *Xiao Po de shengri*," 307.

53. Lao She wrote (and abandoned) this autobiographical novel about Manchu-Han relations in Beijing (set amidst the Boxer Rebellion against the Qing at the turn of the twentieth century) in the 1960s before his suicide during the Cultural Revolution. For a treatment of this novel and Lao She's "doubly-peripheral condition" in London and China, see Prado-Fonts, "Beneath Two Red Banners."

54. Wang Zhefu, *Zhongguo xin wenxue yundong shi*, 224.

55. Besides Malaya, southbound authors also participated in literary activities elsewhere in Southeast Asia. Ai Wu, for example, submitted editorials and short stories to Sinophone newspapers in colonial Rangoon from 1930–31 (Owen Wong, *Zhongguo zuojia yu Nanyang*, 20).

56. Although the remainder of this chapter centers on Yu Dafu, other southbound writers played key roles in Sinophone literary debates in colonial Malaya. Scholars generally divide them into prewar (1927–32), wartime (1937–41), and postwar (1945–48) waves. Besides Yu Dafu, the wartime wave also included Hu Yuzhi (Lin Wanjing, *Zhongguo zuojia zai Xinjiapo,* 10, 107).

57. In early February 1942, Yu Dafu, Hu Yuzhi, and other authors, journalists, and intellectuals fled Singapore in a small motorboat to Bengkalis, an island off the east coast of Sumatra. The subsequent events of Yu Dafu's three years in exile in Sumatra, leading up to his mysterious execution by the Japanese military at the time of its 1945 surrender, are documented in Hu Yuzhi's account, "Yu Dafu's Exile and Disappearance" ("Yu Dafu de liuwang he shizong"), originally published in *Singapore Daily (Xingzhou ribao)* in 1946 after Hu safely returned to Singapore. Taking refuge in the Sumatran village of Payakumbuh, Yu famously masqueraded as a Peranakan businessman under the alias of Zhao Lian. As the only "local" who spoke Japanese, Yu was conscripted by the Japanese military to serve as an interpreter in interrogations of captured enemies. Hu Yuzhi's account suggests the Japanese executed Yu because he directly witnessed evidence implicating them for war crimes. In his final years in Sumatra, Yu Dafu wrote many poems in a flowery classical-style prose: Hu Yuzhi recovered eleven of them after the war and published them under the title "Miscellaneous Poems on War and Exile" (Luanli zashi) in *Singapore Daily* alongside his account. Poems such as "After Singapore Has Fallen, Stranded in a Lone Boat in Sumatra, I Compose this Poem to Find the Will to Go On" ("Xingzhou ji xian, e Sudao kun guzhou zhong, fuci jianzhi," 1942) express dislocation by invoking the persona of an ancient scholar-official banished from the imperial Chinese capital (Hu, "Yu Dafu de liuwang," 9, 64–67; Yu Dafu, *Yu Dafu wenji di shi juan*, 464).

58. See Chapter 3.

59. Yeo, *Zhanqian Xin Ma wenxue*, 13–19.

60. Quoted in ibid., 21.

61. This refers to the publication of Xu Dishan's "Birds of a Feather." See Chapter 1.

62. Yeo, *Zhanqian Xin Ma wenxue*, 33.

63. Quoted in ibid., 39.

64. Ibid.

65. Quoted in ibid., 43.

66. Mo, *Local Colour*, 1.

67. In their inaugural statement in November 1922, the editors of *South Seas Periodical (Nanyang qikan)* included Burma, Siam, Borneo, Java, and Sumatra in their definition of the Nanyang (Yeo, *Zhanqian Xin Ma wenxue*, 30).

68. Quoted in Yeo, *Zhanqian Xin Ma wenxue*, 99–100.

69. Mo, *Local Colour*, 1–2.

70. Yeo, *Zhanqian Xin Ma wenxue*, 71; Kenley, *New Culture*, 168–72.

71. Miao Xiu, *Ma Hua wenxue shihua*, 3, 412; Yeo, *Zhanqian Xin Ma wenxue*, 82.

72. Yeo, *Zhanqian Xin Ma wenxue*, 96.

73. Sun Yizhong, "Yu Dafu zhanshi dui Xing Ma wenxue de gongxian," 146.

74. Miao Xiu, *Ma Hua wenxue shihua*, 416–17.

75. Yu Dafu, *Yu Dafu Nanyang suibi*, 64–67.

76. Ibid., 66–67.

77. Quoted in Lin Wanjing, *Zhongguo zuojia zai Xinjiapo*, 122.

78. Yu Dafu, *Yu Dafu Nanyang suibi*, 80.

79. Ibid., 158.

80. Miao Xiu, *Ma Hua wenxue shihua*, 418. Educated in colonial Singapore's Anglophone education system, Miao Xiu (1920–80) was one of Malaya's first homegrown bilingual writers. In addition to succeeding Yu Dafu as editor of *Singapore Daily*'s literary supplements following the Pacific War, he later wrote the acclaimed novels *Under the Singapore Roof (Xinjiapo wuding xia*, 1951) and *Savage Night Voyage (Can yexing*, 1976) (*Singapore Literary Pioneers Gallery Guide*, 43–46).

81. Yu Dafu, *Yu Dafu Nanyang suibi*, 255.

82. Ibid., 257–60.

83. Xu Jingfeng, "Malu gongren," 16.

84. Bi Xia, "Sichang de yiri ye," 19.

85. By 1948, due to colonial policies unfavorable to leftist writers in Malaya, many members of the postwar generation of southbound writers (including Hu Yuzhi) were forced to return to China. As permanent émigrés, those who stayed were absorbed into the local literary tradition (Lin Wanjing, *Zhongguo zuojia zai Xinjiapo*, 67).

CHAPTER 3

1. Lim Kien Ket, "Weishenme Ma Hua wenxue?" 5.

2. Groppe, *Sinophone Malaysian Literature*, 61–63. Alison Groppe analyzes the spoken-language strategies of realist authors in the 1940s and 1950s such as Tie Kang, Miao Xiu, and Zhao Rong, the latter of whom compiled a dictionary in 1979 of "nonstandard" Sinophone literary terms from Singapore and Malaysia as part of "an effort to legitimize and preserve their use in literary language" (ibid., 68–70).

3. My use of "minor literature" draws primarily from its first defining condition as "that which a minority constructs in a major language" (Deleuze and Guattari, *Kafka*, 16). This "minor usage" deconstructs the major language from the outside, reterritorializing it with the history and experience of a new place. In Sinophone Malaysian literature, standard Chinese (based on spoken Mandarin, the national majority language of China) is reterritorialized and transformed by the "minor" experience of Malaysia (a smaller nation where Malay is the national majority language). Several scholars have debated the applicability of "minor literature" to the Sinophone Malaysian context. See Tee, *Malaixiya Huayu yuxi wenxue*, 25–29; Ng, "Minor Sinophone Literature," 15–28; and Groppe, *Sinophone Malaysian Literature*, 93–98.

4. "Secondary diaspora" refers to the remigration from an initial settlement to a new one, such as the remigration of French Canadians (Acadians) to Louisiana, where they became known as Cajuns (Chaudenson, *Creolization*, 134).

5. Though this chapter focuses solely on Ng Kim Chew's short fiction, the work of Choong and Chan also engages in recuperating creolized Malaysianness. While all three authors write in different literary genres, all come from the same postcolonial generation, all began publishing only after their arrival in Taiwan in the late 1980s, and all are active literary critics and professors at Taiwanese universities. For Choong Yee Voon (Zhong Yiwen, 1969-), her collection of prose memoirs entitled *Wild Peninsula (Ye bandao*, 2007) narrates her childhood experiences living in a kampong on an oil palm plantation near Ipoh and demonstrates a belated appreciation for her formative cross-cultural experiences. As for her husband, Chan Tah Wei (Chen Dawei, 1969-), his volume of poetry *Approaching the Ramayana (Kaojin Luomoyanna,* 2005) addresses the cross-cultural and religious frictions in his hometown of Ipoh. For analysis of these works, see Bernards, "Beyond Diaspora," 319–23.

6. Here, I emphasize this as specific to narratives about Peninsular Malaysia (West Malaysia). A more ecocritical dynamic characterizes much of the Sinophone literature on Malaysian Borneo (East Malaysia). See Chapter 4.

7. Chinese Malaysians account for 36 percent and Indian Malaysians for 11 percent of the population in West Malaysia (Demery and Demery, *Adjustment and Equity*, 19).

8. Kuhn, *Chinese Among Others*, 102, 148.

9. Demery and Demery, *Adjustment and Equity*, 20; Kuhn, *Chinese Among Others*, 147.

10. This attitude originates with European colonists finding Malays unwilling to labor under exploitative conditions. Working in a mine or on a plantation provided little incentive to abandon traditional livelihoods in fishing and subsistence agriculture. The British "myth of the lazy native" provided a rationale for the importation of coolie labor from China and India, creating a racialized labor division (Alatas, *Myth of the Lazy Native*; Hirschman, "Making of Race," 345–47).

11. The early 1920s Retrenchment Commission made preference for Malays an absolute rule in government services (Roff, *Origins of Malay Nationalism*, 18, 94, 116).

12. Reid, *Chinese and Malay Identities*, 2–8.
13. Roff, *Origins of Malay Nationalism*, 110.
14. Ibid., 127.
15. Andaya and Andaya, *History of Malaysia*, 282.
16. In the still relatively moderate political climate between 1957 and 1969, Sinophone literature—its direct ties to mainland China now severed—transformed and experienced renewed vigor, as an independent Malaysia initially represented a "liberated new world." Student-run literary journals such as *Banana Winds (Jiao feng)*, established in Singapore in 1955 and relocated to Kuala Lumpur in 1957, and *Students Weekly (Xuesheng zhoubao)* became the source of a "modern" (*xiandai*) Sinophone Malaysian literature (Lin Ye, "Jiefang de xin shijie," 105–8).
17. Chiu, "Empire of the Chinese Sign," 600.
18. Conservative government reports estimate the riots left nearly two hundred dead, more than four hundred injured, and around six thousand Kuala Lumpur residences destroyed or damaged (Andaya and Andaya, *History of Malaysia*, 298).
19. Kuhn, *Chinese Among Others*, 306.
20. The NEP aimed to redress economic inequity by raising the *bumiputera* share of gross domestic product from 4 percent in 1970 to 30 percent by 1990 (Cho, *Malaysian Economy*, 261).
21. Tee, *Malaixiya Huayu yuxi wenxue*, 23; Chiu, "Empire of the Chinese Sign," 597.
22. Chong, "Ma Hua wenxue," 14–15; Tee, *Malaixiya Huayu yuxi wenxue*, 22–23.
23. Lim Kien Ket, "Weishenme Ha Hua wenxue?" 21.
24. Khor, *Nanfang xuanhua*, 164.
25. This does not imply that Sinophone literature disappeared from Malaysia, only that a new trajectory—namely a modernist one that helped resignify the Nanyang imagination—developed through ties to Taiwan.
26. Tee, *Nanyang lunshu*, 135.
27. Tee, "Wenhua huigui," 10. Their "cultural return" may be exaggerated, as Jing Tsu points out: "Professions of cultural belonging are frequently strategic rather than sentimental" (*Sound and Script*, 177), especially when such pronouncements are necessary for securing university scholarships.
28. Sung-sheng Chang, *Modernism*, 7–13; Sung-sheng Chang, *Literary Culture*, 9.
29. Sung-sheng Chang, *Modernism*, 150.
30. Yip, *Envisioning Taiwan*, 27–29.
31. Tu Wei-ming defines "cultural China" as a diasporic projection of China as a civilization (akin to Europe) with continental roots in the Central Plains yet tied to the centripetal force of China as a "geopolitical concept" ("Cultural China," 1–17).
32. Ng, "Ma Hua wenxue quancheng," 20–24; Tee, *Nanyang lunshu*, 127–28; Lim Kien Ket, "Weishenme Ma Hua wenxue?" For an overview of these debates, see Groppe, *Sinophone Malaysian Literature*, 27–29. Written in a Romanized script, Baba Malay generally follows Malay grammatical

structure but draws heavily from Hokkien and English vocabulary. Literature in Baba Malay declined in the late colonial era: as the preferred bureaucratic middlemen of the British, the Babas were Anglophone-educated, and their written medium predominantly became English. By labeling them "Straits Chinese," the British also racialized the Babas as "Chinese," effectively erasing the creolized "third space" they forged within the larger community (Skinner, "Creolized Chinese Societies," 91).

33. Ng, "Ma Hua wenxue quancheng," 20–21.

34. Ng, "Sinophone/Chinese," 75–79; Tee, *Malaixiya Huayu yuxi wenxue*, 25.

35. Ng, "Sinophone/Chinese," 76–77. Writers sometimes invent new characters: this is common in Cantonese literature from Hong Kong.

36. Shu-mei Shih identifies this as an existential condition of Sinophone writing (*Visuality and Identity*, 5).

37. Tee, *Malaixiya Huayu yuxi wenxue*, 25.

38. Ng, "Ma Hua wenxue quancheng," 25. This accusation is reminiscent of judgments of Caribbean creoles as "bad varieties" of French. "Bazaar Huawen" evokes its pidgin qualities: the word "pidgin" likely derives from the English word "business," as these were contact languages employed in the marketplace or bazaar (Chaudenson, *Creolization*, 16–17).

39. Ng, *Ma Hua wenxue yu Zhongguo xing*, 135. Similarly, Lim Kien Ket argues that Sinophone Malaysian literature no longer need address its distinction from Chinese literature, but should rather explicate its relationship to the non-Sinophone literary traditions of Malaysia ("Weishenme Ma Hua wenxue?" 27).

40. David Wang, "Huai haizi Huang Jinshu," 12, 21.

41. Yu Dafu, *Yu Dafu Nanyang suibi*, 66–67. I discuss Yu's essay, entitled "Some Questions," at greater length in Chapter 2.

42. Ng, *Meng yu zhu yu liming*, 18–20. Jawi refers to Malay as written in the Arabic script prior to its Romanization during European colonization.

43. Ibid., 18–19.

44. Ibid., 14–16.

45. For more on Chang and Li, see Chapter 4.

46. Ng, *Meng yu zhu yu liming*, 16–21.

47. Ibid., 31–32.

48. The specter of Yu Dafu not only haunts this story, but several Ng Kim Chew stories, including "Death in the South" ("Si zai nanfang," 1992) and "Supplement" (Buyi, 2001). For analysis of these stories (and Yu's presence in them), see Groppe, "Dis/Reappearances of Yu Dafu," and also Tsu, *Sound and Script*, 174–203.

49. Ng, *Meng yu zhu yu liming*, 33.

50. Ibid., 38.

51. Ibid., 39.

52. Ng, *You dao zhi dao*, 325–27, 334.

53. Ibid., 339–44.

54. Ibid., 339–55. Luring coolies to gamble and accrue debt was indeed a colonial strategy to ensure their indentured servitude (Kuhn, *Chinese Among Others*, 121).

55. Ng, *You dao zhi dao*, 356–57.

56. This resonates with Ng's sentiments in his literary criticism, in which he calls the Sinophone Malaysian cultivation of diasporic Chineseness a "performance of cultural melancholia" and a postcolonial "ritual of trauma" ("Dongnan Ya Huaren," 119).

57. Ng, "Ala de zhiyi," 236–43, 255.

58. Ibid., 238.

59. Ibid., 241–46.

60. Ibid., 243–44.

61. Ibid., 257.

62. Ibid., 251–52.

63. Ibid., 247–55, 264.

64. Ibid., 257–58.

65. Ibid., 236.

66. For analysis of this story, see Bernards, "Beyond Diaspora," 321–22.

67. Ng, *Tu yu huo*, 62.

68. Ibid., 63–67. The Orang Asli, or "aboriginal people," is a general Malay term applied to the indigenous, nonseafaring, forest-dwelling peoples of Peninsular Malaysia who are composed of several "culturally and linguistically distinct groups" with a total population of roughly 150,000 (Wawrinec, "Tribality and Indigeneity," 96).

69. Ng, *Tu yu huo*, 65. The Kadazan are an indigenous Dayak people from Borneo, and the nipah virus was a respiratory infection that broke out on Peninsular Malaysian pig farms in 1999.

70. Ibid., 71–74.

71. Krishnan, *Reading the Global*, 95–100. Munsyi is variably spelled "Munshi" or "Musyi," thus suggesting that the protagonist Liu Cai/Musyi Abdullah from "The Will of Allah" also embodies the spirit of this historical figure.

72. For a translation and separate analysis of the citation, see Groppe, *Sinophone Malaysian Literature*, 146–47.

73. Ng, *You dao zhi dao*, 247.

74. Ibid., 245–49.

75. Ibid., 253–56.

76. Ibid., 261–64. For additional analysis of these passages, see Groppe, *Sinophone Malaysian Literature*, 140–45.

77. Ng, *You dao zhi dao*, 266. A *songkok* is a traditional hat worn by Malay men.

78. Tee, *Nanyang lunshu*, 141–45.

79. For an account of the incident and its representation in Taiwanese literature, see Sylvia Lin, *Representing Atrocity.*

CHAPTER 4

1. Choong Yee Voon calls Borneo the "most important landmark" for rainforest writing in Sinophone literature (*Wujin de zhuixun*, 188).

2. Divided into the volumes *Upstream (Suliu*, 2008) and *Mountain (Shan*, 2010), *River's End* tells the story of a Chinese Malaysian teenage boy who

joins a group of Westerners for a longboat safari up the Kapuas River (Borneo's longest river) from Pontianak in Indonesian West Kalimantan to the heart of the island's interior. It is a haunting tale of excessive sex and bloody violence against the backdrop of the politically volatile mid-1960s in Indonesia as well as the Chinese Hungry Ghost Festival, observed mainly by settler communities in Southeast Asia.

3. Sung-sheng Chang describes Li Yongping's fiction as "the apex of the development of modernist aestheticism" in Taiwan (*Modernism*, 17). In *Sinophone Malaysian Literature*, Alison Groppe provides a very detailed reading and interpretation of the "reflective nostalgia" in Li Yongping's *The Snow Falls in Clouds*, including episodes that take place in the Borneo rainforest (187–232).

4. "Dayak" is a loose term for all the indigenous groups of Borneo.

5. See Chapter 3.

6. Huggan and Tiffin, *Postcolonial Ecocriticism*, 3–5.

7. "Blue water colonialism" typically describes the direct rule over indigenous populations and the occupation of their lands by a small group of colonists far from the imperial metropole. By contrast, settler colonialism presumes that "the native population is swamped by a large mass of colonial settlers" who come to constitute "cultural majorities" (Weaver, "Indigenousness and Indigeneity," 223; Johnston and Lawson, "Settler Colonies," 372).

8. Huggan and Tiffin, *Postcolonial Ecocriticism*, 8, emphasis in the original.

9. Veracini, *Settler Colonialism*, 8, emphasis in the original.

10. Johnston and Lawson, "Settler Colonies," 364.

11. Lawson, "Comparative Studies," 157.

12. Veracini, *Settler Colonialism*, 3, emphases in the original.

13. Kuhn, *Chinese Among Others*, 83–84.

14. Ibid., 84; Ward, "Hakka Kongsi in Borneo," 363–64.

15. Li Yongping's literary aesthetic of *titto* (*zhitu*), a Taiwanese term that the author uses to celebrate the hardy pioneering spirit of his Hakka ancestors in Borneo, is a fine example of this. *Titto*, written with "two ancient and rare characters that combine the sun and moon character elements with that of walking or running," is a concept Li evokes to connect his own migratory trajectory (from Borneo to Taiwan) to the "long history of Hakka migration" (Groppe, *Sinophone Malaysian Literature*, 189–90).

16. Huggan and Tiffin, *Postcolonial Ecocriticism*, 14.

17. Edouard Glissant uses the term "opacity" to describe the right of the colonized subject not to be transparent, thoroughly knowable, and reductively translatable through the "vehicular language" and epistemology of the colonizer (*Poetics of Relation*, 111–20).

18. Huggan and Tiffin, *Postcolonial Ecocriticism*, 13.

19. Sung-sheng Chang, *Literary Culture*, 91.

20. Yu Kwang-chung, *Shou ye ren*, 25 (this follows Yu's own translation from the bilingual volume).

21. In *Ecoambiguity*, Karen Thornber notes that despite its more general concern "with the plight of rural individuals" as "victims of Taiwan's

increasingly capitalist, urban, and materialist culture," Taiwanese nativism "does not neglect damage to nature," as many of the island's nature writers who emerged in the market-driven literary environment of the 1980s and 1990s are indebted to the nativist movement (90).

22. Sung-sheng Chang, *Literary Culture*, 8.

23. Choong, *Wujin de zhuixun*, 175–76.

24. As the third-largest island in the world, Borneo's territory is largely split between Indonesia and Malaysia, with the tiny but wealthy oil sultanate of Brunei occupying two slivers of land in the northern portion of the island. For Indonesia and Malaysia, Borneo represents a frontier far removed from the seats of national power in Javanese Jakarta and peninsular Kuala Lumpur. Groups loyal to the Sultan of Sulu in the southern Philippines still claim the Malaysian state of Sabah as their own. The ongoing territorial conflicts in Sabah date back to treaties signed between the Dutch, the British North Borneo Company, the Sultan of Brunei, and the Sultan of Sulu, which transformed the territory into the British colony of North Borneo in the late nineteenth century.

25. As the main producers of the nation's petroleum, Sabah and Sarawak have "contributed significantly to Malaysia's trade surplus," yet they have "gained little from the industry" and have "experienced net outflows of public funds" (Wee, *Regional Disparities*, xiii–xv).

26. Pan Yutong, *Ye dian*, 231–47.

27. Choong, *Wujin de zhuixun*, 177–79.

28. Pan Yutong, *He'an chuanshuo*, 204–9, 236–37.

29. Ibid., 104–5.

30. Ibid., 106–7.

31. Pan Yutong, *Jing shui da xue*, 267.

32. Ibid., 267, 274–75.

33. World Wildlife Foundation, *Borneo*, 6–10.

34. Between 1998 and 2003, the annual growth rate of oil palm areas was nearly eight percent in Sarawak and Sabah (ibid., 7).

35. Pan Yutong, *He'an chuanshuo*, 73

36. Ibid., 57, 63.

37. Pan Honghui, "Yulin zhi ge," 39.

38. Tsu, *Sound and Script*, 206, 213.

39. Sarawak's inception as a state began in 1841 when the Sultan of Brunei offered land concessions along the Sarawak River to James Brooke, a British "merchant-adventurer," in exchange for leading military campaigns against the Ibans, the most populous of Sarawak's Dayak groups. Thus began a hundred years of rule under the "White Rajas." After Malaya gained independence in 1957, Britain negotiated the inclusion of Singapore and its Borneo colonies in the "Malaysian merger," lest they fall into the hands of a communist-friendly Indonesia under President Sukarno. Although Sarawak and Sabah elected to join Malaysia, Brunei worried about the potential redistribution of its oil profits and refused to join, remaining a protectorate of the British until 1984. Aware of Malaya's designs on Borneo as early as 1961, Sukarno denounced Malaysia a "neocolonial" plot by the British and declared a policy

of Konfontasi or "Confrontation" that involved five years of violent skirmishes along the Sarawak-Kalimantan border, ending only with the bloody "counter-coup" that toppled Sukarno and decimated the Indonesian Communist Party (PKI) in 1965 (Andaya and Andaya, *History of Malaysia*, 128; Bernards, "Ambivalent Boundaries," 91). This tumultuous historical period serves as an important backdrop to Chang Kuei-hsing's novels on Borneo.

40. This is how Edouard Glissant, in *Caribbean Discourse*, describes the symbolic force of the forest in the fiction of Gabriel García Márquez (82–83). For many Sinophone literary critics, Chang Kuei-hsing's novels draw comparisons to those of Márquez.

41. Chang Kuei-hsing, *Hou bei*, 12.

42. David Wang, "Zai qun xiang yu hou dang de jiaxiang," 26.

43. Chang Kuei-hsing, *Sailian zhi ge*, 11–12.

44. Ibid., 17–18.

45. Ibid., 28–36.

46. E. K. Tan, *Rethinking Chineseness*, 112–39.

47. Chang Kuei-hsing, *Qun xiang*, 60.

48. Ibid., 91.

49. Ibid., 70, 146.

50. Ibid., 129.

51. Ibid., 30.

52. I borrow this phrasing from Edouard Glissant, who posits "Relation" as a "third dynamic" of cross-cultural interaction between cultures: whereas the first two dynamics trace an "arrowlike projection" of movement between a hierarchically configured imperial center and colonial periphery (or vice-versa), the third dynamic is "curved," making "every periphery into a center" (*Poetics of Relation*, 29).

53. Bachner, "Reinventing Chinese Writing," 191–92.

54. Chang Kuei-hsing, *Qun xiang*, 181; Bernards, "Plantation and Rainforest," 335. Both E. K. Tan and Andrea Bachner point out how the novel functions as a metanarrative on language and script as mediation and translation (E. K. Tan, *Rethinking Chineseness*, 117; Bachner, "Reinventing Chinese Writing," 193–94).

55. David Wang, "Zai qun xiang yu hou dang de jiaxiang," 28. According to Mikhail Bakhtin's definition, "heteroglossia" is "the base condition governing the operation of meaning in any utterance," an act that requires one to "appropriate the words of others and populate them with one's own intention" (*Dialogic Imagination*, 428).

56. Bachner, "Reinventing Chinese Writing," 185.

57. Elsewhere, I have analyzed the symbolic spaces of the plantation and the rainforest in *Monkey Cup*. See Bernards, "Plantation and Rainforest."

58. Chang Kuei-hsing, *Wo sinian de changmian zhong de Nanguo gongzhu*, 45. In my translations from the novel, I have used Valerie Jaffee's 2007 translation as a reference and guide, but have made several modifications. All citations below refer to Chang's original work.

59. Chang Kuei-hsing, *Wo sinian de changmian zhong de Nanguo gongzhu*, 46, 231.

60. Ibid., 230.
61. Ibid., 97, 231.
62. Ibid., 187.
63. Ibid., 92.
64. Ibid., 45.
65. As Alison Groppe explains, Li Yongping creates a similar chain of resemblances in *The Snow Falls in Clouds*: the adult male narrator wanders the streets of Taipei, telling stories of Kuching to a young girl who at times interrupts the narration with her own questions and comments (*Sinophone Malaysian Literature*, 195–230).
66. Chang Kuei-hsing, *Wo sinian de changmian zhong de Nanguo gongzhu*, 126.
67. Ibid., 122.
68. Ibid., 222–30.

CHAPTER 5

1. See Chapter 3.
2. Kuhn, *Chinese Among Others*, 148.
3. The state assigns such racial designations to every citizen: it is the second item of information (after one's name) on the National Registration Identity Card (NRIC). Recent census statistics define the nation as 75 percent Chinese, 13 percent Malay, 9 percent Indian, and 3 percent "Other."
4. PuruShotam, *Negotiating Multiculturalism*, 7, 17, 221.
5. Chua, *Communitarian Ideology*, 1.
6. George, *Singapore*, 174.
7. Lee Kuan Yew, *From Third World to First*, 155–56.
8. PuruShotam, *Negotiating Multiculturalism*, 12.
9. Singapore's bilingual education policy, first implemented in 1966, evolved over the first decade of independence to mandate, by the late 1970s, that the compulsory "second-language" subject (with few exceptions) be one's "mother tongue" (PuruShotam, *Negotiating Multiculturalism*, 177).
10. Recalling that "the best ministers in my early cabinets were not born in Singapore" but in Malaya, China, and India, Lee Kuan Yew claims that Singapore only thrives because it is "useful to the world" as a beacon attracting foreign talent (*From Third World to First*, 665, 690).
11. Heng and Devan, "State Fatherhood," 357.
12. The National Library Board's *Singapore Literary Pioneers Gallery Guide* includes short biographies of Singapore's foundational authors in the four official languages, with descriptions in the original languages and English translations on the facing pages (only English is provided for the Anglophone writers).
13. Wong Meng Voon, *Xinjiapo Huawen wenxue*, 240.
14. Poon, Holden, and Lim, introduction to *Writing Singapore*, xxii.
15. In Edwin Thumboo's ambitious anthology *The Fiction of Singapore*, non-Anglophone works appear only in English translation, reinforcing English as common medium. The section introductions are written by different

specialists in each literary tradition. Only Thumboo's general introduction briefly assesses their differences: each of Singapore's official literatures is "intrinsically bound to both the antecedents of the respective ethnic groups and the English using community" (i–ii).

16. Shirley Lim, *Writing S.E./Asia in English*, 137.

17. Nirmala PuruShotam suggests that multiracialism has made it "nearly impossible" for one to identify oneself as "Singaporean" without reference to being "Singaporean-hyphen-Chinese," "Singaporean-hyphen-Malay," or "Singaporean-hyphen-Indian" (*Negotiating Multiculturalism*, 215).

18. Singaporean English, or "Singlish," is a local Anglophone creole that mixes English with Hokkien and Malay vocabulary and grammatical patterns, while also drawing upon words from Teochew, Tamil, Cantonese, Hakka, and Mandarin.

19. See Chapter 2.

20. Wong Meng Voon, *Xinjiapo Huawen wenxue*, 268; Wong Meng Voon, "Singapore Chinese Literature," xi–xii.

21. Lee Kuan Yew, *From Third World to First*, 145–49.

22. Ibid., 186.

23. Lee Kuan Yew, *Singapore Story*, 402.

24. Ibid., 332.

25. Lee Kuan Yew, *From Third World to First*, 147–51.

26. In 1981, the Nanyang campus reopened as the Nanyang Technological Institute, with its emphasis on science and technology clearly aimed at dissociating the school from the political orientation of its namesake. Ten years later, the institution's status was upgraded from an institute to a university. In 2005, some faculty members of NTU and alumni of the old Nanyang petitioned to revert the school's name to Nanyang University, but the move was postponed.

27. Another example is *South Seas Commercial News* (*Nanyang shangbao*, aka *Nanyang Siang Pau)*, which according to Lee Kuan Yew "turned rabidly pro-communist and pro-Chinese language and culture" in 1970, painting Lee and the PAP as a government of "pseudo foreigners who forget their ancestors." Lee argues that such newspapers "catered to their readers' communal interests and did not have any Singapore identity" (*From Third World to First*, 148, 186).

28. In 1995, Yeng opened the Grassroots Book Room (Caogen Shushi), a bookstore that has doubled as a publisher of Sinophone Singaporean literature. Yeng retired and sold the store in 2014.

29. George, *Singapore*, 140.

30. Yeng, *Bu cunzai de qingren*, 36–38.

31. Ibid., 38.

32. Ibid., emphasis added.

33. Ibid., 39.

34. Lee Kuan Yew, *From Third World to First*, 173–74.

35. George, *Singapore*, 140.

36. Yeng, *Yi ge xiang wo zheyang de nanren*, 62.

37. Ibid., 17, 24–25, 168.

38. Ibid., 30, 150. The parrot is a common motif in Yeng's fiction. In a satirical work of miniature short fiction entitled "Libel" ("Feibang," 2003) whose publication was censored by the Singaporean government, a parrot at a bird shop escapes from its cage and flies to a nearby street where a demonstrator is speaking out against the PAP. After mimicking the demonstrator's slogan—"Overthrow dictatorship!"—the parrot is sentenced to one year in prison for libel. For not "properly rearing" the parrot, the bird shop owner is fined SGD$50,000 and sentenced to six months in prison (Yeng, *Bu cunzai de qingren*, 122).

39. Yeng, *Yi ge xiang wo zheyang de nanren*, 44.

40. Ibid., 195.

41. Ibid., 177–97.

42. Yeng, *Guji de lian*, 25.

43. Ibid., 131–32.

44. Ibid., 13–14.

45. Yeng, *Saodong*, 65–66, 247.

46. Ibid., 49, 250–51, 263. During the Emergency period (1948–60), the British forcibly resettled Chinese Malayan "squatters" (many of whom lost their property during the Japanese occupation) into quarantined "New Villages," allowing officials to monitor their movement and enforce strict food controls to cut off the Malayan Communist Party's sustenance and support (Andaya and Andaya, *History of Malaysia*, 273–74). In *Unrest*, Weikang recalls that, as an adolescent, he was once cruelly interrogated by the British police simply because he brought a can of food back to Chaah (Yeng, *Saodong*, 59–60).

47. Yeng, *Saodong*, 3–4, 11.

48. Ibid., 13–14, 149–51.

49. Literally meaning "united morning newspaper," *Lianhe zaobao* is Singapore's largest Sinophone newspaper, created from a 1983 merger between *South Seas Commercial News* and *Singapore Daily*.

50. Chia is the younger brother of the acclaimed author Xi Ni Er (Chia Hwee Pheng [Xie Huiping], 1957-), whose penname is a transliteration of the English "senior." Xi Ni Er is a master of the miniature short story (*weixing xiaoshuo*) genre (Wong Meng Voon, *Xinjiapo Huawen wenxue*, 302–9).

51. Chia, *Chonggou Nanyang tuxiang*, 74.

52. Ibid., 124.

53. Ibid., 74.

54. For an account and analysis of the massacre, see Cribb, *Indonesian Killings*. For an analysis of how the massacre targeted Chinese Indonesians, see Coppel, *Indonesian Chinese*.

55. Chia, *Chonggou Nanyang tuxiang*, 69–84.

56. Ibid., 68–70, 87.

57. Ibid., 94.

58. Ibid., 107–9.

59. Chua, *Communitarian Ideology*, 5–6, 158, 162.

60. Lee Kuan Yew, *From Third World to First*, 153.

61. Heng and Devan, "State Fatherhood," 351.

62. PuruShotam, *Negotiating Multiculturalism*, 69.

63. Lee Kuan Yew, *From Third World to First*, 154. Lee was aware of the absurdity in proposing Mandarin as the "Chinese mother tongue," admitting that the language was "totally alien" to him growing up. Baba Malay was his "home language," and his grandfather was a Hakka immigrant (*Singapore Story*, 26–35, 152, 355).

64. Full diplomatic relations between Singapore and China were not established until 1990, as Lee Kuan Yew fulfilled a promise to ASEAN not to recognize Beijing until Indonesia did likewise (Tu, "Cultural China," 22).

65. Lee Kuan Yew, *From Third World to First*, 155, 665, 690.

66. Several critics have exposed the contradiction in the campaign's promotion of Mandarin as simultaneously indispensable to globalization and only necessary as a "mother tongue" for the racial majority, as it denies minorities the right to partake of this necessary resource for upward mobility and promotes a racial possessiveness toward Mandarin in the classroom. Nevertheless, the Speak Mandarin Campaign has achieved its intended results: government estimates suggest 87 percent of Chinese Singaporeans were able to speak Mandarin by 1992, a glaring contrast to the 0.5 percent who claimed it their mother tongue in 1965 (George, *Singapore*, 162; PuruShotam, *Negotiating Multiculturalism*, 199; Heng and Devan, "State Fatherhood," 363).

67. The title of the Singaporean novel *Foreign Bodies* (1997) by Hwee Hwee Tan alludes to the processes of "East-West" cross-contamination against which "Asian values" and "Speak Good English" purport to defend. In defiance of these campaigns, Mei, the novel's protagonist, asserts: "[W]e didn't speak 'broken' English because we lacked the ability to speak the Queen's English; we spoke Singlish, because with all its contortions of grammar and pronunciation, its new and localized vocabulary, Singlish expressed our thoughts in a way that the formal, perfectly enunciated, anal BBC World Service English never could. Besides, who wants to talk like some O level textbook, instead of using our own language, our home language, the language of our souls?" (8).

68. For example, in Lim's *The River's Song* (a novel set against the backdrop of the postcolonial state's campaign to clean up the Singapore River and drive out riverside tenants), Ping, the protagonist and daughter of "Chinatown's Pipa Queen," discovers after her mother's death that the father she never knew was Indian. Helping Ping to overcome the shock of her discovery, her former lover, Weng, tells her: "Chinese, Indian or Chindian, your roots are here—in this river" (284).

69. Suchen Lim, *Fistful of Colours*, 31.

70. Holden, "Interrogating Multiculturalism," 281.

71. Suchen Lim, *Fistful of Colours*, 19, 241.

72. Ibid., 144.

73. Ibid., 127, 141–42, 147.

74. Ibid., 58–59.

75. Ibid., 258.

76. Ibid., 68–69.

77. Ibid., 76.
78. Ibid., 79, 247.
79. Ibid., 70, 105–8.
80. Ibid., 165, 248–52.
81. Ibid., 32. The generic male nickname Ah Beng and its female counterpart Ah Huay (or Ah Lian) pejoratively denote "someone who is not highly educated, culturally crass, usually speaks Hokkien and Mandarin, and uses Singlish in certain social settings" (Quah, "Performing Multilingualism," 100).
82. Suchen Lim, *Fistful of Colours*, 77–78.
83. Ibid., 186.
84. Ibid., 188–90.
85. Ibid., 225.
86. Ibid.
87. Terms include *huan-na* (Hokkien: mixed Southeast Asian blood), *ulu* (Malay: upcountry, upstream), and *dhoby* (Tamil: washerman).
88. Suchen Lim, *Fistful of Colours*, 18.
89. Built in the early 1930s, the Tanjong Pagar Railway Station was, until its recent closure, the southern terminus of the Keretapi Tanah Melayu (KTM), or Malaysian national railway (Gill, *Guide to the Murals*, 7, 31). Following an agreement (and exchange) between Singapore and Malaysia in 2011, Singapore gained control of the territory occupied by the station and the railroad tracks, as Malaysia moved station operations northward to the Woodlands Checkpoint. The agreement stipulates that the Tanjong Pagar station shall be preserved by the National Heritage Board.
90. Suchen Lim, *Fistful of Colours*, 297–98.
91. Portions of this mural are featured on the front and back cover of this book.
92. Gill, *Guide to the Murals*, 20, 24.

CHAPTER 6

1. "Thai exceptionalism" is a claim made by Thai scholars to avoid comparison with other postcolonial societies. The essays in *The Ambiguous Allure of the West*, a volume coedited by Rachel Harrison and Peter Jackson, challenge this claim, arguing that Thailand's semicolonial, or "crypto-colonial," history is analytically useful for comparative colonial and postcolonial studies.
2. Anderson, *Spectre of Comparisons*, 328. Adun Rattanamankasem further claims that the Sino-Thai are "the minority with the fewest number of problems" (*Kamnoet khon Taečhiu*, 164).
3. "Tai" refers to a large ethno-linguistic group (with multiple subgroupings) spanning several nations in Southeast Asia, including southwestern China, Burma, Thailand, and Laos. This chapter refers to the Tai majority in Thailand as the "Tai-Thai" or "Tai-Siamese," depending on historical period.
4. Thongchai, *Siam Mapped*, 14–17.

5. Adun Rattanamankasem identifies two historical "types" of Sino-Thai: those with and those without a Tai-Thai parent (usually the mother) (*Kamnoet khon Taečhiu*, 146).

6. The integration of Chinese settlers in the Philippines (periodically the target of violence under the Spanish) is another "success story," especially with its historical formation of a highly influential mestizo community. See Skinner, "Creolized Chinese Societies."

7. See Anderson, introduction to *In the Mirror*.

8. This term is also commonly spelled Lukjin or Lookjin.

9. Adun, *Kamnoet khon Taečhiu*, 150.

10. Baker and Pasuk, *History of Thailand*, 264–65.

11. Anderson, *Imagined Communities*, 101.

12. Baker and Pasuk, *History of Thailand*, 265.

13 Ibid.

14. Nidhi, *Pen and Sail*, 78.

15. Adun, *Kamnoet khon Taečhiu*, 150.

16. Nidhi, *Pen and Sail*, 78–80. Much of Nidhi's book traces how the commercial values of the Sino-Thai mercantile class influenced the cultural and literary aesthetics of the Siamese nobility in Bangkok prior to 1850.

17. Keyes, *Thailand*, 133.

18. Ibid.; Skinner, *Chinese Society in Thailand*, 127.

19. As Benedict Anderson writes, the "prime models" of national modernization for King Chulalongkorn (Rama V, r. 1868–1910) "were not the United Kingdom or Germany, but rather the colonial *beamtenstaaten* of the Dutch East Indies, British Malaya, and the Raj" (*Imagined Communities*, 99–100).

20. Kuhn, *Chinese Among Others*, 80.

21. Kasian, "Imagined Uncommunity," 76.

22. Ibid., 77–79.

23. Adun, *Kamnoet khon Taečhiu*, 168–71; Baker and Pasuk, *History of Thailand*, 93. Although Teochews predominated, Hakkas and Hainanese were also well represented among the arriving population.

24. Kasian, "Imagined Uncommunity," 78.

25. Baker and Pasuk, *History of Thailand*, 96, 271.

26. Baker and Pasuk, introduction to *Pridi by Pridi*, xi–xiv.

27. Phibun demonized Pridi as a communist and attempted to scapegoat him in the assassination of King Ananda Mahidol (Rama VIII) in 1946, leading to Pridi's permanent exile from the country (Ibid., ix–xiv).

28. Adun, *Kamnoet khon Taečhiu*, 154.

29. Baker and Pasuk, *History of Thailand*, 39, 124–25.

30. Kasian, "Imagined Uncommunity," 78, 82. Some evening schools persisted, especially in the peninsular south, where some parents also sent their children across the border to Malaya (particularly Penang) to receive Sinophone education (Adun, *Kamnoet khon Taečhiu*, 151–54).

31. Baker and Pasuk, *History of Thailand*, 146.

32. Ibid., 168.

33. Anderson, *Spectre of Comparisons*, 162.

34. Ibid., 173, 180.
35. Baker and Pasuk, *History of Thailand*, 140.
36. Smyth and Manas, introduction to *The Sergeant's Garland*, xvi.
37. Most notably, this includes the attacks on student protesters at Thammasat University in October 1976 by the Thai military and "Village Scout" militias (Baker and Pasuk, *History of Thailand*, 193–94).
38. Ibid., 205–6.
39. Suchit, *Čhek pon Lao*, 11–12.
40. Chan and Tong, "Rethinking Assimilation," 151.
41. Ibid., 164.
42. Kuhn, *Chinese Among Others*, 80.
43. Fang, "Taiguo Huawen wenyi," 63.
44. Ibid., 57.
45. Li Qing, introduction to *Tai Hua wenxue*, 3; Wu Yiqi, "Taiguo Huawen wenxue," 320.
46. In addition to Hong Kong, most critical interest in Sinophone Thai literature comes from scholars and conferences held at the University of Amoy in Xiamen, an institution that earned its elite reputation through the investments and contributions of Overseas Chinese (Huaqiao) and "Repatriated Overseas Chinese" (Guiqiao), particularly from Southeast Asia.
47. Fang Siruo calls this the foundational period of modern Sinophone Thai literature, identifying popular fiction as its representative genre ("Taiguo Huawen wenyi," 62–64).
48. Shen Yiwen's collection, *Daybreak: Selected Thai Short Fiction (Liming: Taiguo duanpian xiaoshuo xuan*, 1974), includes a story by Lao Khamhom (penname of Khamsing Srinawk, 1930-), arguably the foremost author of the Literature for Life movement.
49. *Stormy Yaowarat Road* was the second sequential novel Fang organized. The first, *Biography of a Ruined Man (Pobishe waizhuan;* serialized in the late 1950s), is a critique of materialism: its title is Teochew slang for a bankrupted man (Weng, "*Pobishe waizhuan*," 407–9).
50. Nian, *Tai Hua xiezuo ren*, 3–4, 34, 61, 69–71, 221–22; Fang, "*Fengyu Yaohuali* de dansheng," i–x; Weng, "*Pobishe waizhuan*," 412.
51. Li Hong et al., *Fengyu Yaohuali*, 120, 250.
52. Ibid., 35, 85, 189.
53. Weng, "*Pobishe waizhuan*," 408–14.
54. Li Jun's name is likely an allusion to the rebel in the classical Chinese saga, *The Water Margin*, who escapes persecution in China to become lord of Siam.
55. Li Hong et al., *Fengyu Yaohuali*, 66–67.
56. Ibid., 126.
57. Ibid., 251.
58. Another excellent example is the novel *The Alleyway (Louxiang*, 1980) by Ba Er (penname of Yan Bi, 1914-[?]). A snapshot of Bangkok Sino-Thai society at the end of the 1970s, *The Alleyway* captures a fleeting moment at the "tail end of a rainy season in the Nanyang" (11), critically reflecting upon the heroin abuse that was a growing epidemic among urban Thai youth at the

time. At the end of the novel, the working-class community pools together their resources to send one of their troubled teens to a Buddhist temple that serves as a rehabilitation center.

59. Buddhist monks played an unprecedented role in the social activism of the 1970s, largely appealing to the national conscience over the issue of rural poverty (Anderson, *Spectre of Comparisons*, 167).

60. Weng, "*Pobishe waizhuan*," 412.

61. Chen Xianmao, "Taiguo Huawen wenxue," 329.

62. Ibid., 328–29.

63. Li Hong et al., *Fengyu Yaohuali*, 48, 50, 99.

64. Adun, *Kamnoet khon Taečhiu*, 294–98. Adun's study includes a glossary of Teochew vocabulary derived from Thai (302–12).

65. Li Hong et al., *Fengyu Yaohuali*, 94.

66. This is the same *nai* in Fang Siruo's Sinophone penname, Nai Fang, which, appropriating the Thai meaning of the term, means "Mr. Fang."

67. Li Hong et al., *Fengyu Yaohuali*, 131.

68. I have gleaned these terms from several Thai-language novels: in addition to Botan's *Before the Fog Lifts* and Praphatson Sewikun's *Through the Pattern of the Dragon* (the two works examined in this chapter), Chitra Konanthakiat's *Papa (Apa*, 2008) and Kantima's *Last Petal of the Peony (Botan klip sutthai*, 2008) describe analogous circumstances with similar language. The phrase "a sleeping mat and a pillow" is a popular Thai metaphor describing the poor conditions in which Chinese immigrants arrived in Siam (Adun, *Kamnoet khon Taečhiu*, 140). Most of these novels are based on true stories: Chitra's *Papa*, for example, fictionalizes the biographies of several ridiculously wealthy Sino-Thai business magnates and their humble Teochew origins, including Chin Sophonpanich (1910–88), founder and former CEO of Bangkok Bank and Bangkok Insurance, and Vanich Chaiyawan, chairman of Thai Life, the nation's second-largest life insurance company (*Apa*, 20, 102).

69. Traditionally, the *čhao sua* were powerful Sino-Thais who traded "on behalf of the king and senior courtiers" and who by royal patronage amassed incredible wealth and status in eighteenth- and nineteenth-century Bangkok (Baker and Pasuk, *History of Thailand*, 34).

70. Kasian, "Imagined Uncommunity," 86.

71. Kepner, *Lioness in Bloom*, 43.

72. This is now the Southeast Asian Writers (S.E.A. Write) Award.

73. Botan, *Čhotmai čhak Mưang Thai*, 629. An English translation of the novel by Susan Kepner is available from Silkworm Books.

74. Adun, *Kamnoet khon Taečhiu*, 291–92.

75. Botan, *Kon sai mok lưan*, 3–4.

76. Ibid., 57.

77. In Thai, *samunphrai* commonly denotes herbs, vegetables, and fruits considered to possess health benefits.

78. Botan, *Kon sai mok lưan*, 486.

79. Barang, postscript to *Time in a Bottle*, 248–52.

80. Praphatson, *Lot lai mangkon*, 7.

81. Ibid., 17.
82. Ibid., 306.
83. Ibid., 69.
84. Ibid., 171.
85. Ibid., 42.

CONCLUSION

1. Brenda Chan, "Home, Identities," 121; Tai, "Big Little Nyonya."
2. Rudolph, *Reconstructing Identities*, 2, 273.
3. Kon, "Emily of Emerald Hill," 317.
4. Tai, "Big Little Nyonya."
5. Ibid.
6. *The Little Nyonya* is not the first award-winning Singaporean television drama whose predominant Mandarin dialogue displaces nonstandard Sinitic languages associated with a "Chinese subgroup" in postcolonial Singapore, despite the deep local lineages and widespread usage of these languages. The Mandarin family melodramas *The Teochew Family* (*Chaozhou jiazu*, 1995), *The Guest People* (*Kejia zhi ge*, 1997), and *Hainan Kopi Tales* (*Qiongyuan kafeixiang*, 2000) respectively allegorize the histories of Teochew, Hakka, and Hainanese migration and settlement in Singapore and other areas of Southeast Asia, including Cambodia and Indonesia.
7. Yung, "Territorialization," 137.
8. The hemispheric concept of the "Global South" emerged in the 1970s to draw attention to the economic dominance of (post)colonial societies in the South by an imperial North (Dirlik, "Global South").
9. Lionnet, "Continents and Archipelagoes," 1508.
10. Kuhn, *Chinese Among Others*, 296.
11. For example, see Tzu-hui Celina Hung's discussion of the *Mano Po* films in "Hunxue(yu)hua mailuo zhong de Huayu yuxi yanjiu."
12. Regarding the Philippines (in conjunction with post–Cultural Revolution China), see Caroline Hau's discussion of Bai Ren's *Adrift in the South Seas* (*Nanyang piaoliuji*) in "The Question of Foreigners."
13. Brent Hayes Edwards, for example, argues for a concept of "African diaspora" based not on "a principle of unity," but rather on heterogeneity within "a complex past of forced migrations and racialization" (*Practice of Diaspora*, 13).
14. See Hall, "West and the Rest."

BIBLIOGRAPHY

Adun Rattanamankasem อดุลย์ รัตนมั่นเกษม. *Kamnoet khon Taečhiu: Wiwatthanakan čhak adit thưng patčhuban* กำเนิดคนแต้จิ๋ว วิวัฒนาการจากอดีตถึงปัจจุบัน [The origins of the Teochew people: Evolution from past to present]. Bangkok: Samnakphim Saengdao, 2008.

Ai Wu 艾蕪. *Nan xing ji* 南行記 [Travels in the south]. Beijing: Zuojia Chubanshe, 1963.

Alatas, Syed Hussein. *The Myth of the Lazy Native*. Abingdon, Oxon, UK: Frank Cass, 1977.

Amrith, Sunil S. *Migration and Diaspora in Modern Asia*. Cambridge: Cambridge University Press, 2011.

Andaya, Barbara Watson, and Leonard Y. Andaya. *A History of Malaysia*. 2d ed. Basingstoke, UK: Palgrave, 2001.

Anderson, Benedict. *Imagined Communities: Reflections on the Origin and Spread of Nationalism*. London: Verso, 1991.

———. Introduction to *In the Mirror: Literature and Politics in Siam in the American Era*, edited and translated by Benedict R. O'G. Anderson and Ruchira Mendiones, 9–87. Bangkok: Editions Duang Kamol, 1985.

———. *The Spectre of Comparisons: Nationalism, Southeast Asia and the World*. London: Verso, 1998.

Ang, Ien. *On Not Speaking Chinese: Living Between Asia and the West*. London: Routledge, 2001.

Ashcroft, Bill, Gareth Griffiths, and Helen Tiffin. *The Empire Writes Back: Theory and Practice in Post-Colonial Literatures*. London: Routledge, 2002.

Ba Er 巴爾. *Louxiang* 陋巷 [The alleyway]. Bangkok: Dapeng Chuban, 1980.

Bachner, Andrea. *Beyond Sinology: Chinese Writing and the Scripts of Culture*. New York: Columbia University Press, 2014.

———. "Reinventing Chinese Writing: Zhang Guixing's Sinographic

Translations." In *Global Chinese Literature: Critical Essays*, edited by Jing Tsu and David Der-wei Wang, 177–96. Leiden, Netherlands: Brill, 2010.

Baker, Chris, and Pasuk Phongpaichit. *A History of Thailand*. Cambridge: Cambridge University Press, 2005.

———. Introduction to *Pridi by Pridi: Selected Writings on Life, Politics, and Economy*, by Pridi Banomyong, i–xxvi. Chiang Mai, Thailand: Silkworm Books, 2000.

Bakhtin, M. M. *The Dialogic Imagination: Four Essays*, translated by Caryl Emerson and Michael Holquist. Austin: University of Texas Press, 1981.

Barang, Marcel. Postscript to *Time in a Bottle*, by Praphatsorn Seiwikun, 241–52. Bangkok: Thai Modern Classics, 1996.

Barlow, Tani E. "On 'Colonial Modernity.'" In *Formations of Colonial Modernity in East Asia*, edited by Tani E. Barlow, 1–20. Durham, NC: Duke University Press, 1997.

Bergère, Marie-Claire. *Sun Yat-sen*, translated by Janet Lloyd. Stanford, CA: Stanford University Press, 1994.

Bernards, Brian. "Ambivalent Boundaries: Nanyang Chinese and Ethnic Violence in Borneo." *Stanford Journal of East Asian Affairs* 9, no. 1 (2009): 88–101.

———. "Beyond Diaspora and Multiculturalism: Recuperating Creolization in Postcolonial Sinophone Malaysian Literature." *Postcolonial Studies* 15, no. 3 (2012): 311–29.

———. "Plantation and Rainforest: Chang Kuei-hsing and a South Seas Discourse of Coloniality and Nature." In *Sinophone Studies: A Critical Reader*, edited by Shu-mei Shih, Chien-hsin Tsai, and Brian Bernards, 325–38. New York: Columbia University Press, 2013.

Bi Xia 碧霞. "Sichang de yiri ye" 私娼的一日夜 [A day and night in the life of an unlicensed prostitute]. *Xingzhou ribao* 星洲日報 [Singapore daily], August 30, 1941, Chen xing fukan 辰星副刊 [Morning star supplement] section, early edition.

Botan โบตั๋น. *Čhotmai čhak Mưang Thai* จดหมายจากเมืองไทย [Letters from Thailand]. Bangkok: Chomromdek, 1999.

———. *Kon sai mok lưan* ก่อนสายหมอกเลือน [Before the fog lifts]. Bangkok: Chomromdek, 1987.

———. *Letters from Thailand*, translated by Susan F. Kepner. Chiang Mai, Thailand: Silkworm Books, 2002.

———. *Phuying khon nan chư Bunrot* ผู้หญิงคนนั้นชื่อบุญรอด [That woman's name is Boonrawd]. Bangkok, Chomromdek, 1981.

Bowen, John. "The Contributions Development of Southeast Asian Studies in the United States." In *The Politics of Knowledge: Area Studies and the*

Disciplines, edited by David Szanton, 386–425. Berkeley: University of California Press, 2004.

Cao Xueqin. *The Story of the Stone: A Chinese Novel in Five Volumes*. Vol. 1, *The Golden Days*, translated by David Hawkes. London: Penguin Books, 1973.

———. *The Story of the Stone: A Chinese Novel in Five Volumes*. Vol. 2, *The Crab-Flower Club*, translated by David Hawkes. London: Penguin Books, 1977.

Casanova, Pascale. *The World Republic of Letters*, translated by M. B. DeBevoise. Cambridge, MA: Harvard University Press, 2007.

Casino, Eric S., and Myongsup Shin. "South China Sea or 'Asian Mediterranean Sea': Re-conceptualizing a Common Regional Zone." *International Area Review* 2, no. 1 (1999): 43–64.

Chan, Brenda. "Home, Identities and Transnational Appeal: The Case of Singaporean Television Dramas." *Critical Studies in Television* 6, no. 2 (2011): 114–26.

Chan Kwok Bun, and Tong Chee Kiong. "Rethinking Assimilation and Ethnicity: The Chinese in Thailand." *International Migration Review* 27, no. 1 (1993): 140–68.

Chan Tah Wei (Chen Dawei) 陳大爲. *Kaojin Luomoyanna* 靠近儸摩衍那 [Approaching the Ramayana]. Taipei: Jiuge Chubanshe, 2005.

Chang Kuei-hsing (Zhang Guixing) 張貴興. *Hou bei* 猴杯 [Monkey cup]. Taipei: Lianhe Wenxue, 2000.

———. *My South Seas Sleeping Beauty: A Tale of Memory and Longing*, translated by Valerie Jaffee. New York: Columbia University Press, 2007.

———. *Qun xiang* 群象 [The elephant herd]. Taipei: Maitian Chuban, 2006.

———. *Sailian zhi ge* 賽蓮之歌 [Siren song]. Taipei: Maitian Chuban, 2002.

———. *Wo sinian de changmian zhong de Nanguo gongzhu* 我思念的長眠中的南國公主 [My South Seas sleeping beauty]. Taipei: Maitian Chuban, 2001.

Chang, Sung-sheng Yvonne. *Literary Culture in Taiwan: Martial Law to Market Law*. New York: Columbia University Press, 2004.

———. *Modernism and the Nativist Resistance: Contemporary Chinese Fiction from Taiwan*. Durham, NC: Duke University Press, 1993.

Chaudenson, Robert. *Creolization of Language and Culture*, translated by Salikoko S. Mufwene. London: Routledge, 2001.

Chen Chen 陳忱. *Shuihu houzhuan* 水滸後傳 [Water margin: A sequel]. 2 Vols. Taipei: Fengyun Shidai Chubanshe, 1987.

Chen Xianmao 陳賢茂. "Taiguo Huawen wenxue zhong de Chaoshan wenhua tezheng" 泰国华文文学中的潮汕文化特征 [The Teochew-Swatow cultural features of Sinophone Thai literature]. In *Haiwai Huawen wenxue shi* 海外华文文学史 [A history of Sinophone literature overseas], vol. 2, edited by Chen Xianmao 陳賢茂, 328–42. Xiamen: Lujiang Chubanshe, 1999.

Chia Joo Ming (Xie Yumin) 謝裕民. *Chonggou Nanyang tuxiang* 重构南洋图像 [Reconstructing an image of the South Seas]. Singapore: Full House Communications, 2005.

Chitra Konanthakiat จิตรา ก่อนันทเกียรติ. *Apa* อาปา [Papa]. Bangkok: Samnakphim Chitra, 2008.

Chiu, Kuei-fen. "Empire of the Chinese Sign: The Question of Chinese Diasporic Imagination in Transnational Literary Production." *The Journal of Asian Studies* 67, no. 2 (2008): 593–620.

Cho, George. *The Malaysian Economy: Spatial Perspectives.* London: Routledge, 1990.

Chong Fah Hing (Zhuang Huaxing) 莊華興. "Ma Hua wenxue yu Malai wenxue: ruhe dingwei?" 马华文学与马来文学：如何定位？ [Sinophone Malaysian literature and Malay literature: How can their positions be determined?]. *Renwen zazhi* 人文杂志 [Journal of humanities] 44, no. 11 (2000): 14–18.

Choong Yee Voon (Zhong Yiwen) 鍾怡雯. *Wujin de zhuixun: dangdai sanwen de quanshi yu piping* 無盡的追尋：當代散文的詮釋與批評 [An eternal pursuit: Interpretation and criticism of contemporary prose]. Taipei: Lianhe Wenxue, 2004.

———. *Ye bandao* 野半島 [Wild peninsula]. Taipei: Lianhe Wenxue, 2007.

Chow, Kai-wing. "Narrating Nation, Race, and National Culture: Imagining the Hanzu Identity in Modern China." In *Constructing Nationhood in Modern East Asia*, edited by Kai-wing Chow, Kevin M. Doak, and Poshek Fu, 47–83. Ann Arbor: University of Michigan Press, 2001.

Chow, Rey. *Primitive Passions: Visuality, Sexuality, Ethnography, and Contemporary Chinese Cinema.* New York: Columbia University Press, 1995.

Chow Tse-tsung. *The May Fourth Movement: Intellectual Revolution in Modern China.* Stanford, CA: Stanford University Press, 1975.

Chua, Beng-Huat. *Communitarian Ideology and Democracy in Singapore.* London: Routledge, 1995.

———. "Southeast Asia in Postcolonial Studies: An Introduction." *Postcolonial Studies* 11, no. 3 (2008): 231–40.

Clifford, James. *Routes: Travel and Translation in the Late Twentieth Century.* Cambridge, MA: Harvard University Press, 1997.

Coppel, Charles A. *Indonesian Chinese in Crisis.* Kuala Lumpur: Oxford University Press, 1983.

Cribb, Robert. *The Indonesian Killings of 1965–1966*. Clayton, Victoria, Australia: Centre of Southeast Asian Studies, 1990.

Deleuze, Gilles, and Félix Guattari. *Kafka: Towards a Minor Literature*, translated by Dana Polan. Minneapolis: University of Minnesota Press, 1986.

DeLoughrey, Elizabeth M. *Routes and Roots: Navigating Caribbean and Pacific Island Literatures*. Honolulu: University of Hawai'i Press, 2007.

Demery, David, and Lionel Demery. *Adjustment and Equity in Malaysia*. Paris: Development Centre of the Organisation for Economic Cooperation and Development, 1992.

Dirlik, Arif. "The Global South: Predicament and Promise." *The Global South* 1, no. 1 (2007): 12–23.

Edwards, Brent Hayes. *The Practice of Diaspora: Literature, Translation, and the Rise of Black Internationalism*. Cambridge, MA: Harvard University Press, 2003.

Emmerson, Donald K. "'Southeast Asia': What's in a Name?" *Journal of Southeast Asian Studies* 15, no. 1 (1984): 1–21.

Eriksen, Thomas Hylland. "Creolization in Anthropological Theory and in Mauritius." In *Creolization: History, Ethnography, Theory*, edited by Charles Stewart, 153–77. Walnut Creek, CA: Left Coast Press, 2007.

Fan Chuo 樊綽. "Man shu" 蠻書 [Book of the southern barbarians]. In *Si ku quan shu* 四庫全書 [The imperial catalog], vol. 464, 1–41. Taipei: Taiwan Shangwu Yinshuguan, 1986.

Fang Siruo 方思若. "*Fengyu Yaohuali* de dansheng yu zuozhe qunxiang" 《風雨燿華力》的誕生與作者群像 [The birth of *Stormy Yaowarat road* and a portrait of the authors]. In *Fengyu Yaohuali: Jielong xiaoshuo* 風雨燿華力：接龍小說 [Stormy Yaowarat road: A sequential novel], by Li Hong 李虹 et al., i–x. Hong Kong: Dipingxian chubanshe, 1983.

———. "Taiguo Huawen wenyi huigu yu qianzhan" 泰國華文文藝回顧與前瞻 [Sinophone Thai literature: Review and outlook]. In *Taiguo Huawen zuojia xiehui wenji* 泰國華文作家協會文集 [The collected works of the Sinophone Thai Writers Association], edited by Taiguo Huawen zuojia xiehui 泰國華文作家協會, 55–71. Bangkok: Taiguo Huawen Zuojia Xiehui Chuban, 1991.

Fanon, Frantz. "On National Culture," translated by Constance Farrington. In *The Fanon Reader*, edited by Azzedine Haddour, 158–87. London: Pluto Press, 2006.

Farquhar, Mary Ann. *Children's Literature in China: From Lu Xun to Mao Zedong*. Armonk, NY: M. E. Sharpe, 1999.

Finlay, Robert. "Portuguese and Chinese Maritime Imperialism: Camões's

Lusiads and Luo Maodeng's *Voyage of the San Bao Eunuch*." *Comparative Studies in Society and History* 34, no. 2 (1992): 225–41.

Fiskesjö, Magnus. "On the 'Raw' and the 'Cooked' Barbarians of Imperial China." *Inner Asia* 1, no. 2 (1999): 139–68.

Furnivall, J. S. *Colonial Policy and Practice: A Comparative Study of Burma and Netherlands India*. Cambridge: Cambridge University Press, 1948.

George, Cherian. *Singapore, the Air-conditioned Nation: Essays on the Politics of Comfort and Control, 1990–2000*. Singapore: Landmark Books, 2000.

Ghosh, Durba, and Dane Kennedy. Introduction to *Decentring Empire: Britain, India, and the Transcolonial World*, edited by Durba Ghosh and Dane Kennedy, 1–15. Hyderabad, India: Orient Longman, 2006.

Gill, Simryn. *Guide to the Murals at Tanjong Pagar Railway Station, Singapore*. Singapore: Simryn Gill & Singapore Biennale, 2006.

Glissant, Edouard. *Caribbean Discourse: Selected Essays*, translated by J. Michael Dash. Charlottesville: University Press of Virginia, 1989.

———. *Poetics of Relation*, translated by Betsy Wing. Ann Arbor: University of Michigan Press, 1997.

Goldberg, David Theo. "Heterogeneity and Hybridity: Colonial Legacy, Postcolonial Heresy." In *A Companion to Postcolonial Studies*, edited by Henry Schwarz and Sangeeta Ray, 72–86. Malden, MA: Blackwell, 2005.

Goldman, Merle. Introduction to *Modern Chinese Literature in the May Fourth Era*, edited by Merle Goldman, 1–14. Cambridge, MA: Harvard University Press, 1977.

Groppe, Alison M. "The Dis/Reappearances of Yu Dafu in Ng Kim Chew's Fiction." *Modern Chinese Literature and Culture* 22, no. 2 (2010): 161–95.

———. *Sinophone Malaysian Literature: Not Made in China*. Amherst, NY: Cambria Press, 2013.

Guo Qifu 郭其福, ed. *Wu wang guochi: Zaichuang huihuang* 勿忘国耻·再创辉煌 [Never forget national humiliation: Recreating glory]. Wuhan, China: Wuhan Daxue Chubanshe, 1996.

Hall, Stuart. "Cultural Identity and Diaspora." In *Identity: Community, Culture, Difference*, edited by Jonathan Rutherford, 222–37. London: Lawrence and Wilshart, 1990.

———. "The West and the Rest: Discourse and Power." In *Formations of Modernity*, edited by Stuart Hall and Bram Gieben, 275–332. Oxford: The Open University / Polity Press, 1992.

———. "When Was the 'Post-Colonial'? Thinking at the Limit." In *The Post-Colonial Question: Common Skies, Divided Horizons*, edited by Iain Chambers and Lidia Curti, 242–60. London: Routledge, 1996.

Hanyu da cidian 漢語大詞典 [A comprehensive Chinese dictionary]. Vol. 1, edited by Luo Zhufeng 羅竹風. Hong Kong: Sanlian Shudian, 1987.

Harrison, Rachel V., and Peter A. Jackson, eds. *The Ambiguous Allure of the West: Traces of the Colonial in Thailand*. Hong Kong: Hong Kong University Press; Ithaca, NY: Cornell University Southeast Asia Program Publications, 2010.

Hau, Caroline. "The Question of Foreigners: Bai Ren's *Nanyang Piaoliuji* and the Re/making of Chinese and Philippine Nationness." In *Southeast Asia Over Three Generations: Essays Presented to Benedict R. O'G. Anderson*, edited by James T. Siegel and Audrey R. Kahin, 189–222. Ithaca, NY: Cornell University Southeast Asia Program Publications, 2003.

Hau'ofa, Epeli. "Our Sea of Islands." In *A New Oceania: Rediscovering Our Sea of Islands*, edited by Eric Waddell, Vijay Naidu, and Epeli Hau'ofa, 2–17. Suva, Fiji: School of Social and Economic Development, University of the South Pacific / Beake House, 1993.

Heng, Geraldine, and Janadas Devan. "State Fatherhood: The Politics of Nationalism, Sexuality, and Race in Singapore." In *Nationalisms and Sexualities*, edited by Andrew Parker, Mary Russo, Doris Sommer, and Patricia Yaeger, 343–64. New York: Routledge, 1992.

Hirschman, Charles. "The Making of Race in Colonial Malaya: Political Economy and Racial Ideology." *Sociological Forum* 1, no. 2 (1986): 330–61.

Ho Sok Fong (He Shufang) 賀淑芳. "Bie zai tiqi" 別再提起 [Never mention it again]. In *Bie zai tiqi: Ma Hua dangdai xiaoshuo xuan, 1997–2003* 別再提起：馬華當代小説選, 1997–2003 [Never mention it again: Selected contemporary Sinophone Malaysian fiction, 1997–2003], edited by Tee Kim Tong (Zhang Jinzhong) 張錦忠 and Ng Kim Chew (Huang Jinshu) 黃錦樹, 287–94. Taipei: Maitian Chuban, 2004.

Hobsbawm, E. J. *The Age of Empire, 1875–1914*. New York: Vintage, 1987.

Holden, Philip. "Interrogating Multiculturalism and Cosmopolitanism in the City-State: Some Recent Singapore Fiction in English." *Mobilities* 5, no. 2 (2010): 277–90.

Hsia, C. T. *A History of Modern Chinese Fiction*. 3d ed. Bloomington: Indiana University Press, 1999.

Hu Yuzhi 胡愈之. "Yu Dafu de liuwang he shizong" 郁达夫的流亡和失踪 [Yu Dafu's exile and disappearance]. In *Liuwang zai chidao xianshang* 流亡在赤道线上 [Exiled on the equator], by Hu Yuzhi 胡愈之 and Shen Cijiu 沈兹九, 41–78. Beijing: Shenghuo, Dushu, Xinzhi Sanlian Shudian, 1985.

Huang Jianli. "Umbilical Ties: The Framing of Overseas Chinese as the Mother of Revolution." In *Sun Yat-sen, Nanyang and the 1911*

Revolution, edited by Lee Lai To and Lee Hock Guan, 75–129. Singapore: ISEAS Publications, 2011.

Huggan, Graham, and Helen Tiffin. *Postcolonial Ecocriticism: Literature, Animals, Environment*. London: Routledge, 2010.

Hung, Tzu-hui Celina (Hong Zihui) 洪子惠. "Hunxue(yu)hua mailuo zhong de Huayu yuxi yanjiu" 混血(語)化脈絡中的華語語系研究 [Sinophone studies through the lens of creolization]. *Zhongshan renwen xuebao* 中山人文學報 [Sun Yat-sen journal of humanities] 35 (2013): 47–67.

Jiang Chuncai 江春才. "Lao She *Xiao Po de shengri* de 'yinhan duzhe' tansuo" 老舍《小坡的生日》的"隐含读者"探索 [An investigation of the "implied reader" in Lao She's *Little Po's Birthday*]. In *Xin Ma Huawen zuojia zuopin lunji* 新马华文作家作品论集 [Essays on the works of Sinophone Singaporean and Malaysian writers], vol. 2, edited by Li Xuanlou 李選樓, 17–43. Singapore: Xinjiapo Wenyi Xiehui, 2006.

Johnston, Anna, and Alan Lawson. "Settler Colonies." In *A Companion to Postcolonial Studies*, edited by Henry Schwarz and Sangeeta Ray, 360–76. Malden, MA: Blackwell, 2005.

Kantima กานติมา. *Botan klip sutthai* โบตั๋นกลีบสุดท้าย [Last petal of the peony]. Bangkok: Samnakphim Phưandi, 2008.

Karl, Rebecca. *Staging the World: Chinese Nationalism at the Turn of the Twentieth Century*. Durham, NC: Duke University Press, 2002.

Kasian Tejapira. "Imagined Uncommunity: The *Lookjin* Middle Class and Thai Official Nationalism." In *Essential Outsiders: Chinese and Jews in the Modern Transformation of Southeast Asia and Central Europe*, edited by Daniel Chirot and Anthony Reid, 75–98. Seattle: University of Washington Press, 1997.

Kellman, Steven G. *The Translingual Imagination*. Lincoln: University of Nebraska Press, 2000.

Kenley, David L. *New Culture in a New World: The May Fourth Movement and the Chinese Diaspora in Singapore, 1919–1932*. London: Routledge, 2003.

Kepner, Susan F. *The Lioness in Bloom: Modern Thai Fiction About Women*. Berkeley: University of California Press, 1996.

Keyes, Charles F. *Thailand: Buddhist Kingdom as Modern Nation-State*. Boulder, CO: Westview Press, 1987.

Khoo Joo Ee. *The Straits Chinese: A Cultural History*. Amsterdam: The Pepin Press, 1996.

Khoo Kheng-Hor. *Nanyang: The Lure of the Southern Ocean to Lands of Opportunity and Danger.* Subang Jaya, Selangor, Malaysia: Pelanduk Publications, 2007.

Khor Boon Eng (Xu Wenrong) 許文榮. *Nanfang xuanhua: Ma Hua wenxue de zhengzhi dikang shixue* 南方喧哗：马华文学的政治抵抗诗学 [Uproar in the south: The poetics of political resistance in Sinophone Malaysian literature]. Skudai, Johor, Malaysia: Nanfang Xueyuan Chubanshe; Singapore: Bafang Wenhua Chuangzuoshi, 2004.

Kleeman, Faye Yuan. *Under an Imperial Sun: Japanese Colonial Literature of Taiwan and the South*. Honolulu: University of Hawai'i Press, 2003.

Kon, Stella. "Emily of Emerald Hill." In *Writing Singapore: An Historical Anthology of Singapore Literature*, edited by Angelia Poon, Philip Holden, and Shirley Geok-lin Lim, 297–326. Singapore: National University of Singapore Press, 2009.

Krishnan, Sanjay. *Reading the Global: Troubling Perspectives on Britain's Empire in Asia*. New York: Columbia University Press, 2007.

Kuhn, Philip A. *Chinese Among Others: Emigration in Modern Times*. Lanham, MD: Rowman & Littlefield, 2008.

Langao zhuren 蘭皋主人. *Qilou chongmeng* 绮楼重梦 [Revisiting the silken chambers]. Beijing: Beijing Daxue Chubanshe, 1990.

Lao She 老舍. *Er Ma* 二马 [Mr. Ma and son]. Chengdu: Sichuan Renmin Chubanshe, 1980.

———. "Wo zenyang xie *Xiao Po de shengri*" 我怎样写《小坡的生日》 [Why I wrote *Little Po's Birthday*]. In *Lao She ertong wenxue zuopin xuan* 老舍儿童文学作品选 [Selected works of Lao She's children's literature], by Lao She 老舍, 303–08. Changsha, China: Hunan Wenyi Chubanshe, 2013.

———. "Xiao Po de shengri" 小坡的生日 [Little Po's birthday]. In *Lao She quanji: di er juan / xiaoshuo er ji* 老舍全集：第二卷 / 小说二集 [The complete works of Lao She, volume two: Fiction part two], by Lao She 老舍, 1–141. Beijing: Renmin Wenxue Chubanshe, 1999.

Lawson, Alan. "Comparative Studies and Post-Colonial 'Settler' Cultures." *Australian-Canadian Studies* 10, no. 2 (1992): 153–59.

Lee Kuan Yew. *From Third World to First: The Singapore Story, 1965–2000*. New York: HarperCollins, 2000.

———. *The Singapore Story: Memoirs of Lee Kuan Yew*. Singapore: Times Editions; Singapore Press Holdings, 1998.

Lee, Leo Ou-fan. *The Romantic Generation of Modern Chinese Writers*. Cambridge, MA: Harvard University Press, 1973.

Li Hong 李虹, Chen Qiong 陳瓊, Bai Ling 白翎, Nai Fang 乃方, Shen Yiwen 沈逸文, Hong Ying 紅櫻, Li Xu 李栩, Yi Fei 亦非, and Yi She 亦舍. *Fengyu Yaohuali: Jielong xiaoshuo* 風雨燿華力：接龍小說 [Stormy Yaowarat Road: A sequential novel]. Hong Kong: Dipingxian Chubanshe, 1983.

Li Qing 犁青. Introduction to *Tai Hua wenxue* 泰華文學 [Sinophone Thai literature], edited by Li Qing, 3. Hong Kong: Wenxue Shijie, 1991.

Li Yongping 李永平. *Dahe jintou* 大河盡頭 [River's end]. Vol. 1, *Suliu* 溯流 [Upstream]. Taipei: Maitian Chuban, 2008.

———. *Dahe jintou* 大河盡頭 [River's end]. Vol. 2, *Shan* 山 [Mountain]. Taipei: Maitian Chuban, 2010.

———. *Yuxue feifei: Poluozhou tongnian jishi* 雨雪霏霏：婆羅洲童年記事 [The snow falls in clouds: Recollections of a Borneo childhood]. Taipei: Tianxia Yuanjian Chuban, 2002.

Lim Kien Ket (Lin Jianguo) 林建國. "Weishenme Ma Hua wenxue?" 爲什麽馬華文學？ [Why Sinophone Malaysian literature?]. In *Chidao huisheng: Ma Hua wenxue duben* 赤道回聲：馬華文學讀本 [Equatorial echoes: A Sinophone Malaysian literary reader], edited by Chan Tah Wei (Chen Dawei) 陳大爲, Choong Yee Voon (Zhong Yiwen) 鍾怡雯, and Woo Kam Lun (Hu Jinlun) 胡金倫, 3–32. Taipei: Wanjuanlou Chubanshe, 2004.

Lim, Shirley Geok-lin. *Writing S.E./Asia in English: Against the Grain, Focus on Asian English-Language Literature.* London: Skoob Books Publishing, 1994.

Lim, Suchen Christine. *Fistful of Colours.* Singapore: SNP Editions, 2003.

———. 2013. *The River's Song.* Twickenham, UK: Aurora Metro Books.

Lin, Sylvia Li-chun. *Representing Atrocity in Taiwan: The 2/28 Incident and White Terror in Fiction and Film.* New York: Columbia University Press, 2007.

Lin Wanjing 林萬菁. *Zhongguo zuojia zai Xinjiapo jiqi yingxiang, 1927–1948* 中国作家在新加坡及其影响, 1927–1948 [Chinese writers in Singapore and their influence, 1927–1948]. Singapore: Wanli Shuju, 1978.

Lin Ye 林也. "Jiefang de xin shijie: Xin Ma xiandai wenxue de fazhan" 解放的新世界：新马现代文学的发展 [A liberated new world: The development of modern Singaporean and Malaysian literature]. In *Dongnan Ya Huawen wenxue yu Zhongguo xiandai wenxue* 东南亚华文文学与中国现代文学 [Sinophone Southeast Asian literature and modern Chinese literature], by Zhuang Zhongqing 庄鐘慶 et al., 105–24. Xiamen, China: Xiamen Daxue Chubanshe, 1991.

Lionnet, Françoise. *Autobiographical Voices: Race, Gender, Self-portraiture.* Ithaca, NY: Cornell University Press, 1989.

———. "Continents and Archipelagoes: From *E Pluribus Unum* to Creolized Solidarities." *PMLA* 123, no. 5 (2008): 1503–15.

Lu Xun. *The Real Story of Ah-Q and Other Tales of China: The Complete Fiction of Lu Xun*, translated by Julia Lovell. London: Penguin, 2009.

———. *Selected Stories of Lu Hsun*, translated by Yang Hsien-yi and Gladys Yang. New York: W. W. Norton, 2003.

Lu Yongheng 陸永恆. *Zhongguo xin wenxue gailun* 中國新文學概論 [An overview of Chinese new literature]. Guangzhou, China: Kewen Yinwuju, 1932.

Ma Huan. *Ying-yai Sheng-lan: "The Overall Survey of the Ocean's Shores" [1433]*, translated by Feng Ch'eng-Chün. Bangkok: White Lotus Press, 1997.

Majumdar, R. C. *Ancient Indian Colonization in South-East Asia*. 2d ed. Baroda, India: B. J. Sandesara, 1963.

Miao Xiu 苗秀. *Ma Hua wenxue shihua* 馬華文學史話 [A historical narrative of Sinophone Malayan literature]. Singapore: Qingnian Shuju, 1968.

Mo Yimei. *Local Colour in Malayan Chinese Fiction: A New Approach (1920–1937)*. Bochum, Germany: Brockmeyer, 1992.

Moore-Gilbert, Bart. "Spivak and Bhabha." In *A Companion to Postcolonial Studies*, edited by Henry Schwarz and Sangeeta Ray, 451–66. Malden, MA: Blackwell, 2005.

Mullaney, Thomas S. *Coming to Terms with the Nation: Ethnic Classification in Modern China*. Berkeley: University of California Press, 2011.

Murray, David A. B., Tom Boellstorff, and Kathryn Robinson. "East Indies/West Indies: Comparative Archipelagoes." *Anthropological Forum* 16, no. 3 (2006): 219–27.

Nair, Supriya. "Creolization, Orality and Nation Language in the Caribbean." In *A Companion to Postcolonial Studies*, edited by Henry Schwarz and Sangeeta Ray, 236–51. Malden, MA: Blackwell, 2005.

Naoto, Sudo. *Nanyo-Orientalism: Japanese Representations of the Pacific*. Amherst, NY: Cambria Press, 2010.

Ng Kim Chew (Huang Jinshu) 黃錦樹. "Ala de zhiyi" 阿拉的旨意 [The will of Allah]. In *Yuanxiang ren: zuqun de gushi* 原鄉人：族群的故事 [Man of the ancestral land: Stories of ethnicity], edited by David Der-wei Wang (Wang Dewei) 王德威 and Ng Kim Chew (Huang Jinshu) 黃錦樹, 235–65. Taipei: Maitian Chuban, 2004.

———. "Dongnan Ya Huaren shaoshu minzu de Huawen wenxue—zhengzhi de Malaixiya ge'an: lun Da Ma Huaren bendi yishi de xiandu" 東南亞華人少數民族的華文文學——政治的馬來西亞個案：論大馬華人本地意識的限度 [The Sinophone literature of the Chinese Southeast Asian minority—the case of political Malaysia: On the limits of the local consciousness of Chinese Malaysians]. In *Chongxie Ma Hua wenxue shilun wenji* 重寫馬華文學史論文集 [Collected essays on the rewriting of Sinophone Malaysian literary history], edited by Tee Kim Tong (Zhang Jinzhong) 張錦忠, 115–32. Puli, Taiwan: Jinan Daxue Dongnan Ya Yanjiu Zhongxin, 2004.

———. "'Ma Hua wenxue' quancheng: Chulun Malaixiya de 'Huaren wenxue' yu 'Huawen wenxue'" 「马华文学」全称：初论马来西亚的「华人文学」与「华文文学」 [The full title of "Sinophone Malaysian literature": A preliminary discussion of Malaysia's "literature by Chinese" and "literature in Chinese"]. In *Ma Hua wenxue daxi: pinglun, 1965–1996* 马华文

学大系: 评论, 1965–1996 [Compendium of Sinophone Malayan literature: Criticism, 1965–1996], edited by Dai Xiaohua 戴小華 and Yun Lifeng 雲里風, 19–28. Johor Bahru, Malaysia: Caihong Chuban, 2004.

———. *Ma Hua wenxue yu Zhongguo xing* 馬華文學與中國性 [Sinophone Malaysian literature and Chineseness]. Taipei: Yuanzun Wenhua, 1998.

———. *Meng yu zhu yu liming* 夢與豬與黎明 [Dream, swine, and aurora]. Taipei: Jiuge Chuban, 1994.

———. "Minor Sinophone Literature: Diasporic Modernity's Incomplete Journey," translated by Andy Rodekohr. In *Global Chinese Literature: Critical Essays*, edited by Jing Tsu and David Der-wei Wang, 15–28. Leiden, Netherlands: Brill, 2010.

———. "Sinophone/Chinese: 'The South Where Language Is Lost' and Reinvented," translated by Brian Bernards. In *Sinophone Studies: A Critical Reader*, edited by Shu-mei Shih, Chien-hsin Tsai, and Brian Bernards, 74–92. New York: Columbia University Press.

———. *Tu yu huo: Tanah Melayu* 土與火 [Land and fire: Malay land]. Taipei: Maitian Chuban, 2005.

———. *You dao zhi dao / Ke bei: Dari Pulau Ke Pulau* 由島至島 / 刻背 [From island to island / Back inscriptions]. Taipei: Maitian Chuban, 2001.

Nian Lamei 年臘梅. *Tai Hua xiezuo ren jianying* 泰華寫作人剪影 [Sketches of Sinophone Thai authors]. Bangkok: Bayin Chubanshe, 1990.

Nidhi Eoseewong. *Pen and Sail: Literature and History in Early Bangkok*, translated by Chris Baker et al. Chiang Mai, Thailand: Silkworm Books, 2005.

Ooi Keat Gin. Introduction to *Southeast Asia: A Historical Encyclopedia, from Angkor Wat to East Timor*, edited by Ooi Keat Gin, 1–110. Santa Barbara, CA: ABC-CLIO, 2004.

Pan Honghui 潘弘輝. "Yulin zhi ge: Zhuanfang Zhang Guixing" 雨林之歌—專訪張貴興 [Song of the rainforest: A special interview with Chang Kuei-hsing]. *Ziyou shibao* 自由時報 [Liberty times], February 21, 2001, Ziyou fukan自由副刊 [Liberty supplement] section.

Pan Yutong 潘雨桐. *He'an chuanshuo* 河岸傳說 [Riverbank legends]. Taipei: Maitian chuban, 2002.

———. *Jing shui da xue* 静水大雪 [Still waters, heavy snows]. Johor Bahru, Malaysia: Caihong Chuban, 1996.

———. *Ye dian* 野店 [The country shop]. Johor Bahru, Malaysia: Caihong Chuban, 1998.

Patke, Rajeev, and Philip Holden. *The Routledge Concise History of Southeast Asian Writing in English*. London: Routledge, 2009.

Poon, Angelia, Philip Holden, and Shirley Geok-lin Lim. Introduction to *Writing Singapore: An Historical Anthology of Singapore Literature*, edited by Angelia Poon, Philip Holden, and Shirley Geok-lin Lim, xxi–xxvi. Singapore: National University of Singapore Press, 2009.

Prabhu, Anjali. *Hybridity: Limits, Transformations, Prospects*. Albany: State University of New York Press, 2007.

Prado-Fonts, Carles. "Beneath Two Red Banners: Lao She as a Manchu Writer in Modern China." In *Sinophone Studies: A Critical Reader*, edited by Shu-mei Shih, Chien-hsin Tsai, and Brian Bernards, 353–63. New York: Columbia University Press, 2013.

Praphatson Sewikun ประภัสสร เสวิกุล. *Lot lai mangkon* ลอดลายมังกร [Through the pattern of the dragon]. Bangkok: Samnakphim Nanmi, 2008.

PuruShotam, Nirmala Srirekam. *Negotiating Multiculturalism: Disciplining Difference in Singapore*. Berlin: Mouton de Gruyter, 2000.

Qin Xianci 秦賢次. "Xu Dishan nianbiao" 許地山年表 [Xu Dishan's chronology]. In *Xu Dishan xiaoshuo xuan* 許地山小說選 [Selected fiction of Xu Dishan], by Xu Dishan 許地山, 383–402. Taipei: Hongfan Shudian, 2001.

Quah Sy Ren. "Performing Multilingualism in Singapore." In *Between Tongues: Translation and/of/in Performance in Asia*, edited by Jennifer Lindsay, 88–103. Singapore: Singapore University Press, 2006.

Reid, Anthony. *Chinese and Malay Identities in Southeast Asia*. PROSEA Research Paper No. 34. Taipei: Academia Sinica Program for Southeast Asian Area Studies, 2000.

Riep, Steven. "Xu Dishan (Luo Huasheng)." In *Chinese Fiction Writers, 1900–1949*, edited by Thomas Moran, 250–56. Detroit: Thomson Gale, 2007.

Roff, William. *The Origins of Malay Nationalism*. Kuala Lumpur: Oxford University Press, 1994.

Rudolph, Jürgen. *Reconstructing Identities: A Social History of the Babas in Singapore*. Aldershot, UK: Ashgate, 1998.

Rush, James R. *Opium to Java: Revenue Farming and Chinese Enterprise in Colonial Indonesia, 1860–1910*. Ithaca, NY: Cornell University Press, 1990.

Said, Edward. *Orientalism*. New York: Vintage, 1979.

Schafer, Edward H. *The Vermilion Bird: T'ang Images of the South*. Berkeley: University of California Press, 1967.

Schwarcz, Vera. *The Chinese Enlightenment: Intellectuals and the Legacy of the May Fourth Movement of 1919*. Berkeley: University of California Press, 1986.

Sears, Laurie J. "Postcolonial Identities, Feminist Criticism, and Southeast Asian Studies." In *Knowing Southeast Asian Subjects*, edited by Laurie J. Sears, 35–74. Seattle: University of Washington Press; Singapore: National University of Singapore Press, 2007.

Shen Yiwen 沈逸文, trans. *Liming: Taiguo duanpian xiaoshuo xuan* 黎明：泰國短篇小說選 [Daybreak: Selected Thai short fiction]. Hong Kong: Wanye Chubanshe, 1974.

Shih, Shu-mei. "The Concept of the Sinophone." *PMLA* 126, no. 3 (2011): 709–18.

———. *Visuality and Identity: Sinophone Articulations across the Pacific*. Berkeley: University of California Press, 2007.

Singapore Literary Pioneers Gallery Guide. Singapore: National Library Board, 2006.

Skinner, G. William. *Chinese Society in Thailand: An Analytical History*. Ithaca, NY: Cornell University Press, 1957.

———. "Creolized Chinese Societies in Southeast Asia." In *Sojourners and Settlers: Histories of Southeast Asia and the Chinese*, edited by Anthony Reid, 51–93. Honolulu: University of Hawai'i Press, 1996.

Smyth, David, and Manas Chitakasem. Introduction to *The Seargeant's Garland and Other Stories*, translated by David Smyth and Manas Chitakasem, ix–xxii. New York: Oxford University Press, 1998.

Stewart, Charles. "Creolization: History, Ethnography, Theory." In *Creolization: History, Ethnography, Theory*, edited by Charles Stewart, 1–25. Walnut Creek, CA: Left Coast Press, 2007.

Suchit Wongthet สุจิตต์ วงษ์เทศ. *Čhek pon Lao* เจ๊กปนลาว [A mixed Lao-Chinaman]. Bangkok: Silapa Wathanatham, 1987.

Sun, Lixin. "Chinese Maritime Concepts." *Asia Europe Journal* 8, no. 3 (2010): 327–38.

Sun Yizhong 孫逸忠. "Yu Dafu zhanshi dui Xing Ma Huawen wenxue de gongxian" 郁达夫战时对星马华文文学的贡献 [Yu Dafu's wartime contributions to Sinophone Singaporean and Malayan literature]. In *Dongnan Ya Huawen wenxue yu Zhongguo xiandai wenxue* 东南亚华文文学与中国现代文学 [Sinophone Southeast Asian literature and modern Chinese literature], by Zhuang Zhongqing 庄鐘慶 et al., 146–60. Xiamen, China: Xiamen Daxue Chubanshe, 1991.

Tai, Elizabeth. 2009. "Big Little Nyonya." *The Star Online*, November 22, 2009, accessed March 11, 2011. http://ecentral.my/news/story.asp?file=/2009/11/22/tvnradio/5149808& sec=tvnradio.

Tan, E. K. *Rethinking Chineseness: Translational Sinophone Identities in the Nanyang Literary World*. Amherst, NY: Cambria Press, 2013.

Tan, Hwee Hwee. *Foreign Bodies*. New York: Washington Square Press, 1997.

Tang Tao. *History of Modern Chinese Literature*. Beijing: Foreign Languages Press, 1993.

Tee Kim Tong (Zhang Jinzhong) 張錦忠. *Malaixiya Huayu yuxi wenxue* 馬

來西亞華語語系文學 [On Sinophone Malaysian literature]. Petaling Jaya, Selangor, Malaysia: Youren Chuban, 2011.

———. *Nanyang lunshu: Ma Hua wenxue yu wenhua shuxing* 南洋論述：馬華文學與文化屬性 [South Seas discourse: Sinophone Malaysian literature and cultural attributes]. Taipei: Maitian Chuban, 2003.

———. "Wenhua huigui, lisan Taiwan yu lüxing kuaguoxing: 'Zai Tai Ma Hua wenxue' de anli" 文化回归，离散台湾与旅行跨国性：「在台马华文学」的案例 [Cultural return, diasporic Taiwan and traveling transnationalism: The case of "Sinophone Malaysian literature in Taiwan"]. In *Qiandao Nanyang* 千岛南洋 [South Seas archipelago], by Lim Chin Chown (Lin Xingqian) 林幸謙, 8–26. Selangor Darul Ehsan, Malaysia: Malaiya Tushu Youxian Gongsi, 2005.

Teng, Emma Jinhua. *Eurasian: Mixed Identities in the United States, China, and Hong Kong, 1842–1943*. Berkeley: University of California Press, 2013.

Thongchai Winichakul. *Siam Mapped: The History of the Geo-body of a Nation*. Honolulu: University of Hawai'i Press, 1994.

Thornber, Karen Laura. *Ecoambiguity: Environmental Crises and East Asian Literatures*. Ann Arbor: University of Michigan Press, 2012.

Thumboo, Edwin. Introduction to *The Fiction of Singapore*, edited by Edwin Thumboo, i–xx. Singapore: Unipress, 1990.

Ting, Helen. "The Battle Over the Memory of the Nation: Whose National History?" In *Controversial History Education in Asian Contexts*, edited by Mark Baildon, Loh Kah Seng, Ivy Maria Lim, Gül İnanç, and Junaidah Jaffar, 41–57. Abingdon, Oxon, UK: Routledge, 2014.

Trivedi, Harish. "The Postcolonial or the Transcolonial? Location and Language." *Interventions: International Journal of Postcolonial Studies* 1, no. 2 (1999): 269–72.

Tsu, Jing. *Sound and Script in Chinese Diaspora*. Cambridge, MA: Harvard University Press, 2010.

Tsu, Jing, and David Der-wei Wang, eds. *Global Chinese Literature: Critical Essays*. Leiden, Netherlands: Brill, 2010.

Tu Wei-ming. "Cultural China: The Periphery as Center." In *The Living Tree: The Changing Meaning of Being Chinese Today*, edited by Tu Weiming, 1–34. Stanford, CA: Stanford University Press, 1991.

Turnbull, C. M. *A History of Singapore: 1819–1988*. 2d ed. Singapore: Oxford University Press, 1989.

Veracini, Lorenzo. *Settler Colonialism: A Theoretical Overview*. Houndmills, Basingstoke, UK: Palgrave Macmillan, 2010.

Wade, Geoff. "The Zheng He Voyages: A Reassessment." In *China and Southeast Asia*, vol. 2, *Southeast Asia and Ming China (from the*

Fourteenth to the Sixteenth Century), edited by Geoff Wade, 118–41. London: Routledge, 2009.

Wagner, Rudolph. "The Canonization of May Fourth." In *The Appropriation of Cultural Capital: China's May Fourth Movement*, edited by Milena Doleželová-Velingerová and Oldřich Král, 66–120. Cambridge, MA: Harvard University Asia Center, 2001.

Wang, David Der-wei (Wang Dewei) 王德威. *Fictional Realism in Twentieth-Century China: Mao Dun, Lao She, Shen Congwen*. New York: Columbia University Press, 1992.

———. "Huai haizi Huang Jinshu: Huang Jinshu de Ma Hua lunshu yu xushu" 壞孩子黃錦樹：黃錦樹的馬華論述與敘述 [Ng Kim Chew, enfant terrible: Ng Kim Chew's Sinophone Malaysian discourse and narrative]. In *You dao zhi dao / Ke bei: Dari Pulau Ke Pulau* 由島至島 / 刻背 [From island to island / back inscriptions], by Ng Kim Chew (Huang Jinshu) 黃錦樹, 11–35. Taipei: Maitian Chuban, 2001.

———. "Zai qun xiang yu hou dang de jiaxiang: Zhang Guixing de Ma Hua gushi" 在群象與猴黨的家鄉: 張貴興的馬華故事 [In the homeland of elephant herds and monkey gangs: Chang Kuei-hsing's Sinophone Malaysian stories]. In *Wo sinian de changmian zhong de Nanguo gongzhu* 我思念的長眠中的南國公主 [My South Seas sleeping beauty], by Chang Kuei-hsing (Zhang Guixing) 張貴興, 9–38. Taipei: Maitian Chuban, 2001.

Wang Gungwu. "Early Ming Relations with Southeast Asia: A Background Essay." In *The Chinese World Order: Traditional China's Foreign Relations*, edited by John King Fairbank, 34–62. Cambridge, MA: Harvard University Press, 1968.

Wang Zhefu 王哲甫. *Zhongguo xin wenxue yundong shi* 中國新文學運動史 [History of the Chinese new literature movement]. Hong Kong: Xianggang Yuandong Tushu Gongsi, 1965.

Ward, Barbara E. "A Hakka Kongsi in Borneo." *Journal of Oriental Studies* 1, no. 2 (1954): 358–70.

Wawrinec, Christian. "Tribality and Indigeneity in Malaysia and Indonesia." *Stanford Journal of East Asian Affairs* 10, no. 1 (2010): 96–107.

Weaver, Jace. "Indigenousness and Indigeneity." In *A Companion to Postcolonial Studies*, edited by Henry Schwarz and Sangeeta Ray, 221–35. Malden, MA: Blackwell, 2005.

Wee Chong Hui. *Regional Disparities and Federalism in Malaysia*. Kuala Lumpur: University of Malaya Press, 2006.

Weng Luanbo 翁鑾波. "*Pobishe waizhuan* he *Fengyu Yaohuali*" 《破毕舍外传》和《风雨耀华力》 [*Biography of a ruined young man* and *Stormy Yaowarat road*]. In *Haiwai Huawen wenxue shi* 海外华文文学史 [A history of Sinophone literature overseas], vol. 2, edited by Chen Xianmao 陳賢茂, 407–19. Xiamen: Lujiang Chubanshe, 1999.

Widmer, Ellen. "*Honglou meng* Sequels and Their Female Readers in Nineteenth-Century China." In *Snakes' Legs: Sequels, Continuations, Rewritings, and Chinese Fiction*, edited by Martin W. Huang, 116–42. Honolulu: University of Hawai'i Press, 2004.

———. *The Margins of Utopia:* Shui-hu hou-chuan *and the Literature of Ming Loyalism*. Cambridge, MA: Council on East Asian Studies, Harvard University Press, 1987.

Witchard, Anne. *Lao She in London*. Hong Kong: Hong Kong University Press, 2012.

Wong Meng Voon (Huang Mengwen) 黃孟文. "Singapore Chinese Literature in the Post-Independence Era." In *An Anthology of Singapore Chinese Literature*, edited by Wong Meng Voon and Wong Yoon Wah, ix–xvi. Singapore: Singapore Association of Writers, 1983.

———. *Xinjiapo Huawen wenxue shi chugao* 新加坡华文文学史初稿 [A preliminary history of Sinophone Singaporean literature]. Singapore: Xinjiapo Guoli Daxue Zhongwen Xi, Bafang Wenhua, 2002.

Wong, Owen (Huang Aoyun) 黃傲雲. *Zhongguo zuojia yu Nanyang* 中國作家與南洋 [Chinese writers and the South Seas]. Hong Kong: Kehua Tushu Chuban, 1986.

Wong Yoon Wah (Wang Runhua) 王潤華. "Chongxin huanxiang: Cong huanxiang Nanyang dao Nanyang huanxiang—cong danyuan de Zhongguo huanxiang dao Dongnan Ya bentu duoyuan huanxiang" 重新幻想：從幻想南洋到南洋幻想——從單元的中國幻想到東南亞本土多元幻想 [Fantasizing anew: From fantasizing the South Seas to a South Seas fantasy—from a singular Chinese fantasy to a local and pluralized Southeast Asian fantasy]. In *Dangdai wenxue yu renwen shengtai* 當代文學與人文生態 [Contemporary literature and the ecology of the humanities], edited by Wu Yeow Chong (Wu Yaozong) 吳燿宗, 13–28. Taipei: Wanjuanlou, 2003.

———. *Post-Colonial Chinese Literatures in Singapore and Malaysia*. Singapore: Department of Chinese Studies, National University of Singapore; River Edge, NJ: Global Publishing, 2002.

Woodside, Alexander. *Vietnam and the Chinese Model: A Comparative Study of Vietnamese and Chinese Government in the First Half of the Nineteenth Century*. Cambridge, MA: Harvard University Council on East Asian Studies, 1988.

World Wildlife Foundation. *Borneo: Treasure Island at Risk*. Frankfurt: WWF Germany, 2005.

Wu Jin 吳進. *Redai fengguang* 熱帶風光 [Tropical scenery]. Hong Kong: Xuewen Shudian, 1953.

Wu Yiqi 吴奕錡. "Taiguo Huawen wenxue gaishu" 泰国华文文学概述 [An overview of Sinophone Thai literature]. In *Haiwai Huawen wenxue shi* 海外华文文学史 [A history of Sinophone literature overseas], vol. 2, edited by Chen Xianmao 陳賢茂, 310–28. Xiamen: Lujiang Chubanshe, 1999.

Xu Dishan 許地山. *Xu Dishan xiaoshuo xuan* 許地山小說選 [Selected fiction of Xu Dishan]. Taipei: Hongfan Shudian, 1984.

Xu Jingfeng 許靜風. "Malu gongren" 馬路工人 [Road construction worker]. *Xingzhou ribao* 星洲日報 [Singapore daily], September 6, 1941, Chen xing fukan 辰星副刊 [Morning star supplement] section, early edition.

Xu Zhimo 徐志摩. *Xu Zhimo quanji: sanwen, xiaoshuo, shiji, riji* 徐志摩全集：散文, 小說, 詩輯, 日記 [The complete works of Xu Zhimo: Essays, fiction, poetry, diaries]. Taipei: Shiyi Wenhua, 2001.

———. *Xu Zhimo wenji (er): xiaoshuo ji* 徐志摩文集（二）：小說集 [The collected works of Xu Zhimo, vol. 2: Fiction]. Shanghai: Shangwu Yinshuguan, no date.

Yamada, Teri Shaffer, ed. *Virtual Lotus: Modern Fiction of Southeast Asia*. Ann Arbor: University of Michigan Press, 2002.

Yeng Pway Ngon (Ying Pei'an) 英培安. *Bu cunzai de qingren* 不存在的情人 [The nonexistent lover]. Taipei: Tangshan Chubanshe, 2007.

———. *Guji de lian* 孤寂的臉 [A lonely face]. Singapore: Caogen Shushi, 1989.

———. *Saodong* 騷動 [Unrest]. Taipei: Erya Chuban, 2002.

———. *Yi ge xiang wo zheyang de nanren* 一個像我這樣的男人 [A man like me]. Taipei: Tangshan Chubanshe, 2004.

Yeo Song Nian (Yang Songnian) 楊松年. *Zhanqian Xin Ma wenxue bendi yishi de xingcheng yu fazhan* 战前新马文学本地意识的形成与发展 [The formation and development of local consciousness in prewar Singaporean and Malayan literature]. Singapore: Xinjiapo Guoli Daxue Zhongwen Xi; River Edge, NJ: Global Publishing, 2001.

Yip, June. *Envisioning Taiwan: Fiction, Cinema, and the Nation in the Cultural Imaginary*. Durham, NC: Duke University Press, 2004.

Yu Dafu 郁達夫. "Chenlun" 沉沦 [Sinking]. In *Xiandai xiaoshuo yidai zongshi: Yu Dafu xiaoshuo quanji* 现代小说一代宗师：郁达夫小说全集 [Master of modern fiction: Yu Dafu's complete fiction], edited by Yue Qi 樂齊, 1–35. Beijing: Zhongguo Wenlian Chuban, 1996.

———. *Yu Dafu Nanyang suibi* 郁達夫南洋隨筆 [Yu Dafu's jottings in the South Seas]. Taipei: Hongfan Shudian, 1978.

———. *Yu Dafu wenji di shi juan: shici* 郁達夫文集第十卷：詩詞 [The collected works of Yu Dafu, vol. 10: Poetry]. Hong Kong: Shenghuo, Dushu, Xinzhi Sanlian Shudian, 1984.

Yu Kwang-chung (Yu Guangzhong) 余光中. *Shou ye ren: Zhong Ying duizhao shiji* 守夜人：中英對照詩集 [The night watchman: A bilingual selection of poems], translated by Yu Kwang-chung. Taipei: Jiuge Chubanshe, 1992.

Yung, Sai shing. "Territorialization and the Entertainment Industry of the Shaw Brothers in Southeast Asia." In *China Forever: The Shaw Brothers and Diasporic Cinema*, edited by Poshek Fu, 133–53. Urbana: University of Illinois Press, 2008.

Zhou Zuoren 周作人. *Zhongguo xin wenxue de yuanliu* 中國新文學的源流 [The origins of Chinese new literature]. Beijing: Renwen Shudian, 1934.

INDEX